KUP'S CHICAGO

*The first requisite to happiness is that
a man be born in a famous city.*

—EURIPIDES

Irv Kupcinet

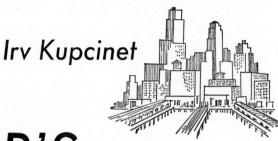

KUP'S
CHICAGO

THE WORLD PUBLISHING COMPANY

CLEVELAND AND NEW YORK

Published by The World Publishing Company
2231 West 110th Street, Cleveland 2, Ohio

Published simultaneously in Canada by
Nelson, Foster & Scott Ltd.

Library of Congress Catalog Card Number: 62-9046

FIRST EDITION

WP962

To my wife Essee, daughter Karyn,
and son Jerry, I humbly dedicate this book.
Without their compassion and understanding,
I never could have met the demands of
a daily column, which too often
deprived me of their companionship.
Without the column, there would be no book.
Perhaps all would have profited—
family, column, and book—had I stuck
to my last and become a beachcomber.

Contents

Illustrations

ILLUSTRATIONS

KUP'S CHICAGO

1. Me and My Home Town

For nearly twenty years, or ever since I began writing "Kup's Column" in the Chicago *Times,* now the *Sun-Times,* I've been following my town's daily drama and recording some of its history, checking its blood pressure, taking its pulse. In that time I have come to know many of its faces intimately, and it has many—from the stockyards to plush executive suites, from the slums and skid row to the Gold Coast. I've become acquainted with its politicos and merchant princes, its financial wizards and writers, and with the educators, clergy, sports heroes, hoodlums, and other conspicuous citizens and celebrities of our community. I've reported murders, scandals, marriages, premières, and national political conventions (of which Chicago has had more than any other city— twenty-three). I've been amused, intrigued, outraged, enthralled, and exasperated by Chicago. And I've come to love this American giant, viewing it as the most misunderstood, most underrated city in the world. There is none other quite like it, my "City of Big Shoulders."

Chicago is America's second largest city, the nation's convention capital, crossroads for air and rail transportation, steelmaker and "stacker of wheat." It's the town of Jane Addams, Carl Sandburg, Nelson Algren, James T. Farrell, Montgomery Ward, Adlai Stevenson, P. K. Wrigley, Mike Todd, Sally Rand, and Al Capone.

13

It's where one mayor, "Big Bill" Thompson, threatened to "bust King George on the snoot," and where four decades later another mayor, Richard J. Daley, played host to Queen Elizabeth as two million citizens cheered; where the violent days of newspaper history, later dramatized into *The Front Page* were actually lived; where the skyscraper was originated and a river was made to run backward; where both the Atomic Age and the hootchy-kootchy dance were introduced; and where they still argue over the truth of a rumor that the city's name means "skunk."

"Reeking, cinder-ridden, joyous," one of its most famous writers, Ben Hecht, called it. "Exciting, impressive, one of the most beautiful cities in the world," said one of its visitors, Germany's Prince Otto von Bismarck.

It's all this and more, is Chicago.

Just 130 years ago it was a frontier town so swampy and nondescript that a visitor, asking the way to Chicago, was told, "You're in it, stranger, you're in it." Today it is a metropolis of 3,800,000 persons (7,000,000 including its suburbs), with a financial district (LaSalle Street) second in importance only to Wall Street; a "Little White Way" (Randolph and Rush Streets) exceeded in entertainment variety and vigor only by the "Great White Way" of Broadway and the Strip in Las Vegas; and a concentrated shopping district (State Street) second to none. Everyone knows of its stockyards and steel mills, but it is the bustling capital of mail-order, paint, sporting goods, electronics, candy, cosmetics, and job-printing industries.

It has beauty—a twenty-nine-mile shoreline along Lake Michigan, framed by more parks than any other city in the world, and one of the most photographed of all skylines. It has squalor—slums, segregation, and the back-alley world of what Nelson Algren has termed "the nameless nobodies." It has culture—a renowned symphony orchestra led by Fritz Reiner; more colleges and universities (58) than any other city; a Lyric Opera which plays regularly to capacity audiences; and one of the best art museums in America.

It has a future—*Fortune* magazine, in a recent study, prophesied the day will come when Chicago, already a vast commercial, industrial, and residential complex stretching over fifty miles along the sandy southwestern curve of Lake Michigan, will become a four-hundred-mile city, running from Detroit to Chicago to Milwaukee. The authors of the *Fortune* study, Edwin Darby of the *Sun-Times* and William Clark of the *Tribune*, summed up their article with these glowing words: "The Chicago of 1962 is as new as the city that emerged from a decade of furious construction after the fire of 1871 leveled 18,000 of the city's buildings. . . . Celebrating the 125th anniversary of its founding this year [1962], Chicago is a city of constant and booming change and growth—a living city." The man on the street, taking cognizance of the tremendous amount of building, perhaps summed it up more succinctly: "We'll have a helluva city—once they finish it."

It has crime—a syndicate so well publicized that a farm boy was once quoted as saying, "Good-bye, God, we're going to Chicago." Less publicized is the fact that it also has more theological institutions than any other city in the nation.

And some say it has the biggest line of ballyhoo anywhere, an accusation which stuck it with a nickname in 1893 during a squabble over a World's Fair. "Don't pay any attention to the nonsensical claims of that Windy City," said New York editor Charles A. Dana. "Its people couldn't build a World's Fair if they won it." Editor Dana thereby initiated an intercity feud that has grown with the years. But the "Windy City" did build that World's Fair, the Columbian Exposition of 1893. It built that, and much more.

It filled swamps with dirt from its South Side, jacked up streets, sidewalks, and buildings, and in sixty years did what Paris required six hundred and fifty to achieve—it passed the million mark in population. And as any recent visitor can testify, Chicago is still a boom town. In the past decade it has built more factories than any other city—by a margin of more than one and a half billion dollars in valuation. Its steel-making capacity now equals that of Britain and exceeds that of Asia's workshop, Japan.

It is the world's leading inland port, handling more traffic annually than the Panama Canal; it is the world's leading rail terminal (22 lines moving 239,000 passengers a day); and the biggest air center (nearly one fourth of America's passenger traffic). In the mail-order business (led by Sears, Roebuck and Company, Montgomery Ward, Spiegel, and Aldens), it accounts for more than nine tenths of all United States sales in the field.

Chicago boasts the world's tallest hotel (the forty-two-story Morrison) and the largest (the 3,000-room Conrad Hilton); and the biggest commercial building (Merchandise Mart), convention hall (McCormick Place), indoor arena (Chicago Stadium), grain-trading pit (Board of Trade), produce market (South Water Street), and air terminal (O'Hare International Airport).

Its daily transportation activity includes more than 1,200 airplane landings and take-offs, 1,000 passenger train arrivals and departures, 32,000 freight car movements, and 28,000 truck loadings and unloadings. Nearly $2,500,000 in retail sales are rung up every working hour—some $40,000 a minute.

There is a birth every five and a half minutes and a marriage every twelve. More daily commuters—865,000—funnel into its business district than occupy the entire city of Dallas or Milwaukee or Washington, D.C. An average of 12,000 visitors attend the ten or more conventions and trade shows daily in progress.

Fabulous, ordinary, beautiful, ugly, progressive, backward, cultured, rough-edged, Chicago is a city I'd like you to know better.

I would like you to see not merely what is visible en route between Midway Airport or O'Hare Field and the Loop, or what can be crammed into a weekend or the after hours of a convention. I would like to take you to little-known places, down obscure streets and byways, behind the scenes with the people and places and stories that make up the time-never-stops world of my Chicago.

Along the way we'll puncture a few myths. There is a story that Chicago's name means "onion" or "skunk." Actually, its name derives from the Indian word *chicagou*, which meant "anything powerful or great." Nor is it true that Chicago is the crime capital of the nation. FBI statistics now award that dubious distinction to Los Angeles.

"Hog Butcher for the World," sang Chicago's favorite poet, Carl Sandburg. Not so today. Thanks to modern transportation, Kansas City and Omaha now share the lead in cattle slaughtering;

and due to Chicago's rapid growth and diversification, meat-packing is only one of its many industries.

I would be remiss in my loyalty to my home town if I failed to dispel the canard inspired by Charles Dana that Chicago is the nation's "Windy City." Not long ago a Chicago advertising executive, Harry Cohen, launched a campaign to explode this ancient fallacy. His gust of statistics from the United States Weather Bureau showed that eighteen other cities are windier. And guess what city topped the list. Dana's New York—with an average hourly wind speed of 14.5 mph, as compared to Chicago's zephyr-like 9.8.

The chalk-white Wrigley Building, the twin lions outside the Art Institute, the outdoor market on Maxwell Street, the Water Tower that survived the Chicago Fire, the quaintness of Chinatown, the eccentrics of "Bughouse Square"—they are all symbols of the Chicago I love.

But Chicago isn't my only love. My job itself is another—an assignment that has encompassed and provided more glamour and adventure than I ever dreamed I could be a part of. So we won't stop with Chicago and its suburbs. We'll examine the kaleidoscope of events which make up the unique world of a big-city columnist: events which include a private audience with Pope Pius XII in the Vatican; visits with Presidents Franklin Delano Roosevelt and Harry S. Truman in the White House; the coronation of Queen Elizabeth II of England. My job has taken me to Alaska and the Far East on Christmas trips with Bob Hope; to Palestine and the Displaced Persons Camp in Europe on a "Mission of Mercy" with Chicago philanthropists; into the lives and homes of movie and TV stars.

And I would like to share with you the experiences of my television show, *At Random*, now in its fourth year on Chicago's CBS station, WBBM-TV. *At Random*, "a conversational show for controversial people," is syndicated and seen in a dozen cities. Every Saturday I assemble a small group of articulate persons from various professions for a free exchange of ideas that continues from midnight into the early hours of Sunday morning. Former Presidents, future Presidents, Senators, governors, foreign dignitaries, authors, educators, producers, playwrights, and stars of sports and show business—all have participated in the informal, no-holds-barred discussions that comprise *At Random*. I also do football broadcasts every Sunday during the season. Football and journalism long have been twin obsessions with me. Through my high school and college years they complemented each other to the exclusion of practically all other interests. My playing days ended after a brief fling at professional football with the Philadelphia Eagles. However a few years later I was not only covering football and other sports for the old Chicago *Times*, but also officiating in the National Football League. As a matter of fact, the most running I ever did in my football career was on a Sunday late in 1940, when I was one of the officials in the unforgettable championship game in which the Chicago Bears slaughtered the Washington Redskins, 73-0.

When my officiating and sportswriting days ended, I moved into the radio booth to do the "color" on the Bears' broadcasts, beside one of the nation's stellar sportscasters, Jack Brickhouse.

In addition to sharing my Chicago, my sports and television experiences, you will also get to know some of the secrets of a columnist. And along the way, I hope you get to know *me*—how I operate, my passions (many), and prejudices (few). You will find, for example, that I love action—things to do, places to go, and, especially, people to see. (Didn't Shakespeare say that "the people are the city"?) That I dislike sleeping, the suburbs, and quiet evenings at home. On second thought, I had better revise that last statement. After twenty years of night-club reporting, I now relish, on occasion, a quiet evening at home when I can read a book or watch a special television program.

You will also learn that I respect quality, whether it is in writing, performing, or the clothes I wear; that I love the theater, the movies, good night-club acts, and sports events; that I like golf but play a 95 game; that I enjoy deep-sea fishing and have one sailfish that didn't get away, stuffed and hanging on a wall in my office; that I like steaks or hamburgers with beefsteak tomatoes, and Scotch-and-water. And also that I love jazz, comedians, blondes, brunettes, redheads, and eggheads; that I enjoy the quips in Ann Landers' column, and a year with four real seasons. (California and Florida as a bland year-round diet you and the birds can have.)

My feeling for the town has been growing since July 31, 1912, when I was born into the West Side home of my parents, Max and Olga Kupcinet. My father was a bakery driver. In addition to my beloved mother the household included three older Kups: Ben, Joe, and Sophie. Brother Ben, the eldest, is the only other member of the family ever associated with a newspaper—he is a pressman for the Chicago *Tribune*; Joe is a veteran physical education teacher and high school football coach in Chicago (his Taft High School team won the city championship in 1960); and my sister, Mrs. Sophie McKerr, is a widow living in Hollywood, Florida. The apartment in which we all grew up at Sixteenth and Kedzie was certainly not plush; we weren't wealthy, but as they say on *This Is Your Life*, we "got along."

Because of shifting population, the old neighborhood today is all Negro. In my youth it was a real melting pot—Polish, Bohemian, Irish—but it was largely Jewish.

Nearby was huge Douglas Park. And there were holiday parades, street-cleaning wagons which shot water to both sides and behind, vaudeville shows, movies, and countless other attractions. And there was the Loop. I still recall the first time I landed there. A group of us had played hooky from school and taken a ride atop the double-decker Douglas Park bus, an incomparable thrill in those days.

Clanging trolleys rounded the bend from Kedzie onto Sixteenth Street right in front of our home. I will always remember Kedzie Avenue and those trolleys. It was the scene of an accident that almost snuffed out my life. Crossing the street when I was about four years old, at what was then Carlisle Avenue and now is Fifteenth Place, I suddenly stooped to pick up a penny. (Even then I was the frugal type.) The next thing I knew I was lying underneath a streetcar. Fortunately, it was the old, high-built "Toonerville Trolley" type which was part of the Chicago scene for so long, and there was safe clearance for one small Kupcinet beneath it. I remember hands reaching under the trolley to pull me to safety after the streetcar had been jacked up. The damage was comparatively slight, even though I wound up with a gash that required six stitches. I never did get the penny, but somehow I've had an unduly warm relationship with Jack Benny over the years.

In our own little world of those early days, there was no football to match our games on the cement sidewalk. (It was man to man, and you had to plunge through your opponent to gain three squares in four downs.) And there were no political rallies like those of the 24th Ward Democratic organization, most powerful in the nation and able to deliver ten-to-one majorities in every election. The 24th Ward was bossed by a man we assumed at that time to be second only to God, Jacob M. Arvey, about whom I'll have more to say later. The appearances of Arvey and other leaders such as the late Sidney Deutch and Arthur X. Elrod, both of whom rose to high rank in local government, and Abraham Lincoln Marovitz, now a prominent judge, at the weekly Amateur Boxing Nights in the old Edmille Club at Kedzie and Roosevelt were as much a highlight of the evening as the ring appearances of such local heroes as Barney Ross, later a world champion.

And were there any baseball stars but the White Sox? Those were the days of Red Faber, Eddie Collins, Ray Schalk, Hollis ("Sloppy") Thurston, Bib Falk, and Johnny Mostil. The White Sox pennant hanging in our flat was almost a shrine, at least until we were old enough to venture to the North Side and discover Wrigley Field and the Cubs. The North Side was another world to us—the home of the rich and the aristocratic.

The West Side was rough. Stories of beatings and slayings were not uncommon, although none ever occurred on our block. I saw my first gun fight when I was twelve. I had attended the Central Park Theater with a group of boys. As we were leaving the theater, we heard a series of gunshots from the rear of the building. We raced outside. There, sprawled in the filth and rot of the alleyway, lay a gunman, killed by a bullet that had pierced his head. The blood gushing from the wound and the grotesque position of the legs left an impression on me that is as vivid today as it was then.

Brutal though it was, Chicago was still a wonderful place in which to be young. I remember the days when I would arise with my father at three in the morning—now my bedtime—to help him on his bakery route, just as my brother Joe had done before me. I would help my father hitch up the team of horses, load the wagon with bakery goods, and then clip-clop off on his route with him. We wouldn't get home until three in the afternoon. One of our proudest moments came when the bakery finally retired the horses and we began traveling in style in a truck.

My father was not one for preaching, but the simple, hard life he led bespoke far more eloquently the lessons in living we had to learn. His long and unusual working hours did not allow him to spend as much time with his children as he would have liked. His influence on us was indirect rather than direct, yet none of us suffered.

"How did you become a columnist?" I am often asked.

The trail began on my first day at Harrison High School. The get-acquainted tour for freshmen led us to the student printing shop, next to Mrs. Theresa Josi's journalism class. Here the editorial staff and printers were putting the weekly *Harrison Herald* to bed. I was fascinated. The idea that students could write, edit, and print a newspaper touched a responsive chord in me. I determined there and then that I would study journalism and become a newspaperman. At the age of thirteen my course was set. My enthusiasm caught Mrs. Josi's attention and I became the first freshman accepted in the journalism class.

I learned the rudiments of journalism from Mrs. Josi, but another teacher, Wilfrid Smith, at *Harrison High* was to help me further toward my career. He was then teaching a civics course, serving as head basketball coach, and helping Bob Daugherty coach football. Since he was also working on the *Tribune* sports desk and playing professional basketball and football, "Smitty" was the idol of almost every athlete at Harrison. He took pains to give me tips on sportswriting, and he taught me a great deal about football. He is now one of the most powerful figures in the athletic world as sports editor of the *Tribune*.

On graduation from Harrison High in February 1930, I went
to Northwestern University on a football scholarship—but not
before I spent six months working as a car cleaner for the Pullman
Company in the Illinois Central Railroad Yards, at a wage rate
of forty cents per hour. Those were the Depression days and jobs
were hard to find. Thanks to my sister Sophie, who was secretary to
R. J. Ruddy, a Pullman Company executive, I had been able to
work in the yards during my summer vacations from high school.

The money I saved in that six-month period was important
to me, but the lessons I learned on the job, I now believe, were
more important. Car-cleaning was essentially a Negro occupation.
I was thrust into an all-black world. I worked and ate with
Negroes, made friends with them, and gained firsthand knowledge
of their problems. Unconsciously, in those formative years, I
developed an understanding of human beings that was to help me
later on.

I attended Northwestern for two years, during which I played
football, covered sports for *The Daily Northwestern*, and worked
as an assistant to Walter Paulison, the University's veteran sports
publicity director. Two years later I transferred to the University
of North Dakota. The late Jack West, athletic director and
football coach, lured me there with a "prize" offer: I would
become his publicity director. I was probably the only college
football player who had his own office and secretary. My salary
in those Depression days? Twenty-five dollars a month!

But the experience was invaluable. I would write five or six
stories per week and hand them to my secretary for mimeo-
graphing and mailing. On Fridays I would call on sports editors
with a sheaf of publicity material under my arm. On Saturdays
I would put on my uniform to play quarterback in the games I
had been publicizing. This arrangement was not only better
than sweeping out the gym, but also led me to friendships that
have lasted through the years. My friendship with Los Angeles
columnist Vincent X. Flaherty is one of those. He was then
writing a sports column in Washington, D.C. (University of
North Dakota, 7—George Washington University, 0.)

After my college days I played professionally with the Philadelphia Eagles for a short time. Then I was ready to pursue my chosen profession. With my college journalism training and publicity experience, I felt confident that I could handle a metropolitan newspaper job. Marvin McCarthy, sports editor of the old Chicago *Times*, apparently shared this confidence. He hired me on the recommendation of a Tau Delta Phi fraternity brother of mine, Herbert Simons, who was then covering baseball for the *Times*. My starting salary as a sports copyreader: $32.50 per week.

Sports thrive on the unexpected. I remember that when I played for the Philadelphia Eagles in 1935, the team was in serious financial difficulty. Bert Bell, owner of the Eagles who later became National Football League Commissioner, had an inspiration for bolstering the box-office receipts. One of the most publicized sports figures of that era was a player named Alabama Pitts. Alabama had been the number one baseball and football star at his former institution, Sing Sing Prison. Bell signed him as a halfback for the Eagles. A few days before the season opened, Bell summoned the players to a meeting to announce it. He sketched Pitts' career for us and requested that we treat him as we did any other player. He explained, too, that he hoped Pitts would become a box-office attraction, which would benefit us all. As the meeting broke up, Bell called me aside and said, quite straight-faced, "By the way, Kup, I have a special assignment for you. You have the honor of being Alabama's roommate. Sleep well, my boy." With that, he walked away.

As it developed, I had no reason not to sleep well. Alabama was a quiet, unobtrusive roommate who seldom talked at all. I was never sure whether this was the result of his years in prison, or an inferiority complex caused by his having been thrust into a group of college men. At any rate, Alabama didn't last long with the club. After the publicity of his signing had faded, he was found wanting for lack of weight (165 pounds) and experience, and he was released. (I was sorry to read, several years later, that Pitts had been killed in a saloon fight.)

Later that season a serious shoulder injury retired me from pro football. I almost suffered far more serious injuries in 1937,

while covering the baseball spring-training season in Florida
as a sportswriter. Among the teams training on the west coast
of Florida was the St. Louis Cardinals. The late Jack Miley,
then sports columnist for the New York *Daily News*, was riding
Dizzy Dean and his wife. Few sportswriters were more deft with
the written barb than Miley, and the Deans were getting the
full treatment.

One day Mrs. Dean spotted Miley in the lobby of the Tampa
Terrace Hotel. She pointed to him and said to Dizzy, "There's
that fat sonuvabitch. Give him his lumps." Then, as I stood
at Miley's side, an innocent bystander, Dizzy and Miley got
embroiled in a name-calling contest. As the argument grew more
heated, some eighteen members of the St. Louis club, still in
uniform after an exhibition game, trudged into the lobby. Dizzy,
Miley, and I were surrounded. By this time the verbal exchange
between Miley and Dizzy had grown so vicious that one of the
players lashed out with a spiked shoe he was carrying in his
hand. He had taken off his shoes so as not to slice up the
hotel rug; he spared the rug but not Miley. This was the signal
for a free-for-all, with the players taking swings at the two sportswriters. The result: a two-inch gash on Miley's forehead, a black
eye for Kupcinet, a number of broken lamps and smashed potted
palms for the Tampa Terrace. And front-page headlines in the
newspapers.

After Dizzy was traded to the Chicago Cubs, he and I made
up our differences and became friends. But each year at spring-
training time, the "Battle of the Tampa Terrace" has been revived
by Vince Flaherty in his column. And each year, according to
Flaherty's version, I get braver and braver. The last time Vince
revived the story, he had me annihilating—single-handedly—
the entire St. Louis gang. The fact is, I would have been over-
matched against the bat boy.

As a reporter, assistant sports editor, and columnist, I remained on the sports beat until 1943. In that year the late editor
of the *Times*, Richard J. Finnegan, called me into his office.
With him was Managing Editor Russ Stewart, who is now vice-
president of the newspaper division of Fields Enterprises.

"We're starting a new man-about-town column," Mr. Finnegan said, "and Russ thinks you're the man for it. I agree with him. How do you feel about it?"

I leaped at the opportunity. I liked writing sports, but I felt ready to branch out. I enjoyed going around town, visiting night clubs, mingling with show-business personalities, and talking to people in all walks of life.

On January 18, 1943, I wrote my first "Kup's Column," a name which Stewart had selected. "Kupcinet," he had reasoned, "was too difficult a name to inflict on the public. Kup could easily be remembered." The lead item in that first column concerned the disciplinary problems Irving Berlin was having with the cast of *This Is the Army*, then playing in Chicago. Ever since that day I've been fighting a daily deadline six times a week. But I wouldn't trade the excitement of writing the column for any other job in the world. One *does* meet such interesting people, not to mention the bores, boors, and brutes who also inhabit my little world.

Many of the celebrities I write about have become deep, personal friends, and I like to feel that they would be my friends even if I didn't write the column. (I like to feel that way. I don't know that it is true.)

Bob Hope is among my closest friends in show business. I met "Ol' Ski Nose" through his press agent, Mack Millar, shortly after I started writing the column. Over the years Bob and I have discovered that we like many of the same things—travel, golf, football, night life, and playing benefits. And we like people who like travel, golf, football, night life, and playing benefits. I have traveled with Hope over a large part of the globe as he makes his annual Christmas tours to entertain our GIs.

Down through the years, I have developed friendships and acquaintances with most of the big names of show business, from A for Adams (Edie and Joey) to Z for Zimbalist (Efrem). Many of these have become close personal friends, which poses a problem for a columnist. Not all the items and references can be favorable. But a newspaperman must adhere to the philosophy that in almost all instances, his profession comes first, regardless of personal consequences. I have lost a few friends because of this ticklish problem. I hope I have gained the respect of many more. These relationships often involve my family. As readers of my column know, this includes my lovely, red-haired wife Essee; our twenty-year-old daughter Karyn, now an actress in Hollywood; and our seventeen-year-old son Jerry, a student in the East. When there is a career setback, marital breakup, or any other problem among our celebrity friends, we feel it deeply. We understand the tremendous conflicts and pressures under which most celebrities labor.

Essee, for example, was one of the late Diana Barrymore's dearest friends. She was one of the last to see alive this luckless member of the great acting family. It was during one of Essee's trips to New York to see Karyn, then appearing in a play in the East. Diana, after having apparently conquered alcoholism, suffered a relapse. The cooling of her romance with Tennessee Williams and the loss of a role on which she had set her heart, the lead in the touring company of *Sweet Bird of Youth*, were too much for her to combat. Other problems were piling up. At one time during this visit, she told Essee, "You're spending a week here with your daughter. Do you realize that's more than I spent with my mother in a lifetime?"

One of the last things Essee did before leaving Diana was to remove a drink from her hand. But for the "poor little rich girl" who revealed everything in her autobiography, it was too little too late. We never have forgotten her.

From the outside looking in, a columnist's job appears to be all glamour and glitter. It isn't. There is also a good deal of hard work. Considerable responsibility is involved in writing a big-city column. Aside from reporting gossip, quips, and anecdotes, the columnist should make an effort to educate and inform readers on the important problems of the day. A column must have a conscience, and the columnist should be willing to take a stand on important issues. In my column you will find considerable critical comment about racial and religious bigotry, whether it occurs in Chicago or Little Rock. You will find items defending freedom of expression. (For years I have fought against Chicago's notorious movie censorship.) You will also find items criticizing television for its failure to live up to its potentials. You will find me speaking out in favor of improved educational facilities, public health institutions, and prisons, even if this means higher taxation. And you will find me campaigning for tighter law enforcement— criticizing first those citizens who are so willing to corrupt policemen with bribes. And you will find me discussing the more intelligent approaches to our juvenile problems.

Another guideline, laid down by my first editor, Mr. Finnegan, is that a column, like a newspaper, must have a "heart." This means a willingness to take time to help the less fortunate members of society, the sick and the poor. In the past two decades the list of causes in "Kup's Column" has been, I think, a lengthy one. It includes veterans' welfare, funds to further medical research and to help the widows and children of firemen and policemen. Hundreds of thousands of dollars have been raised through the column, with the help of various show-business celebrities.

Chicago is a big and bustling city. I am only one human being (though at six foot one, weighing 210, a large one). How can I possibly cover it and the rest of my beat, which extends to the Sputniks and beyond?

It's a race, and it usually goes like this:

Every morning at 7:30 I get a wake-up call from the *Sun-Times* switchboard. My apartment, near Lincoln Park on the North Side, is a ninth-floor hideaway of nine rooms, containing eleven phones, four TV sets, a paneled den with bar and bamboo stools, three walls covered with celebrities' pictures, a slot machine (for homesick guests from Las Vegas), a dining room which is a replica of a Pump Room booth, and a hall desk with typewriter for unhappy moments of homework.

By 9:00 A.M. I have showered, shaved, breakfasted, digested the morning *Tribune* and *Sun-Times* (I always find one more digestible than the other), and am heading by taxi for the *Sun-Times-Daily News* Building, at Wabash Avenue and the Chicago River. (Cabbies, incidentally, are among my favorite people and are among the best barometers of man-on-the-street opinion.) I once jokingly described my office as "the only one in town that goes up and down with the Wabash Avenue Bridge." Actually, it is on solid ground, a windowless, two-room layout just off the paper's fourth-floor city room. It's furnished with a leather sofa, TV set, bookshelf, desk, typewriter, and two secretaries: brunette Connie Chancellor, ex-wife of NBC-TV's John (*Today*) Chancellor, and her part-time assistant, blonde Sharon Stelmok, a Northwestern University journalism student.

Awaiting my arrival is a mountain of morning mail, which I sift through as quickly as possible. Next comes a reading of a tear sheet of that day's column, in which I circle various names, especially those of out-of-towners who may not have seen the paper. Each is sent a clipping, a gesture I consider both a courtesy and an aid in maintaining out-of-town contacts which can lead to further column items. This is only one of the four or five daily readings I give the column, for proofreading, updating, or plain self-criticism. (There's not a time when I read it that I don't see how some item could have been sharpened.)

Meanwhile the phone rings incessantly. It may be a celebrity or public official or private citizen with a gripe or tip, a press agent (I must be on the list of ten thousand or more) calling with a potential item, a reader wanting to chat or comment on something. No matter how busy I am or who the caller is, whenever possible I take time to talk. This also is a time when I'm placing calls to Washington, New York, Hollywood, or other points, running down likely stories based on tips, newspaper articles, or items I've picked up on the previous night's rounds. It is not unusual for me to make a couple of dozen long-distance calls a day.

A word about press agents and public-relations men. They are either a columnist's best friend—or worst enemy. Since I do my own reporting, with no "leg men" to assist me, I couldn't begin to cover Chicago and the rest of my beat without the tips and short cuts provided by press agents. They can arrange interviews, call attention to newsworthy items, give important background information, and perform other valuable functions. The great majority do. But inevitably there is a minority who are the bane of a harried columnist's existence. They are the ones who try to plant phony or misleading tips, or supply self-aggrandizing blurbs for publicity-hungry clients seeking a place in the *Sun-Times*. At worst they try to ingratiate themselves by providing witty quotes and quips which are fine—except that they have already appeared somewhere else. Because it is impossible for me to read regularly columns of such colleagues as Earl Wilson, Ed Sullivan, and Hy Gardner in New York, Herb Caen in San Francisco, or Hedda Hopper, Louella Parsons, and Mike Connolly in Hollywood, periodically a press agent manages to palm off as original an excerpt from these various columns. The columnist thus plagiarized has justifiable cause to be miffed. I feel the same when my material turns up elsewhere without credit. When this happens, the press agent himself is the ultimate loser. Once he is pegged as a lifter, he is never trusted again.

Indispensable are those silent heroes, the "amateur" quipsters whose material never stops flowing. One of the best known is Ivan Bunny. Ivan actually is two brothers named Jimmy and Ivan Colitz. Each night they sit down at a typewriter and knock out gags for my column. (Ivan, an auto parts supervisor, wrote professionally at one time for the old Buddy Lester TV show in Chicago.) Al Hamburg, an old high school classmate of mine, is another regular. So are Alex Baruch, South Bend, Indiana, businessman; advertising executive Gil Stern; the pioneer radio announcer Quin Ryan; comedian Jack Herbert; and Sam Tunick, a druggist. (It's easy for me to spot Sam's quips. Every one arrives on a post card.) These wits do it all for laughs—and the pleasure of seeing the best of their material in print.

My deadline for the next morning's first edition is 1:00 P.M. So no later than 11:30 A.M. comes the moment of truth: time to put the column together. Writing, according to my literate friend Red Smith, consists of "placing a blank page in the typewriter and concentrating until little drops of blood appear on your forehead." To me that is no exaggeration. Though I have met more than five thousand column deadlines, I still cannot pull up my swivel chair and bat out the next day's piece with ease. Sometimes getting the words to fall into place is harder than it was for the first column in 1943. I must limit myself to approximately a thousand words and I have always three or four times that amount of material.

I start by making an outline. For each of the nine paragraphs into which the column is divided I earmark the material I think will best develop a smooth continuity. As a rule, the most striking news comes first; a variety of other items follows in the form of quotes, quips, and information about people and places and events; for the finale I choose what I think is the day's best chuckle, in keeping with the old show-business adage, "Always leave 'em laughing." As each paragraph is completed, my secretary checks names for accuracy and sends it off to the copy desk. By 1:00 P.M., wiping the last drops of blood from my forehead, I'm finished.

Then I'm off in pursuit of more material, beginning with a lunch date at Fritzel's, the Tavern Club, or the Pump Room, or a special luncheon or meeting elsewhere. With the help of the headwaiter (another indispensable friend of columnists) I learn who's who for the day, interviewing by phone if I can't make the scene in person. Then it's into the Kupcinet Mambo, table-hopping to buttonhole as many news sources as possible, with time out to greet old friends and fans. In talking, listening, handshaking, and exchanging quips, somehow the news and witticisms pile up. The most interesting I commit to a pocket pad (I fill six a week). But to avoid intruding on conversations, my pencil often doesn't go into action until I'm behind a pillar, or in a taxi, phone booth, or men's room.

At three I'm back in the office to check the final galley proof of the column. Then it's interviews, more phoning, correspondence, and endless miscellany. As other columnists can testify, outsiders have little idea about the ramifications of our job. We need every friend and contact we can make. But friendship is a two-way street. If someone has gone out of his way to help me in an emergency, I naturally will do the same for him, within bounds that won't compromise my integrity. This may involve getting an item of information, arranging an introduction to someone, or doing even more complicated favors. Once a very good friend

phoned from New York and explained that his party hoped to
see Sammy Davis, Jr., at the Copacabana, but couldn't get a
reservation. I called Sammy in New York, and he arranged for
installation of an extra table for my friend.

At 5:00 P.M., with the morning's first edition up from the
pressroom, I pause to give my column another reading. By 6:00,
unless there is a reception or cocktail party to attend, I'm en
route home for dinner, a monitoring of any TV shows of special
interest, and an hour's nap.

About 10:00 P.M. I dress. Then, with or without Essee, depending on how she feels, I begin the evening rounds. The
Pump Room, Chicago's mecca for celebrities, usually comes first.
An hour or two later we're off again. The Chez Paree, alas, is
no more, but there is plenty of life on Rush Street and in the
dining rooms of downtown hotels with floor shows. I'm seldom
home before two or three in the morning. Once there, I spend
some time reading—it might be the two morning newspapers, or
Time, Life, Look, and *Newsweek,* or one of the books on Abraham
Lincoln, current history, and biography, which are always on my
night stand.

Saturday nights I'm out even later than usual. My TV shows
do not end until 3:00 or 4:00 A.M., after which I take my guests
to breakfast—at the intimate Club Alabam, perhaps, or the
Singapore, two of my favorite places. With a Monday column to
check I do not get much extra sleep on Sundays, and even less
during the football season. My broadcasts of the Bears' games
take me from coast to coast, which can mean that I have to catch
an early-morning jet. When that happens I may get no sleep at all.

With this schedule, when is there time for family life?

This worried my first boss, the late *Times* publisher, S. Emory
Thomason. "Everything okay at home?" he'd ask when we met.
"Be sure you spend enough time with your family." Following
his advice was not easy, but by developing such habits as eating
dinner at home almost every night, I've managed to enjoy some
family life, too. Long ago my family became accustomed to my
routine, and to such quirks as my eating dinner in pajamas.

The pajamas habit is the result of a tip from Lou Lurie, ex-Chicago newsboy who made a fortune in real estate and now is known as "Mr. San Francisco."

"When you've been going at a fast pace," he told me, years ago, "get into pajamas as soon as you get home, and don't get dressed again until you have to. You'll feel much more relaxed." It works.

Sounds like a whirl? Or a grind?

It's both. But it is the only way I know to get that column in the newspaper every morning with all the gossip, entertainment, conscience, and heart it deserves. And it is the only way to keep up with Chicago, a city that never sleeps.

2. Capone to the Cardinal

When Chicago became a town in 1833, there were thirteen voters. Twelve voted to incorporate, one was opposed. That's typical—in Chicago there is always an individualist in the crowd. "Independent as a hog on ice" is how Carl Sandburg described it. This spirit of individualism, part of our frontier heritage, is a vital factor in making the city what it is. And what it is, according to the detractors, is merely a 225-square-mile steel and concrete lump on the prairie. But according to one of our favorite sons, writer John Bartlow Martin, now United States Ambassador to the Dominican Republic, Chicago, celebrating its 125th anniversary as a city in 1962, is "the most American of cities."

What makes Chicago special? What does it have that other cities lack?

Nothing. The ingredients are common—but the proportions are different. And, as the Frenchman said, "Vive la différence!" A unique blend of bigness, smallness, brashness, reserve, refinement, and naughtiness, found nowhere else in the world—is Chicago.

It's a city with a stimulating, friendly, going-places atmosphere.

It's a city where things happen: election triumphs and public frauds; political conventions dating from the time of Abraham Lincoln to that of Richard M. Nixon; legendary courtroom

33

scenes, such as Clarence Darrow's impassioned defense of young Nathan Leopold and Richard Loeb; celebrated sports events— including a few scandals, such as the Dempsey-Tunney "long count" or the "Say it ain't so, Joe" Black Sox World Series; revolutionary breakthroughs in scientific fields, such as Lee De Forest's basic inventions in electronics, or the first controlled nuclear coups; and horrible disasters, such as the Great Chicago Fire of 1871, the Iroquois Theater fire of 1903, and the fire that killed 93 children at Our Lady of Angels School in 1958.

But events don't make a city. People do. They are what shapes Chicago's personality and reputation. They are the daily grist for my reportorial mill—and the heroes and heroines of this book.

As befits a city of individualists, there has been an unending parade of interesting people—the "Robber Barons" of the Gilded Age; John "Bet-a-Million" Gates, the steel-and-wire magnate who would literally bet a million dollars on a decision or a card game; saloonkeeper Mickey Finn, whose knockout drink could stiffen a customer for three days; the Everleigh Sisters, possibly the two most genteel madames in the history of vice; and George Wellington ("Cap") Streeter, the steamboat captain who ran aground off the present Gold Coast, and for thirty years enforced a squatter's claim to all land that filled in around him for his own private "District of Lake Michigan."

The Streeter story could have happened only in Chicago. It all began in 1886 when Streeter, trying out a boat with which he planned to run guns to South American revolutionists, hit a sandbar. When he discovered the craft could not be budged, he immediately decided to change from gunrunner into houseboat-dweller. In time, sediment began to form a link between his craft and the shore, and Cap Streeter got an idea that he thought might be even more lucrative than gunrunning. He would claim this "new" land, and all other shoreline formed since 1821, when the State boundaries were established by an official survey which showed the water line to have been much farther inland. He named this strip of beach "The District of Lake Michigan," proclaimed himself the official owner, and appointed a friend of his as

military governor. Asserting that the new territory lay completely
outside of all Federal, State, county, or municipal jurisdiction,
Streeter proceeded to parcel out his claim into lots for sale to
speculators.

Chicago officials of those days tolerated a great deal, but
this was too much. In 1889, five men were sent to oust Streeter,
but the captain, brandishing his rifle, chased them back across
what he called "the city limits." As a result, Streeter was haled
into court. The case dragged on and on. Several policemen, who
were trying on their own initiative to evict the captain, were
doused with scalding water by his wife. Streeter next rallied an
army of friendly drunks and hobos and set up barricades of drift-
wood which it took five hundred policemen to storm. And still
Streeter went free—until the day he defied newly elected mayor
Big Bill Thompson by selling whisky on Sunday. In 1916 police
burned down his shack, and "The District of Lake Michigan" was
finally conquered by the City of Chicago and the State of Illinois.

But these are characters of the past. There is as wide a
variety of fascinating people in Chicago's present—men and
women who continue to maintain *"la différence"* between Our
Town and the rest of the nation. They are the ones I would like
you to meet. Each Friday the thirteenth, for example, a cross
section of eminent Chicagoans meets at the Chicago Athletic
Club or some other downtown site. Among the members are
judges, politicians, businessmen, and sports figures. The name of
this organization: The Anti-Superstition Society. Its purpose: To
spoof silly superstitions and prejudices in any way that comes to
mind. Some members enter the meeting room carrying open
umbrellas. Others walk under ladders, or smash mirrors with
horseshoes, or light three cigarettes on a match. I am fortunate
enough to merit a special distinction in the group: I am the
thirteenth vice-president. I can personally testify that regardless
of what superstition we defy, none of us has been struck by a
lightning bolt yet. (Unless, of course, we travel on an airplane
with Bob Hope.)

And then there are our "little guys," who would do any city
proud. There is Joe Swedie, a factory worker who spends evenings

and weekends showing movies to children in hospitals. There is
Eddie Hamilton, Checker Cabby No. 5000, who offers his passengers free coffee, cigarettes, newspapers, and other comforts
while he cheerfully describes the sights of Chicago—which proves
that no matter what your station in life, a little initiative can
enhance it. And there is Dwight Guilfoil, Jr., a recent "Handicapped American of the Year." Dwight is restricted to a wheel-
chair, but he is the co-founder of a growing electronics firm,
Paraplegics, Inc., which employs other handicapped persons.

There are our eccentrics, such as Lar ("America First") Daly,
the small-businessman who perennially campaigns for office dressed
in an Uncle Sam costume. (He turned up on the Jack Paar Show
in 1960, leading to the revision of broadcasting's equal-time
political rule.) And Jack Muller, the publicity-loving policeman
who enjoys ticketing celebrities' cars and calling newspapers to
announce it. (He has been transferred to a beat where the main
territory is a graveyard.)

There is our high society: the Armours, the Swifts, the Hur-
leys, the Gurleys, and the other blue bloods of Lake Shore
Drive and Astor Street, Lake Forest, Winnetka, and Hinsdale.
They may sponsor debutante cotillions and yacht parties, but
they also endow our universities and colleges, our hospitals and
museums, our Art Institute, Chicago Symphony, Lyric Opera,
and other community assets. They are looked down on by society
in New York and New England and looked up to by the "400" of
St. Louis, Milwaukee, Minneapolis, and other cities of the
Midwest. Many of them winter in the Caribbean and summer on
the Riviera, but for such special gala events as the 1959 St.
Lawrence Seaway visit of Queen Elizabeth II and Prince Philip,
they flock back to Chicago to put on their finery and dance (the
royal reception was in the Conrad Hilton). A handful frequent
the local café society circuit: Jim Kimberly of the paper empire,
Mollie Netcher Bostwick (formerly Bragno) of Chicago's old
Boston Store family, and sportsman Fred Wacker. But the average
Chicagoan rarely sees the glamorous elite as they make their
social rounds.

For all of us who admire beautiful women, this is no small

loss. Many Chicago society wives, including Mrs. Charles Percy, Mrs. Leon Mandel, Mrs. John McGuire, Mrs. Charles Comiskey, and Mrs. Homer Hargrave, Jr., could pass for high fashion models— and prove it regularly, when they appear as volunteer mannequins at the annual Presbyterian-St. Luke's Fashion Show and other exclusive benefits. Many could win contracts as glamour girls. As a matter of fact, many have. Chicago boasts a colony of former actresses of which these names are only a sampling: Colleen Moore (Mrs. Homer Hargrave, Sr.), Martha O'Driscoll (Mrs. Arthur Appleton), Brenda Forbes (Mrs. Merrill Shepard), Colleen Miller (Mrs. Ted Briskin), June Travis (Mrs. Fred Friedlob), Jarma Lewis (Mrs. Ted Bensinger), Linda Cristol (Mrs. Yale Wexler), Edith Luckett (Mrs. Loyal Davis), and skating star Barbara Ann Scott (Mrs. Thomas Van Dyke King).

Barbara Ann, incidentally, still receives dozens of movie, TV, and ice-show offers. But she is the domestic type (her traveling trunk used to include kitchen utensils), and prefers life away from the spotlight. She spends her time operating a beauty salon in suburban Glencoe and cooking for her husband, an ex-Chicago Stadium publicist, who is now number two man in the front office of Joseph P. Kennedy's Merchandise Mart. Her occasional absent-mindedness has earned her the affectionate household nickname of "Gracie."

And then Chicago has its geniuses who are internationally prominent in their professions.

In medicine you will find such notables as Dr. Karl Meyer, head of the huge Cook County Hospital; Dr. Loyal Davis, famed brain surgeon and former president of the American College of Surgeons. And the researchers and specialists at such hospitals as Passavant, Wesley, and Northwestern University's professional schools on the Near North Side, Michael Reese and the University of Chicago clinics on the South, and Presbyterian-St. Luke's, the University of Illinois College of Medicine, and others in the vast West Side Medical Center complex. And the executives of such Chicago-based organizations as the American Medical Association, the International College of Surgeons, the American Hospital Association, and Blue Cross-Blue Shield.

Among the most remarkable of the medical fraternity is Dr.
Morris Fishbein, former spokesman for the American Medical
Association. Ignoring both the clock and calendar, Morris, who
is in his seventies, reads ten books every week and still finds
time to work regularly on one of his own, plays bridge and gin
rummy, supports cultural pursuits ranging from opera to the
Museum of Science and Industry, and takes an active role in three
dozen organizations.

As the home of the American Bar Association and of such
distinguished law schools as De Paul, Northwestern, the University
of Chicago, and Kent College, and as the place where some of
the nation's most significant civil and criminal cases are tried,
it is only natural that Chicago should have an abundance of
noted legal talent.

The Chicago bar includes eminent barristers whose names make
headlines in cases involving everything from corporate affairs
to divorce—Weymouth Kirkland, Albert Jenner, William Kirby,
Stanford Clinton, Russell Topper, Donald Ruben, Harry Busch,
James Dooley, Harold Smith, George Crowley, Frank (Spike)
McAdams, Ben Davis, Edward Rothbart, William Boyden,
Donald Page Moore, Thomas O'Connell, A. Bradley Eben, Norm
Becker, David Levinson, and Arthur Friedlund. It includes Sid
Korshak, whose income from representing Hollywood stars and
other prominent personages is reputed to exceed $700,000 a year,
which makes him probably the number one legal fee-earner in the
nation. It includes such famous criminal lawyers as George Bieber
and Michael Brodkin, known as "B and B," and Charles Bellows.
And Arthur Morse, who is also "father" of college double-header
basketball in Chicago, as well as operator of the Edgewater Beach
Playhouse; and Luis Kutner, who has won release for a number of
wrongly imprisoned men. And William Scott Stewart, the last of a
colorful old school which enlivened Chicago courtrooms for many
years—a group which included Clarence Darrow, Ben Short, W.
W. Smith, George Gunther, Emmett Byrne, and "Ropes" O'Brien.
("Ropes" won that sobriquet for being the assistant state's attorney who sent more men to the gallows than any other prosecutor
of his time.)

Then there is the science field. Big news has come out of the research centers at our universities. It was at the University of Chicago, beneath the grandstand of Stagg Field, that the first uranium reactor was built by the late Enrico Fermi and his brilliant team. (The original atomic pile is buried now and the staff has moved to suburban Argonne National Laboratory, which the university supervises for the Atomic Energy Commission.) Also prominent is the Armour Research Foundation of the Illinois Institute of Technology. The third largest independent, nonprofit research and development lab in the nation, it is a leader in research in rocket fuels, noise abatement and acoustics, ceramics and metals, and the chemical effects of nuclear radiation. I.I.T. holds almost every major patent for the tape recorder. And in this field you will find such well-known pharmaceutical houses as suburban Abbott Laboratories and the safety-testing Underwriters Laboratories.

Two of Our Town's best-known chemists: Dr. Percy Julian, who helped alleviate the suffering of millions through his role in developing cortisone, but who was almost denied free choice of a home in Oak Park because he is a Negro; and octogenarian Otto Eisenschiml, the oil-products researcher, who also is a best-selling Civil War author. With Ralph G. Newman of the Abraham Lincoln Book Shop and other Chicagoans, he helped found the first of the now widely distributed Civil War Round Tables. (Newman, incidentally, with his vast historical knowledge of that period, helps me each February to create one of the most popular "specialties" of my column, a report of a simulated visit with Abe Lincoln on his birthday to obtain his views on past and present affairs.)

Education is another field in which Chicago has distinguished itself, not only in quality, but in quantity. There are 18,000 teachers and 450,000 students in the public schools alone. The Roman Catholic Archdiocese of Chicago administers the largest parochial school system in the nation. And thousands study in the city's dozens of private schools, colleges, seminaries, and universities.

It was here, at the University of Chicago, that the late John Dewey, "Mr. Progressive Education," did some of his most important work. And here also where, a generation later, Dewey's most publicized modern critic, Admiral Hyman G. Rickover, studied in the public high schools. And it is here where Robert M. Hutchins, former "boy wonder" Chancellor of the University of Chicago, tried accepting as collegians bright young students with only two years of high school. (Like football, this program for prodigies no longer is part of the University's policy.) Hutchins's chair is now occupied by Dr. George Wells Beadle, Nobel prize-winning geneticist.

Among the many other important educators are Dr. J. Roscoe Miller, president of Northwestern University; Edward J. Sparling, founder and president of Roosevelt University; Dr. John T. Rettaliata, president of the Illinois Institute of Technology; the Very Reverend C. J. O'Malley, president of De Paul University; the Very Reverend J. F. Maguire, president of Loyola University; and Superintendent of Public Schools Benjamin Willis, who once studied in a one-room school in Maryland and is now the second highest-paid public official in the nation.

In the field of religion, there is Chicago's Mahalia Jackson, a former scrubwoman who is now queen of the gospel singers. She has performed in two hemispheres for kings, presidents, and SRO audiences. But she still lives in a South Side bungalow and sings at her home church, Greater Salem Baptist, at Thirtieth and LaSalle.

Many Chicago men of the cloth have achieved national prominence, including my own rabbi, Dr. Louis Binstock, of Temple Sholom. Among those who are widely respected as leaders in their field are Dr. Preston Bradley, Peoples Church radio minister and author, who just celebrated his fiftieth anniversary in the pulpit; soon-to-retire Rabbi Louis Mann of Sinai Temple, who was a founder of both the National Conference of Christians and Jews and the Hillel Foundation youth organization, which has spread to 239 college campuses; Episcopal Bishop Charles Burrill; Roman Catholic Albert Gregory Cardinal Meyer; and Auxiliary Archbishop Bernard J. Sheil, founder of the Catholic Youth Organization. A gifted athlete who turned down a White Sox contract to enter the priesthood, Archbishop Sheil once, early in his career, had the painful duty of accompanying a former neighbor to the gallows. "Can't someone help people like me *before* we've gone wrong?" the criminal asked. The young priest's answer was the Catholic Youth Organization.

Incidentally, the Roman Catholic Archdiocese of Chicago is the nation's largest. It is greatly to Cardinal Meyer's credit that he has found means to pursue the far-reaching program of helping to integrate into the mainstream of Chicago life the newly arrived Mexicans, Cubans, and Puerto Ricans. That was begun by his predecessor, the late Samuel Cardinal Stritch. Under Cardinal Meyer the program has been expanded to include help for the new arrivals in obtaining jobs, housing, and English language instruction. "If the community shows it cares," he says, "then the newcomers will care about the community." It is an effort other large melting pot centers well might emulate.

And these are only a few of the personalities that make Chicago so exciting. LaSalle Street, State Street, and other business centers harbor some of the nation's most powerful figures in commerce and industry, in labor and management.

These include such union leaders as Bill McFetridge of the Building Service Employes, Bill Lee, Chicago Federation of Labor president, Pat Greathouse of United Auto Workers, Joseph Germano of United Steel Workers, Pat Gorman of the Butchers' Union, and the Musicians' Music Man himself, James Caesar Petrillo.

Although he is now retired from the battles of his American Federation of Musicians, Jimmy Petrillo is still head of Chicago Local No. 10. For many years he was one of the city's—and the nation's—political powerhouses. I vividly remember watching the tough behind-the-scenes convention battle he waged on behalf of Harry S. Truman in 1948, when most of the Democratic Party wanted to get off the Truman bandwagon. But in union affairs Petrillo had no political favorites. One year he threatened to work for the defeat of *any* candidate who used sound trucks instead of live musicians, and he made it clear that his threat applied to *either* party. The political bandwagon had to have a union band.

Despite his tough exterior, Jimmy has revealed a tender heart by sponsoring such activities as an annual Christmas party for the blind at the Sheraton-Blackstone Hotel. For twenty-five years these sightless party guests have been the only ones to "see" Petrillo perform on his favorite instrument, the trumpet, which he learned to play at Hull House.

There is a rumored eccentricity of Petrillo's which I'll confirm. Due to a deathly fear of germs, he shakes hands only by extending a pinky. A perfect "sound-alike" for James Caesar Petrillo is his younger brother, WBBM's musical director (and ardent baseball fan), Caesar James Petrillo.

Then there are the managerial tycoons who have helped to make Chicago the giant of commerce and industry that it is.

You probably know some of the great names from the city's past—Marshall Field, Philip D. Armour, Gustavus Swift, George M. Pullman, Cyrus H. McCormick, Potter Palmer, A. Montgomery Ward, Richard Sears, Alva Roebuck—and yes, Samuel Insull, the light-and-power emperor whose domain crashed under fraud charges in 1931.

These were the momentous names of a momentous age. They built Chicago's railroads, factories, and office buildings. They pulled in its tides of immigrants from farms and foreign countries. They shipped its products around the world.

Whatever they did, they did it big. George Pullman not only built railroad cars, but hired 600 men with 6,000 jacks to raise whole blocks of Loop buildings four feet above the swampy muck, to provide solid footings for the construction of sidewalks—without halting business in any of the structures. Potter Palmer, whose wife was an international society queen, moved the retail center from Lake to State Street and crowned it with a hotel so elegant that the barbershop was paved with silver dollars. Sam Insull, once Thomas A. Edison's private secretary, conceived and built the modern light-and-power business. And McCormick's International Harvester mechanized the farm belt.

"Make no little plans," advised architect Daniel H. Burnham, who planned the city's magnificent park and boulevard system— and Chicagoans never have. Even our civic parasites operated on the grand scale—transportation magnate Charles Yerkes, for one, once tried to slip a $500,000 bribe to a governor of Illinois (and got nowhere). But the sharp promoters were eclipsed by the legitimate builders. A. Montgomery Ward spent hundreds of thousands of dollars in a thirteen-year court battle to preserve the city's lakefront for public use. Julius Rosenwald, of Sears, Roebuck, gave away $63,000,000 for such causes as the Museum of Science and Industry and subsidized five thousand American schools for Negroes.

The big-time spenders are gone now. In fact, wealth and power are spread so thin that it took a *Fortune* magazine survey to reveal to most Chicagoans that one of the nation's richest men is in our midst: John D. MacArthur, owner of Bankers Life & Casualty Company and the youngest of a famous quartet of brothers (the late playwright Charles; Alfred, head of Central Standard Life Insurance Company; and the late Telfer, a suburban newspaper publisher). MacArthur went into business during the Depression, with a capital of $2,500. Since then, he has mail-peddled so many policies at a dollar a month that Bankers Life is now the largest company in its field, owned lock, stock, and fine print by one man. His personal fortune amounts to more than two hundred million dollars.

Yet, despite his tremendous success, John has the reputation of being an eccentric and a tightwad. An eccentric, maybe; a tightwad, no. This I found out when Patrick Hoy, then president of the Ambassador-Sherman Hotels, and I were involved in a fund-raising effort for the George Bernard Shaw Society, one of Chicago's cultural activities. We needed $10,000 immediately. Everyone said that John MacArthur was the last man in town to approach with such a problem, but we decided to take a chance and invite him to join us for lunch in a swank Loop restaurant. MacArthur accepted. And at the appointed time he turned up— wearing an old sweater, baggy pants, and sneakers. Hoy had to use all his influence with the *maître d'hôtel* to obtain a table for this seedy-looking multimillionaire.

(And, after listening to our tale of woe, MacArthur—without a second's hesitation—pledged the necessary $10,000.)

About as wealthy as MacArthur, if not so unconventional, is printing magnate John Cuneo, owner of the Cuneo Press, one of the world's largest printing firms. He is also directly or indirectly in control of many other large corporations, including the National Tea Company. His home—the former Samuel Insull estate, near suburban Libertyville—is one of the showplaces of the State, and the Hawthorn-Mellody Farms Dairy, which is part of it, features one of the most popular zoos in the Chicago area. Cuneo's interests range all the way from business to art, from horsemanship to philanthropy. (He is a Knight of Malta, an honor reserved for individuals distinguished for their activities in Roman Catholic charity work.)

Not many men today are able to lay down the money to set up a huge institution single-handed, as did John D. Rockefeller for the University of Chicago, A. Watson Armour for the Illinois Institute of Technology, or Sears, Roebuck's Max Adler for the lakefront planetarium named for him. But that does not mean that Chicago businessmen are not still research- and education-minded. Only recently, in fact, a committee of Chicago businessmen, led by Chairman David M. Kennedy of the Continental Illinois National Bank, joined with union, educational, and city government officials in organizing a major study of one of the most pressing economic problems of the day—automation. This nationally significant study is the first of its kind to be initiated by a major city. Combining the talents and facilities of the Association of Commerce & Industry, the City Department of Planning, and the Armour Research Foundation of the Illinois Institute of Technology, it is being financed by funds raised largely from such local sources as the People's Gas, Light & Coke Company, Harris Trust and Savings Bank, and the Inland Steel-Ryerson Foundation.

One of the most dramatic demonstrations of this nonconformity came last spring after Chairman Roger Blough of the United States Steel Corporation announced his firm was raising steel prices by $6.00 a ton. One by one, major steel firms also raised their prices. But Chairman Joseph L. Block of Inland Steel Company, the nation's eighth largest steel producer, refused to follow the lead. Vacationing in Japan, he told Chicago *Daily News* correspondent Keyes Beech:

"Even though steel profits are not adequate, we do not feel an advance in steel prices at this time would be in the national interest."

It is this type of independence which has made Inland executives known as community leaders in Chicago, which has given Inland a record of having lost money in only one year (1933) since its founding in 1893, and which led to a retraction of Big Steel's price increase, and one of President Kennedy's most gratifying moments. Joe Block's brother Leigh and his cousin Philip are equally independent as Inland vice-presidents.

This nonconformity also is a reason why the Chicago phone book lists page after page of headquarters for firms whose names have become nationally famous: Kraft, Libby, Quaker Oats, National Tea, Morton Salt, Curtiss, and Wrigley in food products; Motorola, Zenith, Admiral, Webcor, and many more in electronics; Toni, Helene Curtis, Murine, Maybelline, and Alberto-Culver in cosmetics; Bell & Howell and Revere in cameras; Rand McNally, R. R. Donnelley, Cuneo Press, A. N. Marquis (*Who's Who*), and W. F. Hall in printing and publishing; the Burlington Route, Sante Fe, Chicago & North Western in railroading. There, too, are United Air Lines, Fairbanks Whitney Company, Western Electric, Sunbeam, and Hotpoint—even Reuben H. Donnelley, judge of more big-money contests than any other agency.

And it may be why Chicago businessmen are so prominent in government and public service. And why Chicago television sponsors are noted for their excellent programing—Charles Percy, the "boy wonder" chief executive of Bell & Howell, for his documentaries and "think" shows; Bill Gage, of Magikist Services and Products, with Bishop Fulton J. Sheen; and Charles Lubin of the Kitchens of Sara Lee, for classical music and adult drama. Or why Hart Schaffner & Marx, under the late Meyer Kestnbaum, set an outstanding record for good labor-management relations in a fast-changing industry—more than fifty years without a strike. And it is why such men as Brooks (International Harvester) McCormick, of the blue-blood McCormicks, willingly take time to head demanding civic projects. In 1961, thanks to McCormick's talent and hard work, Chicago's annual Crusade of Mercy campaign exceeded its record goal of fifteen million dollars.

You will seldom find Chicagoans making their fortunes in gold, uranium, or wildcat oil wells. It's the better mousetrap and the better way of manufacturing and marketing it that is their specialty.

Nathaniel Leverone, for example, missed an El train once and discovered there were no dependable vending machines on the platform. So he started the Automatic Canteen Company.

General Robert E. Wood, fired from Montgomery Ward & Company for pushing the "radical" idea of operating a chain of retail stores, in addition to the established mail-order trade, sold Sears, Roebuck's board of directors on his idea. Today, Sears, Roebuck is number one in its field. Being number one was nothing new to General Wood. As a young officer, he had played a leading role in construction of the Panama Canal. In World War I, he served as acting chief of the Army Quartermaster Corps—during that time he handled more underwear than did Sears, Roebuck and Montgomery Ward combined. Today he still is number one in his devotion to the Boys Clubs of America, of which he is a chief supporter.

The mail-order business, incidentally, has provided more than its share of colorful Chicagoans. The late Sewell Avery of Montgomery Ward was one of the best known and most controversial. For years, Avery's business philosophy of retrenchment was tested against General Wood's policy of expansion. It was Ward against Sears, providing a battle of giants—fascinating to us on the sidelines. In the end, the results were conclusive: Wood was right, and Sears outdistanced its rival. A rugged individualist of the old school, Avery will long be remembered for the famous World War II newspaper photograph which showed him being carried bodily from his plant by soldiers after he refused to obey a government order to relinquish wartime control of his business. The caption for the photo was equally famous—"This Is the Army, Mr. Avery."

William Wood Prince, heir of Union Stock Yards' Frederick Prince, foresaw changes in the meat industry in time to make his

Armour & Company a leader in diversifying into soaps and other products.

And Adolph Kroch, a great bibliophile, together with his able son, Carl, applied supermarket and modern business principles to hard-cover and paperback book-retailing and became America's number one bookseller.

But it is probably the late Albert Lasker, the father of modern advertising, who has had the most conspicuous effect on the American economy. Lasker, who headed the Lord & Thomas advertising agency, was the first to introduce highly focused description and "sell" into advertising copy.

Through his efforts, dozens of trade names became household words overnight—including "Lucky Strike," "Pepsodent," Kleenex," "Palmolive," "Sunkist," and "Frigidaire." He launched the first major soap opera, and did much to make radio what it was in its golden era, with such drama shows as Mr. *District Attorney*, the long-popular *Your Hit Parade*, and a number of top comedy hours, led by the Bob Hope show for Pepsodent.

One of Bob's favorite Lasker stories is about an exchange he had with the adman in the first week of that show. It seems that Lasker was so impressed with Bob's first broadcast that he suggested that the comedian's original $4,000-a-week contract be raised to $6,000. One of Lasker's assistants rushed up to Bob with the happy news. Robert, ever alert to a good thing, decided to see just how much the traffic would bear, so he replied:

"Tell him thanks, but I'd be very unhappy if the figure weren't $8,000."

When this message was relayed to Lasker, the adman snapped:

"Tell him to be unhappy at $4,000 a week!" and with that, he canceled the raise.

(Lasker later became a good friend of Hope's, but Bob has never forgotten the afternoon he fast-talked himself out of $2,000 a week.)

But as John Gunther has so aptly noted in his biography of Lasker, *Taken at the Flood*, building up a huge advertising agency was only one of the many interests of this Midwestern marvel. Lasker was once part owner of the Chicago Cubs with William

Wrigley, to whom he later sold out. He was instrumental in getting Judge Kenesaw Mountain Landis named Commissioner of Baseball and Will Hays appointed Hollywood movie czar. He assembled one of the great private art collections in America. And through the Albert and Mary Lasker Foundation and the annual Albert Lasker Medical Journalism Awards he has posthumously contributed to advanced medical research.

Among the most prominent of the many famous Lasker trainees is William Benton, once U. S. Senator from Connecticut and now back in Chicago as chairman of the board of the *Encyclopaedia Britannica*, which is edited and published here. In 1921, while Benton was still a Yale undergraduate, he resolved to become a millionaire by the age of thirty-five. Later, after he had worked as Lasker's right-hand man for a time, he faced the boss with a startling question.

"Am I worth enough to you to merit a raise to $50,000 a year?" Benton asked.

"You are," said Lasker. "The raise is yours."

"Then if I'm worth that much to you, I should be worth twice that much to myself," Benton replied. Whereupon he resigned, joined Chester Bowles, organized the Benton & Bowles advertising agency, and reached his million-dollar goal with ease.

Lasker's successor at Lord & Thomas, Fairfax Cone, reorganized the agency as Foote, Cone & Belding. "Fax" is another titan in the field. As shown by his recent speeches on the advertiser's responsibility in helping to upgrade TV programing, he is not afraid to level constructive criticism at his own, sensitive profession. He is also a practice-what-you-preach leader in civic affairs, who has served on Our Town's Board of Education and headed the Community Fund's Crusade of Mercy drive, which won him a "Chicagoan of the Year" award.

Such men as Lasker and Cone—and Freeman Keyes, Mel Brorby, Ed Weiss, Will Grant, George ("There's a Ford in your future") Reeves, and Leo (apples in the reception room) Burnett —have put Chicago agencies in the billion-dollar-a-year class in billings. Chicago's Adman's Row is second only to New York's Madison Avenue.

(Burnett, incidentally, is the 1962-63 president of the Advertising Council, a national, nonprofit organization set up by the industry for public service. "Fax" Cone headed the Council in 1951-52.)

But are today's tycoons mere shadows of those of the "good old days"?

Perhaps they are not as spectacular as some of the great many individualists who preceded them, but as you'll see if you follow me through several present-day executive suites, they are scarcely a line-up of nobodies.

There is J. Patrick Lannan, whose Susquehanna Corporation has won control of such interests as Crowell-Collier and The Macmillan Company, the Milwaukee Road, and Minneapolis-Moline. Lannan's apartments in Chicago, Palm Beach, and New York house one of the finest private art collections in the country. He is also a serious collector of literary autographs and manuscripts, and owns many of the papers of the late Welsh poet, Dylan Thomas. A sincere patron of the arts, he works hard at subsidizing the small, unprofitable cultural magazine, *Poetry*. And, ironically, it was Lannan who was responsible for one of the most violent shocks to American journalism in recent years. After he won control of the Crowell-Collier Publishing Company, *Collier's*, a magazine that had been a family favorite for years, abruptly folded.

There is Max McGraw, the "Toastmaster" manufacturer, who merged his appliance firm with the Thomas A. Edison interests to create the nation's fourth largest electrical products giant: the "new" company dates almost to the beginning of the industry. McGraw also operates the Fin 'n' Feather Farm, near suburban Elgin—one of the most lavish private-membership fish-and-game preserves anywhere.

There is Walter Heller, head of one of the largest financing firms in the nation and a prominent figure in the motion-picture industry.

And William A. (Pat) Patterson, president of United Air Lines. Pat made it the hard way in commercial aviation—from pioneer to president of one of the great systems. Few persons are better liked or more respected. And Pat still retains the rugged individualism that helped develop commercial aviation in this country. He evinced it recently when he joined with a handful of other leading Republicans to support Mayor Richard J. Daley, a Democrat, for re-election. Pat's explanation was simple, and typical of him: "Daley has been a splendid mayor and he is good for Chicago. Party preference takes a back seat in a case like this." That's the way Patterson operates. He wants the best, whether for his passengers or his city.

And then, there are the top executives whose names are more important abroad than in Chicago itself—such as hotel broker Morris DeWoskin, the Caribbean and South American developer who has also boosted Israel through zealous Bonds for Israel sales. And there are the others with almost entirely home-grown fortunes, such as pioneer discount-seller Sol Polk, and prominent auto-dealers Jim (world's largest Ford agency) Moran, and Zollie (world's largest Chevrolet agency) Frank.

One of the phenomena of modern America is the economic rise of the Negro, and this is nowhere more evident than in Chicago, where the Negro population has mushroomed to over 800,000. Chicago has one of the largest groups of Negro millionaires in the country. I wish that there was room to list them all, but let me mention just a few—cosmetics manufacturer S. B. Fuller, who parlayed twenty-five dollars in cash into the S. B. Fuller Products Company, which grosses twenty million dollars a year; real-estate tycoon Dempsey Travis; John H. Johnson, publisher of *Ebony*, *Jet*, and other national magazines; John Sengstacke, publisher of the *Chicago Defender*; Earl B. Dickerson, president of the Supreme Life Insurance Company (largest Negro-owned business in the North); A. W. Williams, head of the United Insurance Company; and Truman Gibson, Sr., another insurance executive, and father of Truman Gibson, Jr., the former boxing impresario.

Some Chicago executives are adventure-lovers. Take the late Commander Eugene F. McDonald, Jr., who started a little electronics firm in a garage in the early days of radio—a little firm called Zenith Radio Corporation! Once, when the Commander was selling automobiles, he drove a new car straight up the steps of a Grant Park statue as a publicity stunt. Another time, he publicized his short-wave radios by traveling north into the Arctic Circle and leading Eskimos in a broadcast songfest. The fishing trips and hunts for pirate treasure on his yacht were legendary. On one unforgettable occasion, he fired a shot across the bow of the yacht of Colonel Leon Mandel. (Fortunately, the peace-loving Mandels didn't return the fire: Mandel's lovely wife, Carola, is a world champion skeet-shooter.)

Another of the many stories still told in yachting circles about Commander McDonald deals with his famous "race" with his friend Burt Massee, who was then president of the Colgate-Palmolive-Peet Company. The race was held not to see who had the faster boat, but the larger. McDonald's first yacht was a 46-footer, which seemed satisfactory until he learned that his rival had a 55-foot craft—whereupon the Commander ordered an 80-footer. Massee retaliated by buying a 90-footer. And so the race went until McDonald acquired the incomparable million-dollar, 185-foot "Mizpah," which he picked up at the bargain-basement price of $375,000, and on which he lived and entertained lavishly in many ports throughout the world.

For years I knew the Commander as a loyal first-nighter at Chicago plays. He was also an early champion of frequency modulation radio (Zenith's WEFM is the nation's oldest FM station). His development of a low-cost hearing aid made him a real benefactor of the hard of hearing. And his was the iron will that carried Zenith successfully through a complicated ten-million-dollar patent infringement case against Radio Corporation of America, General Electric, and Westinghouse. He was also a stalwart campaigner in behalf of pay TV. Before the Commander's death, he personally picked his successor, Zenith's present president, Joseph Wright.

Another adventurer is B. E. ("Ted") Bensinger, whose Brunswick Corporation has become one of the hottest stocks on the New York Exchange. Ted is equally fond of sport, but in a different form. A Yale man with a sharp eye for business organization, he has taken bullfighting lessons in Spain, gone big-game hunting on almost every continent, and at the age of forty-four, he soloed and earned his pilot's license. As befits the head of a bowling equipment firm, he is an accomplished bowler.

But there are also Chicago executives who shun the limelight. One of the most modest men I know is Henry Crown—one of the wealthiest men in the country. Son of a Lithuanian immigrant, Crown once was fired from a four-dollar-a-week job for not being able to differentiate between sand and gravel. Today, his Material Service Corporation is the largest sand-and-gravel supplier in the nation, worth nearly one hundred million dollars. (The company was founded by Henry's late brother, Sol, on $10,000.) And the quiet Henry Crown not only controls Material Service—he has bought and sold the Empire State Building (for a mere sixty-five million dollars), and bankrolled Conrad Hilton in some of his most spectacular deals. He is also a controlling stockholder in the Rock Island Lines, the Hertz Corporation, and General Dynamics, with which Material Service was merged not long ago.

And for all his modesty, Crown is still known among his friends for his unquenchable urge to "think big." When Conrad Hilton was negotiating for Chicago's Palmer House, for example, Crown came to him with a novel suggestion: "Why don't you buy the Stevens, too?" The old Stevens, the largest hotel in the world, is now the Conrad Hilton.

Crown is also known for his "little boy" fascination with gadgets. One afternoon, the door of his private office was closed and his telephone was "plugged" for nearly an hour. His associates, assuming that the boss must be in an extremely important conference, waited around respectfully, reluctant to disturb him. And when someone finally threw open the door and barged in, Crown was discovered with a very important visitor—the late Cook County Board President, Dan Ryan, one of the nation's most powerful politicians. The two big businessmen were squatting on the floor, playing with a little toy train.

Crown also surprised many Chicagoans by appointing hotelman Pat Hoy of the Sherman-Ambassadors Hotel Corporation to succeed him as president of Material Service.

"But I'm a hotelman," Hoy protested. "I know nothing about mixing concrete."

"Maybe not," said Crown. "But without being a cook you've done an excellent job of running the Pump Room." Yielding to Crown's persuasion, Hoy began a new career at the age of forty-six, and made a success of it from the start.

Another Chicago sandman is Jacob Sensibar, a former Indiana farm boy and founder of Construction Aggregates Corporation, the firm which moves more earth than any other in the world. Sensibar has filled in half the land on the lakefront, including much of the Outer Drive, and many of the present beaches. His company has also changed a twenty-million-ton sand dune into a six-mile beach in Los Angeles; scraped out twelve million tons of Coney Island ocean bottom and used it as fill for the New Jersey Turnpike; and reclaimed the two-thousand-year-old Lake Huleh Marshes in Israel, to provide farmland capable of feeding 100,000 persons.

There are dozens of such success stories. But somehow it is still the retail merchant that we think of first when we talk of commerce. And probably no other mile-long stretch anywhere has produced more titans of merchandising than Chicago's State Street.

Massachusetts-born Marshall Field, the most illustrious of all our merchandising magnates, took over his first fledgling store from Potter Palmer toward the end of the Civil War. With nothing much more than a passion for quality and the slogan, "Give the Lady What She Wants," Field and his partner, Levi Z. Leiter, made the store internationally known—and the Field fortune grew into one of the greatest in the world. The firm's holdings include a number of large clothing mills, one of which was once managed by Secretary of Commerce Luther Hodges. And it was Field's money that built the Merchandise Mart, which Joseph P. Kennedy, father of the President, bought shortly after V-J Day. My boss is the great-grandson of the founder. But Marshall Field IV, although the largest stockholder in the store, is less occupied with retail merchandising than with his publishing interests, Field Enterprises, Inc., which I will discuss in a later chapter.

It is not generally known, but one of the Marshall Field organization's largest suburban shopping centers, Old Orchard in Skokie, got its name in an unusual way: Hughston McBain, former board chairman of the store, happened to mention to Mrs. Stanley Field, wife of the executive committee chairman, that construction was ready to begin but a suitable name had not yet been found.

"Why don't you call it Old Orchard?" she suggested.

Recalling that this name had been a tradition in the area, McBain said, "It's a marvelous idea. You must be a student of Chicago history."

"Not exactly," said Mrs. Field. "You see, when Stanley came courting me in Baltimore, years ago, my father just couldn't seem to remember the name 'Field.' So he called him 'Mr. Orchard.' You'd really be naming the center for him." (And, of course, McBain did.)

The Marshall Field store also figures prominently in the success story of its famous competitor, Carson Pirie Scott & Company. Samuel Carson, John Pirie, Robert Scott, and Andrew MacLeish together had operated stores in several locations, but it was not until 1904 that they could gain a permanent foothold on State Street. And then it was only because Field's president, John G. Shedd, arranged for these enterprising partners to meet with the proprietor of a firm about to go out of business down the street at State and Madison—and refused to leave until the deal was consummated.

Shedd later explained: "A top competitor is of great value. We all gain when there are good merchants on State Street."

(The brother of Bruce MacLeish, chairman of Carson Pirie Scott's executive committee, is the poet-playwright and former Librarian of Congress Archibald MacLeish—"the one who got away.")

Goldblatt's, begun by four brothers, Maurice, Nathan, Joel, and Louis, on West Chicago Avenue with five hundred dollars, was almost wiped out early in its history. The original store grew up around a vacant lot, which separated two wings of the building. When construction men began digging in the lot, one wing of the store—its windows snapping like pistol shots—crashed down in a shower of rubble. As the brothers rushed out to sift through the wreckage for salvageable merchandise, two bankers happened along and stopped to watch the desperate merchants as they lifted massive fragments of the old masonry. "If you can work that hard," said one of the bankers, "we'll back you." And thus the business was saved, and today's hundred-million-dollar-plus chain is the result.

During World War II, tragedy struck again when Nathan Goldblatt died of cancer at the peak of his career. Grief-stricken, brother Maurice channeled his energies from business into charity work. Today, the Goldblatt Brothers Foundation is one of the nation's most significant, giving more than one million dollars in a single grant for a University of Chicago cancer research center, named for Nathan. The surviving brothers are national leaders both in the American Heart Association and in the American Cancer Society. The Goldblatts also are given much credit for establishment of the National Heart Institute at the National Institute of Health in Bethesda, Maryland. In 1946 Maurice made a poignant, unrehearsed speech to a Senate committee. Soon afterward, Congress created the new center.

State Street's Wieboldt and Mandel families also are among Chicago's most generous philanthropists. The Wieboldt Foundation, honoring the German immigrant who established the family chain of Chicago neighborhood stores, has given millions of dollars to social agencies and other local organizations. Chief monuments to the Mandel Brothers—whose chain now is merged with Wieboldt's—are Michael Reese Hospital (the late Leon Mandel headed its building committee) and the University of Chicago's Mandel Hall.

The late Morris B. Sachs, the onetime door-to-door salesman whose firm sponsored the famed Sachs Amateur Hour for twenty-four years, also gave generously—not only of his money, but of himself. I'll never forget one charity telethon in which we both participated. Despite his partial physical disability, Morris remained at my side for the entire twenty-four hours. He once produced an entire radio amateur hour with nothing but blind contestants. Chicagoans also will long remember his service as City Treasurer—for which he accepted no pay—and his gallant but unsuccessful primary election campaign for the governorship of Illinois.

For years the "dean" of State Street was clothier Henry C. Lytton, who refused to retire from participation in the operation of the famous shops bearing his name until he was over a hundred years old. I'll always remember the spirit he demonstrated at his centennial celebration in 1946. After posing for pictures which showed him cutting a huge cake model of State Street's stores, he playfully nudged a neighbor, David Mayer of the Maurice L. Rothschild Company, and then took a swing with the knife, which cut the replica of the Rothschild store in two!

Only Mrs. Myrtle Walgreen of the drugstore empire could compare with Lytton for vigorous old age. A globetrotter and a camera enthusiast, she flew her own airplane for years. Next time you pass a drugstore hot lunch counter, you might reflect that it was she who originated the idea, at the first Walgreen outlet at Thirty-ninth and Bowen. "She'd make the soup in big pots at home," says her son Charles, "then carry them over herself!"

What are Chicago tycoons really like?

Some have been ruthless—like the late Sam Insull, whose hunger for power led to his downfall, and forced his son, Samuel, Jr., now an insurance broker, to begin life anew at forty. Some shirk their civic responsibilities, and make all Chicagoans pay in lowered quality of government and city planning. A handful even actively co-operate with syndicate hoodlums, undermining the economy and community of which they're a part.

But as anyone familiar with Chicago knows, Our Town is rich in enlightened and civic-minded businessmen. We have such cultural leaders as William McCormick Blair, Alfred C. Stepan, Jr., and Leonard Spacek of the Lyric Opera. We have such art patrons as Arnold (Maremont Corporation) Maremont, adman Earle Ludgin, Sterling (Morton Salt) Morton, Lou (Ambassador Hotels and rare books) Silver, Nathan (Consolidated Foods Corporation) Cummings, and Leigh (Inland Steel) Block and his wife, the former Mary Lasker, daughter of the late advertising genius. Cummings, one of the wealthiest men in the food business and a great art collector, has even influenced the French cultural scene! General James Gavin, our Ambassador to France, has hung the American Embassy in Paris with hundreds of thousands of dollars' worth of paintings on loan from the Cummings collection—all by Impressionists and other famous French artists. Cummings is also noted for having given several of his executives unusual bonuses—valuable paintings from his collection, in addition to money.

But before concluding this chapter, I also want to speak of another aspect of Chicago life for which, rightly or wrongly, the city has become famous (or infamous)—organized crime, and the G-men and police who oppose it.

Just as Chicago has become big in everything else, it has (if you haven't heard) also been big in crime. Big Jim Colosimo, Johnny Torrio, Al Capone—all were ruthless, powerful syndicate rulers, and all operated in Chicago. They had a supporting cast of hundreds, featuring such "names" as "Machine Gun" Jack McGurn, Paul "The Waiter" Ricca, and Louie "Little New York" Campagna. Their gunmen plotted hundreds of killings—two hundred in one four-year period—including such "spectaculars" as plugging hoodlum Dion O'Banion in his florist shop as he arranged flowers for another criminal's funeral, and machine-gunning his successor, Hymie Weiss, in front of the Near North Side's Holy Name Cathedral (you can still see bullet scars on the building). Early in the thirties there even was one battle at high noon near the "world's busiest corner," State and Madison.

Times have changed since the days of open gang warfare, which culminated in the 1929 Saint Valentine's Day Massacre, when seven members of Bugs Moran's gang were slain in a garage at 2122 North Clark. Hoodlums continue in their insidious rackets and vice, as in almost every other large city. But now underworld disagreements are handled more discreetly. (You've heard of the syndicate's new five-passenger compact car? Rides two in the front seat, two in the rear, and one in the trunk.)

Al Capone, the former New Yorker who once headquartered

in fifty rooms of Chicago's Metropole Hotel, is dead. His brother "Bottles" is busy with a $210,000 back-tax case. His widow Mae and son Albert, now Miami residents, spend most of their time in filing lawsuits connected with movies and TV shows about Scarface Al. As one wag put it: "They want residuals." And pending an appeal to higher courts, for a time Tony Accardo, Capone's syndicate heir, was under Federal sentence for income-tax evasion.

Capone gloried in violence, but Accardo remains the man in the gray flannel suit. While Al loved publicity, and made conspicuous appearances at night clubs and speak-easies with his entourage, Tony shies from it. Except for going deep-sea fishing in Florida, Tony has lived quietly with his family of four in a $600,000-home at 915 Franklin in River Forest (complete with high fence, indoor pool, two bowling alleys, a billiard room, and a one-piece onyx bathtub with gold-plated faucets). His only lavish entertaining is the huge lawn picnics every Fourth of July for "business associates" and their friends, and special affairs such as the marriage last year of his daughter Linda. On that occasion most of the underworld elite turned out, but they scarcely enjoyed it—reporters, photographers, and FBI men in the crowd outnumbered the rice-throwers.

Despite the hoods' having gone "respectable," however, they're no less intolerable a cancer on society than before. (It is no worse in Chicago, I hasten to add, than in any other large city. Senator Kefauver, after all, didn't stop with Chicago in his crime committee hearings.) The annual cost of crime to Our Town, according to ex-FBI man Virgil Peterson, head of the watchdog Chicago Crime Commission, is $750,000,000 a year—more than $200 for every man, woman, and child in the city. The human toll in death, injury, terror, and suffering from racketeers' increasing infiltration into branches of local government, legitimate unions, and business is inestimable.

The financial power and influence wielded by entrenched criminals places a tremendous, unwholesome pressure on agencies of local government and law enforcement. Instead of resisting, a number of businessmen, public officials, and private citizens find it "easier" to give in. (Or they actively contribute to corruption by trying to bribe officials or policemen themselves.) Sometimes, after a reform movement has begun, they discover the job is so complex that the persistence required for a real cleanup dies. That has happened periodically elsewhere as well as in Chicago. But each time, we've taken a few steps forward. We are taking a big one now.

It has come as the result of a scandal you've no doubt heard of: A handful of policemen in one Chicago district not only were looking the other way when burglars burgled, they were actively helping—and getting away with it. As one jokester put it: "Officer, is this a stick-up or a pinch?" But Chicago Mayor Richard J. Daley moved immediately for reform. The man put in charge was Orlando W. Wilson, former University of California criminology dean and adviser in many police cleanups. He is probably the ranking expert now holding office in any police department in the United States.

Nobody I know, including Police Superintendent Wilson himself, believes he will remake the 11,000-man police department into a faultless one, or single-handedly drive every hoodlum from the city. But in approximately two years he already has made vital reforms. He has redrawn the boundaries of the police districts, shaken up the top command to place in power proved young officers, tested and recruited hundreds of new prospects, organized a new internal security unit to check on honesty within the department, introduced new mechanical and electronic devices for detectives' use, revamped and modernized the crime lab, doubled the size of the police auto fleet, changed a sloppy and dishonest method of keeping crime figures into an honest, dependable one, won pay increases for his men, and abolished a number of potential shakedown devices. One patrolman's comment when someone from the Tuberculosis Institute offered him a free chest X ray about sums it up: "No thanks, lady. Since O. W. Wilson took charge, we don't take nothin' for nothin'."

Actually, despite a few notorious incompetents, the Chicago police department has produced many outstanding figures. One, John Reid, is a leading lie-detector expert (now operating his own firm, he has tested more than 20,000 persons from whom he has obtained 5,000 felony confessions, including 150 involving murder). Blonde Lois Higgins, former policewoman (one of America's prettiest) who now heads the Illinois Crime Prevention Bureau, is a widely respected authority on narcotics traffic and enforcement. Frank Pape, a Chicago police captain on leave to head the security force at the Arlington and Washington Park race tracks, has taken on some of the department's toughest assignments (he's been in twenty-six gun battles in which nine men were killed, earning him fifteen extra compensations and twenty-six creditable mentions).

Among Chicago's Federal agents, as any TV viewer knows, there has been a parade of heroes, including the FBI's Melvin Purvis, who set the death trap for John Dillinger outside the Biograph Theater in 1934, and the Treasury Department's Eliot Ness, Chief of Chicago's "Untouchables." His real life, incidentally, was a far cry from the hoked-up version on TV. He was not the hard, steely-eyed character portrayed by Robert Stack on television, but a mild-mannered, witty, warm-hearted guy who seldom carried a gun. "If you don't carry a gun," he told associates, "the hoods won't be so quick to shoot."

As a columnist on the night-club beat, I've often been in the peculiar position of figuratively rubbing elbows with the underworld. Such hoodlums as Marshall Caifano enjoy night life and openly frequent various clubs on Rush Street and elsewhere. Even though they know I'm a columnist, they're usually friendly. On occasion they're even sources of news tips—often more reliable than those of respected citizens.

But I found myself in a terribly uncomfortable situation after one murder a decade ago—in the middle of a gang faction's efforts to convince the world that the facts of their case were not quite as they appeared. South Side policy king, Theodore Roe, had been asked to turn over his territory to the syndicate, but he refused. Moreover, he allegedly had tried to pin the murder of a police lieutenant, William Drury, on Marshall Caifano and three colleagues. So Leonard Caifano, Marshall's elder brother, went calling, allegedly to kidnap Roe. But Leonard ended up dead.

His colleagues held Roe responsible for the slaying. The next body to fall was Roe's.

The police sought Marshall for questioning. Early one morning underworld chums of the late Leonard stopped me in the street on the Near North Side. "Leonard and his pals never intended to kidnap Roe when they curbed his car," they explained. "They just wanted to rough him up—break some bones, you know—for turning stool pigeon. You don't jerk a guy by the lapels if you're going to kidnap him." In other words, they claimed it was all a mistake.

Even in a situation like that, a reporter always has questions to ask. I asked. The key ones they ignored. (And I wasn't pressing *them!*) When one of them said, "We done enough talking," the "interview" was over.

The next day I wrote a column about the incident and the case. That's the last I ever heard of it—including the question of convicting anybody for the killings.

But over the years not all encounters with hoodlums have ended as uneventfully as this for newspapermen. As Chicagoans well know, one of the city's most publicized killings involved a reporter. It was June 9, 1930. Alfred ("Jake") Lingle, a *Tribune* reporter who had covered some of the biggest stories on the police beat, was strolling through the Illinois Central Railroad subway at Michigan Avenue and Randolph en route to a train bound for the Washington Park Race Track. Suddenly a gunman sidled up and fired a single shot at his head. Lingle was killed instantly.

A civic uproar ensued. The *Tribune* posted a $25,000 reward. Two other papers also offered sums, totaling $30,000, for the capture of the killer. Then not long afterward it was discovered that Lingle had been doing something more than covering his beat and pounding out stories on the typewriter. Al Capone had given him a diamond-studded belt. Lingle owned a summer home and a chauffeur-driven limousine. He thought nothing of betting —and losing—a thousand dollars on a horse race.

All this, it developed, resulted from a sinister "secret life" being lived by Jake Lingle as high lieutenant and go-between for the Capone Syndicate. He might have continued his dodge indefinitely. But apparently he became greedy. He demanded too large a cut of several gambling operations. Also he accepted $50,000 "to arrange" a permit for opening a dog track—a promise on which he couldn't deliver. Early death was his reward.

Corruption among Chicago newspapermen, I'm happy to say, is rare. But a kind of "junior Jake Lingle" case did occur in Chicago last winter. Ironically, this involved another *Tribune* reporter, William Doherty of a famous family of Chicago reporters.

One day he went to the home of minor hoodlum Sam DeStefano, ostensibly to check a report that DeStefano had been killed. But the hoodlum was very much alive. So robust in health was he, according to Doherty, that he even threatened the reporter with a gun. Choosing discretion over valor, Doherty fled. He called the police. He called his newspaper. He also called a lawyer and pressed charges against DeStefano.

What happened next came as a shock not only to the *Tribune* but to the entire Chicago press corps. Upon investigation it was found that Doherty had more in common with Lingle than his *Tribune* affiliation. Apparently he, too, had been doing "favors" for the underworld for a fee. The day his case against DeStefano was to come up in court, the *Tribune* announced Doherty's firing. The major charge against DeStefano was, of course, dropped.

But we hadn't heard the last of the glib DeStefano. One day, on a tip from a police official, I printed an item that Sam was threatening reporters who mentioned him unfavorably. The next day DeStefano bent our ear on the telephone for eighteen uninterrupted minutes. As we noted in our column:

"I don't mind listening to DeStefano's fluent flow, but eighteen minutes seemed interminable when deadline is beckoning. And there was no stopping Sam, who was incensed over our item about his threatening reporters. 'I don't threaten nobody. I'm not that type,' said Sam in his Little Lord Fauntleroy voice.

"But when we finally managed to sneak a few words into the one-way conversation and mentioned the name of the reporter so threatened (Sandy Smith of the *Tribune*), DeStefano took a giant step backward. 'Oh, him,' exclaimed Sam. 'That was some time ago. I mean I haven't threatened any reporters LATELY and I wish you would make that clear to your inestimable readers, of whom I am one.' As our favorite comedian, Joe E. Lewis, would have summed up Sam's reaction to our item: he resents it, but he doesn't deny it.

"DeStefano now was warming up to his current difficulties with the law. He had been charged with slugging one Alvin Schultz, who came to DeStefano's home to complain about the exorbitant interest rates on a loan from Sam. 'My ace witness,' DeStefano told us, 'will be artist James Paulus, an associate professor at the Chicago Art Institute. Mr. Paulus was in my home when Schultz came to see me and he will swear that I did not lay a hand on him. Here, Mr. Paulus is in my home now. Talk to him.' Paulus, an artist of considerable reputation, confirmed that he was with De-Stefano to discuss a portrait of him when Schultz came calling and allegedly was sent packing with a nifty shiner. Paulus said he saw or heard nothing to indicate violence had taken place.

"DeStefano returned to the phone. 'I do not engage in fisticuffs at any time,' he insisted. 'It is not the gentlemanly thing to do. In fact, I do not like sitting for this portrait, but my family insists. Mr. Paulus, here, he did portraits of my wife and children and then they said he must do one of me. I told Mr. Paulus that no-body needed another painting or photograph of Sam DeStefano because there are so many at the detective bureau.'

"We asked Sam what he did for a living. 'I do not work any longer,' he replied. 'I am retired.' . . . 'How did you accumulate enough money to retire at the comparatively early age of 52?' . . . 'My finances are an open book and I do not mean the kind of "book" that engages in illegal wagering. I worked hard all my life with never a day off—seven days a week. I owned a 21-apartment building on LaSalle and Superior streets which was a model for cleanliness. I did everything myself—janitor, engineer, plumber. And this gave me a gross income of $23,000 a year.'

"Sam continued: 'And as you may remember from reading the newspapers, I also worked for the city and received remuneration that ranged from $3,000 a year when I started to $6,000 a year when I was fired for telling a little fib. With that kind of income and by living economically—none of that night life and wild spending for me—you can save enough to retire. Provided,' added Sam hastily, 'you make good investments.'

" 'Do you mind revealing what the little fib was that cost you your city job?' . . . 'I have no secrets from you. I lied to the Civil Service Commission about not having a criminal record. (A little job of bank robbery.) If I told the truth, I never could have gotten the job. So I told this little white lie, as you might call it. But I think everybody knew it was a fib, but nobody did anything until the papers started putting the heat on me. Then, suddenly, the lie was discovered and I was bounced. Good-by now and don't write anything nasty about me—or else. Ha ha, you know I'm only kidding.' "

3. Show Biz

The famous Greek philosopher, Spyros Skouras, said it:
"There's more than a little ham in everybody."

I confess that this is true enough of me. I am, I think, a dedicated, lifelong fan of the theater and the world of entertainment—and especially of the wonderful people who make up Show Biz. And one reason show folks fascinate me so is that I am a ham at heart. In watching or listening to a gifted performer, we are really seeing at its finest an extension of talents that we all have in some degree. And make no mistake about it—Americans on the whole love show business. It is as integral a part of our culture as highways and hot dogs. Nowhere else will you find the quantity, diversity, and consistent high quality of popular entertainment that is America's.

For a columnist on a beat like mine, it isn't easy to devote just one short chapter to show business. As I've already indicated, some of my best friends are show people. Hollywood, New York, Las Vegas, Miami Beach, and other show-business centers are almost second homes to me.

Each spring, during the presentation of the Academy Awards, my wife Essee and I take off for Hollywood to participate in the big "countdown" of the film industry—an event usually of tremendous excitement.

65

It has been my privilege and pleasure to attend many of the most important movie premières. This has taken me everywhere: to Hollywood itself, where I was recently master of ceremonies at the première of Mervyn Leroy's *A Majority of One*; to West Germany, where I covered the public debut of Stanley Kramer's superb *Judgment at Nuremberg* (and reported on East-West political tension in Berlin at the same time).

Fittingly for a reporter who once masqueraded as a spear carrier in a Chicago performance of *Aïda*, I have also appeared in two motion pictures—and "appeared" is the word. If you looked sharp, you may have seen me debark from a train in Otto Preminger's *Anatomy of a Murder*, or as one of a group of reporters in a scene in *Advise and Consent*, another Otto Preminger production. Otto, it seems, is the only Hollywood mogul to appreciate my acting.

Such experiences have not only been diverting, they have also instilled in me a hearty respect for everyone connected with the making of a major motion picture. It is long, strenuous work, from the early-morning make-up calls to punch-out time in the late afternoon or evening. It requires patience and a sense of dedication. I have seen Preminger, William Wyler, George Stevens, and other leading directors make and remake a single one- or two-minute scene dozens of times. In recent years motion pictures have reached new heights of technical and dramatic perfection, and for that the skilled and talented workers of Hollywood deserve more credit than they normally receive.

Speaking of films, let me say here that I am often surprised and saddened by certain kinds of criticism leveled at Hollywood. Movies dealing with sex, violence, and delinquency have come under the heaviest fire. Some of this criticism certainly has been justified, for movie-makers have made their share of mistakes. But many of the arrows have been aimed at the wrong target. On the whole, the movies simply mirror our mores, which include violence and delinquency. Our real indignation should be directed toward the society reflected in the films. If we don't approve of the image, why blame the mirror?

It also has been my privilege to visit the homes of many

prominent Hollywood personalities. I could write a whole book about these experiences alone and devote a chapter to each of Jack Benny's beautiful houses—the one in Beverly Hills and the one in Palm Springs. The huge, winding staircase inside the entrance of the Bennys' Beverly Hills mansion, the magnificent bedrooms in which Jack and Mary each have TV sets by their beds, and the movie projection room (a standard feature in many stars' houses) are especially impressive. While Jack and Mary were in New York several years ago, Essee and I lived in their Palm Springs house. Few California properties are more sumptuous.

Another home I think of with affection is the Beverly Hills mansion of Danny and Rosemarie Thomas. When they first moved in, it was a typical Spanish-style house. With each new success of Danny's, they added another wing—until it became apparent that in time this would put the south bedroom somewhere over the Mexican border. Two things I doubt that any visitor to Danny's home will ever forget: the religious figures throughout the house, of which a lighted statue of his patron saint, St. Jude, is noteworthy; and an immense wood carving of *The Last Supper*, which covers one wall of the dining room. The Thomases' dining-room table, incidentally, is U-shaped and so arranged that nobody need turn his back to the wall on which the wood carving hangs. The carving and statuary are conspicuous and moving evidence of Danny's devotion to his religion.

The better I become acquainted with leading show-business personalities, the more I discover that in private life they are usually very different from the public images they present. Frank Sinatra, for example, is generally thought of as a harum-scarum hedonist. Yet Frankie is one of the most generous of entertainers in helping people and causes in which he believes. When the girls' school, Marymount College, moved from Hollywood to another Los Angeles suburb, the administration was astonished to receive a check for $100,000 from Sinatra. When Charlie Morrison, owner of the Mocambo on the Sunset Strip, died heavily in debt several years ago, Frankie played at the Mocambo for a week, gratis, to clear $50,000 for the widow Mary. During

Lee J. Cobb's lean years, Frankie was similarly generous. When Cobb became seriously ill in a strange town, Sinatra not only paid all his medical bills but also phoned him daily to cheer him up. Because Sinatra does his good deeds quietly, however, you seldom hear about them.

And although Marilyn Monroe was married to the brilliant playwright, Arthur Miller, many people still considered her a "dumb blonde." Any amusing repartee attributed to her they dismissed as the concoction of ghost writers and press agents. As other reporters and I can testify, Marilyn was not only highly intelligent, but genuinely witty. Here is an excerpt from an exclusive interview I conducted with her several years ago in Chicago:

"They say you wear nothing underneath your dress but a garter belt. Why?"

"To hold up my stockings, silly boy."

"Have you read Freud?"

"No, I'll wait for the movie."

"Will you hold still for a radio interview?"

"Certainly."

"Mind if it runs about thirty minutes?"

"I don't know you that well."

Zsa Zsa Gabor is even faster with a quip than Marilyn—so much so that Bob Hope once told me she is one of the few women with whom he would hate to compete in an ad-lib contest. Last winter Zsa Zsa's house was burned in the terrible canyon fires in California just a few days before she announced her engagement. I said to her, "Life moves fast for you, doesn't it, Miss Gabor? One week you're burned out of your home and the next week you're engaged."

Replied Zsa Zsa, "Dollink, maybe I'm not as burned out as everybody thought!"

Let us take a slow look at show business in my city.

Stated simply, The Prairie Giant is a glutton for entertainment. Chicagoans love show business in every form: drama, comedy, music, broadcasts, telecasts, night-club acts, the strip tease—you name it, we'll go for it. And when an exciting new trend develops in any of the performing arts, there is a good chance that it originated in Chicago.

This interest of ours is no new phenomenon. Only four years after the city's founding, our isolated, mud-splattered citizens opened their first theater—in a converted hotel dining room. (And now, more than a century and a quarter later, some of Chicago's finest entertainment is still staged in a hotel atmosphere. Today we call it satirical revue.)

Chicago was the home of Florenz Ziegfeld, Jr., and Lillian Russell, and the hub of many music-hall and vaudeville circuits. When America's first musical comedy went on tour, it played what was then an unheard-of 56 nights in Chicago. At one time Chicago vaudeville was so fiercely competitive that when Al Jolson and Eddie Cantor were booked into rival houses here and both became ill, neither would cancel a performance or let the other know of his illness. "I couldn't afford a headline saying, 'Jolson Runs Cantor Out of Chicago,'" Cantor later confessed to Jolson, to which Al roared, "And I only went on out of fear of the same headline—with the names reversed!"

For a time, in silent-movie days, Chicago was the feature film capital of the world. The old Essanay lot on Argyle Street, now the property of Wilding Studios which produces industrial films, was the nation's busiest—with such stars as Gloria Swanson, Wallace Beery, W. C. Fields, Francis X. Bushman, and Charlie Chaplin. Chaplin's bosses had tried to keep him out of contact with competing studios, but it was from Essanay that Chaplin was finally spirited away to Hollywood by a rival who got to him dressed as an extra. It was also from Chicago that former furrier Adolph Zukor moved to help build what became Paramount Pictures, and clothier Carl Laemmle emigrated to found the Universal-International Studios. The lure of California sunshine, plus an antitrust suit that all but wiped out Essanay, ended Chicago's movie-production reign.

Louella Parsons, one of Hollywood's great personalities, has vivid recollections of those early days when Chicago was Movieland. A stage-struck girl from the small Illinois town of Dixon, she came to the Big City to write scenarios for Essanay. When

Francis X. Bushman was a matinee idol, Louella knew what the public was not supposed to know—that he was actually the father of five children. Louella also knew a cross-eyed office boy who confided to her that his great ambition was to be a movie comedian—and he soon was. His name was Ben Turpin. And then one day Louella decided to capitalize on her experience and contacts at Essanay. She walked into the office of William Handy, publisher of the old Chicago *Record-Herald*, and made this suggestion:

"How about a column about the movie stars, what they are like off the screen, whom they go with, what they wear?"

Handy accepted the idea at once, and Chicago gave birth to the first movie column. And when the *Record-Herald* folded, Louella took her idea West to continue making her fortune.

New Orleans may be the birthplace of jazz, but Chicago is the town where it grew up. The old Lamb's Café at Clark and Randolph spelled it, "jass." And Thirty-fifth and State, just a hot note from Comiskey Park, marked the center of the most music-filled neighborhood in the nation. "Just stand there with a horn," someone once said, "and it'll blow by itself." Joe ("King") Oliver, Leon Bismarck ("Bix") Beiderbecke, Louis ("Satchmo") Armstrong, Earle ("Fatha") Hines, and Chicago's own Francis ("Muggsy") Spanier, Ben Pollack, Benny Goodman, and Gene Krupa, all performed in Chicago saloons and speak-easies, transforming jazz from a localized folk art into an international craze.

It was in the old Panther Room of the Sherman Hotel where Fats Waller was asked, "Mr. Waller, what is jazz?"

"Lady," Fats replied, "If you have to ask, don't fool with it."

Nationally famous Chicago ballrooms such as the Aragon and Trianon launched the big sweet bands, including Wayne King, Guy Lombardo, and Lawrence Welk.

Many of the leading network shows in the golden era of radio originated in Chicago—Red Skelton, Dr. IQ, Amos 'n' Andy, Paul Whiteman, Kay Kyser, Ben Bernie, the Quiz Kids, Ma Perkins, the late-afternoon adventure serials which hooked millions of decoder-clutching youths, these were the symbols of its reign. Enduring partnerships were formed, such as that of Garry

Moore and Durward Kirby, who met on the old Ransom Sherman *Club Matinee* program. The excitement of that age is over, but many of its luminaries remain as stars.

Two of the most renowned pioneers of the movie palaces were Chicagoans: the late Abe Balaban and Sam Katz, who with their families built the nation's leading theater chain, Balaban and Katz, and developed the company which was to become Paramount Pictures. It all started while Sam still was in high school and before he graduated, his income averaged four hundred dollars a week. Later his great Chicago Theater set a pattern in grandeur subsequently emulated by New York's Roxy and other great movie houses of the day.

Even at the off-beat Chicago has been "on." It was at the old College Inn that Eddie Shipstad and Oscar Johnson first put their Ice Follies together. And what they didn't do for the frozen slab, Arthur M. (Chicago Stadium) Wirtz and Sonja Henie did. After Sonja's clean sweep of all the world amateur skating titles, Wirtz clearly foresaw the money-making potential of an ice revue with the vivacious Norwegian as star. "Will you turn professional for $3,000 a night?" he wired her. Sonja wired back, "Anyone will turn professional for $3,000 a night." Together both made fortunes; then Sonja's displeasure over Wirtz's seeking to sign Chicagoan Barbara Ann Scott as a co-star led to their split-up.

Many credit "Little Egypt" with originating the hootchy-kootchy dance in Chicago (at the 1893 Columbian Exposition, where the Ferris wheel was introduced for the first time). And Sally Rand unveiled her fan dance at Our Town's centennial celebration, the Century of Progress Exposition, in 1933. Inspired by her press agent, Anne Jesselson, Sally decided to publicize her act by riding *au naturel*, undressed as Lady Godiva—on a horse, which she had had painted white on one side to accommodate the photographers. Though she started out fully clothed, a gateman temporarily upset the plan with a no-horses-in-here order. Sally and Dobbin finally forced a water entrance, via speedboat —and Chicago's most publicized amphibious invasion was history.

One of the modern era's greatest showmen was a Chicago

boy—former West Sider Avram Hirsch Goldbogen (who later changed his name to Mike Todd). He is now buried in our Waldheim Cemetery.

Chicago remembers Mike Todd for many things. It was here that this tireless genius made his first million dollars (on paper), as president of an apartment- and home-building firm, known as the Atlantic and Pacific Construction Company. Mike was eighteen at the time. Unfortunately, the year was 1928. The Depression hit and Mike went broke.

And it was here that Mike got his start in show business. Taking his cue from the success of Sally Rand at the Century of Progress, he conceived the idea of a "Flame Dance" strip tease. When the act was booked into New York's Casino de Paree for $750 a week, Mike was on his way to making a second fortune. Eventually he lost that one, too. But in 1940, he was making headlines again with the world's largest night club, the Michael Todd Theater Café on Chicago's North Side. It had eight thousand seats. Unfortunately, one of Mike's backers was a front man for Frank ("The Enforcer") Nitti of the Capone Syndicate. When Mike discovered this, he promptly quit—wanted no part of the Syndicate. It cost him his bankroll. This was the last enterprise to bear Mike's name in Chicago until his son, Mike, Jr., opened the movie house which is named for him.

The greatest monument to Mike, of course, is the spectacular success of his superb movie, *Around the World in Eighty Days*. In that connection, this story always has appealed to me, not only as being so typical of Mike's flair for the dramatic, but as an illustration of his approach to life on the grand scale. The late Art Cohn told it in his entertaining book, *The Nine Lives of Michael Todd*.

One day during the shooting of the film, while standing on the paddle-wheel steamboat that was bringing Phileas Fogg back to England, Todd noticed that hundreds of sea gulls were following the ship.

"What are they doing?" landlubber Todd asked the first mate.

"Following us for food—the garbage," replied the mate.

Todd was horrified.

"Garbage!" he shouted. "No sea gulls following *my* boat are going to eat garbage. Toss them some decent food. *We* go first class!"

And speaking of off-beat shows, who can forget such TV shows as the old *Garroway at Large,* or *Kukla, Fran & Ollie, Ding-Dong School,* and Studs Terkel's *Studs' Place?* The leisurely, low-pressure pace of "Chicago-style" TV will be remembered as long as there's a glowing tube.

I've emceed many shows at the Chicago Theater. And every visit to my dressing room there conjures up memories of Maurice Chevalier, the Marx Brothers, Mary Pickford, Kate Smith, Mae West, Jack Benny, Danny Kaye, Betty Hutton, Betty Grable, and many others. It was in the Chicago's orchestra pit that Stanley Morner vocalized with the house band before becoming Dennis Morgan of the movies, and where Victor Young once held the baton.

Then there was the Chez Paree. I once referred to it as the most glamorous name in night-club history. "How about the Copacabana?" one of my New York friends asked. "Well, the Chez was in operation longer," I had to reply. "There was no other with a tradition like it." Particularly under the operation of Mike Fritzel and Joey Jacobson during its early and middle years, it was a night club that literally had everything—superb food, thrilling atmosphere, and consistently fine entertainment. The food in most night clubs is—let's face it—pretty ordinary. But people actually went to the Chez just for the pleasure of dining.

In the spring of 1960, the Chez announced that it was closing for the summer, and owners Dave Halper (who is now with the Riviera Hotel in Las Vegas) and Donjo Medlevine (who is now an oil executive) advertised that the club would open as usual in the fall, with Red Skelton as its first attraction. Negotiations with Red proved futile, however. In fact, the owners had difficulty in coming up with any big-name act. That was the end. There was no chance for last visits by Chez Paree regulars, and no last closing. The Chez Paree merely faded into oblivion.

After so many prosperous years, why did it crumple so suddenly?

There were many reasons. One was the steadily growing trend away from the large night clubs of earlier years. The clientele that had once supported such clubs was dropping off; the new generation prefers smaller, more intimate spots.

Television also played a part. It has kept many leading stars so busy that they don't have time for the night-club circuit.

Las Vegas was partly responsible, too. The clubs there are able to pay such enormous salaries that smaller clubs elsewhere in the country cannot match them.

And then there was Uncle Sam. Income taxes are such that once stars make large sums for a few appearances, there is almost no profit to be made by appearing more frequently.

And Chicagoans demand the best. To survive in this town, a club like the Chez had to present the best—regularly. Because it was no longer able to do this, it had to go. But, ah! the warm memories of those many wonderful years.

Yes, Chicago has had a proud show-business tradition; but it is no longer the "Big Apple" it used to be. The concentrations of talent and power which have resulted from the centralization of network TV operations in New York and Hollywood have changed all that. New York and Hollywood are two of my favorite cities, but there are some things they can't do. They are overspecialized, and dominated by pressures and traditions which limit their ability to experiment and change. Promising talent is lost in the shuffle of the big-timers. Except in the world of Off-Broadway, only solid hits will command public support. Show business needs a leavening influence, a creative spur, a showcase for both new and established types of entertainment, which almost all cities except Chicago are too small or too geographically isolated to provide.

Only Chicago has the population, the wealth, the tourist traffic, and the cultural climate to provide the stimulus that is needed. We support the only fully professional theater season away from Broadway. We offer such fine training and proving grounds as the Art Institute's Goodman Theater and Northwestern Uni-

versity's School of Speech, more than thirty suburban and neighborhood stock companies, and the greatest variety of music and
cabaret entertainment between Las Vegas and Broadway. This
makes us the show-business heart of America, and one of the
entertainment capitals of the world. Chicago makes far more
news and permanent contributions to the industry than most
outsiders realize.

Take the legitimate theater. With the rise of TV, with con-
stantly tightening cost squeezes, it has had hard going, even on
Broadway. In Chicago, almost everything possible has worked
against its survival: Monopoly management for years by the
Shubert Theater empire; dingy and uncomfortable theaters; arro-
gant ticket sellers; a notorious racket in ticket-scalping (which
I'm happy to have had a hand in breaking with the "Better Box-
office Break" campaign that got me removed from the Shuberts'
opening-night-tickets lists); and, in some cases, road-show productions far below the quality of the Broadway originals. Yet Chicago remains the number two theater center in the nation. It has
even served as the launching pad for such plays as Chicagoan
Lorraine Hansberry's A Raisin in the Sun and Tennessee Williams'
The Glass Menagerie.

Williams also chose Chicago for the pre-Broadway tryout of
his latest play, The Night of the Iguana. In contrast to the enthusiasm with which Chicago critics had received his earlier plays,
they were lukewarm about this one. Claudia Cassidy of the
Tribune, who had been one of the first critics to recognize
Williams' talent, referred to it as "a bankrupt play." By strenuous
rewriting, Williams turned the play into a Broadway hit. But
Miss Cassidy's criticism continued to rankle him, as he indicated
in some pointed comments about her, and about critics in general, one night on my At Random TV show.

My Fair Lady opened in Chicago with a $650,000 advance
ticket sale and then broke the Chicago record for a run by a
musical (sixty-seven weeks, set by South Pacific in 1951–52).
My Fair Lady ran seventy-four weeks. Music Man played here for
fifty-six weeks, Guys and Dolls for thirty-seven, The King and I
for twenty-five, and Pajama Game for twenty-two—all after long

Broadway runs had removed them from the "new" or "fresh" category. And *Fiorello!* opened with a larger advance sale in Chicago than it had had on Broadway!

And Chicago has been as warm in its welcome to the more serious plays—*The Miracle Worker*, for example, opened with a $100,000 advance; and *A Raisin in the Sun* played to SRO audiences during its entire pre-Broadway run in Chicago.

Of the once-impressive line-up of Loop playhouses, only the Blackstone, the Shubert, the McVickers, and the seldom-used Studebaker remain, augmented by the Arie Crown Theater at McCormick Place and the Civic Theater in the Civic Opera House Building. But in response to this problem—common to other large cities—Chicago has been a pioneer in establishing professional theaters outside the crowded high-rent district, in the city's environs and suburbs. Chicagoan Tony DeSantis, who operates the Martinique Restaurant in suburban Evergreen Park, is a leader in this field: his Drury Lane "summer theater" now presents outstanding stars and plays the year around.

We have established some of the most successful intimate cabarets as worthy successors to the large-capacity, high-overhead supper clubs, which had been killed by TV and rising costs. But perhaps most far-reaching of all has been Chicago's spawning of that sensational new stage trend, improvisational theater. Its most noted exponents: Shelley Berman, Mike Nichols and Elaine May, and the troupe that has been so successful in New York recently, the Second City Players.

The hilarious—the often devastating—Nichols and May, after meeting at the University of Chicago, first appeared on the same stage with the Compass Players—the improvisational troupe that also produced Second City director Paul Sills and Barbara Harris, the new Broadway sensation. Barbara was "discovered" by Richard Rodgers while she was appearing in *From the Second City* at the Royale Theater on Broadway. When Rodgers later teamed up with Alan Jay Lerner to write a new musical, he remembered Barbara and signed her to star in the show. Using news and feature stories from the *Sun-Times*, speeches, advertisements, philosophy and sociology books, Mike and Elaine improvised their sophisticated dialogues in a converted North Side movie house. Through conversation and such media as my column, the word got around. A new trend had begun. Nichols and May, their witty routines honed to razor sharpness, were then booked into New York's Village Vanguard, and then into the Blue Angel. They have been nation-wide delights ever since.

The brilliant improvisational satire of the Second City Players has inspired similar troupes in New York, Washington, and other cities. This troupe began on an almost nonexistent budget as The Playwrights Theater Club on Chicago's Near North Side. Paul Sills, comedian-actor Eugene Troobnik, who is still with the group, and theater buff David Shepard were co-producers. After eighteen months, in 1955, the Chicago Fire Department ordered their theater closed. But the group reopened as the Compass Players, farther north, on Broadway near Devon. By that time, the troupe included not only Nichols and May and Berman, but also Theodore Flicker, impresario of New York's improvisational Premise Players. The Compass folded in 1957. But thanks to Sills and an audience highly receptive to penetrating satire, the troupe bounced back as the Second City Players, when it opened in its present building on North Wells. From there the company of Howard Alk, Severn Darden, Barbara Harris, Paul Sand, Alan Arkin, Andrew Duncan, Mina Kolb, and Eugene Troobnik moved on to Broadway and thence to Greenwich Village, while a second platoon continues to perform nightly in Chicago.

Another new field in which Chicago's franchise is secure is the sharp, sophisticated social comment and satire known as the New Comedy. Mort Sahl, its originator, got his first break at Enrico Banducci's hungry i in San Francisco. But it was Chicago that gave him his big send-off. He was first booked into the Black Orchid on Rush Street—then owned by Al Greenfield, husband of Gertrude Niesen—but he was fired after a few performances, because Greenfield insisted that he wear a coat and tie. Mort held out for his traditional sweater and open-neck shirt. Dressed as he pleased, Mort soon found his real home at Mister Kelly's, another Rush Street club which now is Mecca for the New Comedy.

One night I took Groucho Marx to hear Mort. The king of the quipsters was ecstatic. "The greatest since Will Rogers," said Groucho. "No comedian today has such courage." This was seconded later by Adlai Stevenson and Bill Blair, Jr., our Ambassador to Denmark, who both became devoted admirers of Sahl. When Mort broke up Smilin' Ed Sullivan at a Chicago Press Club Presidents' Dinner, his future was no longer a thing of the future—we were looking at it. ("Right?" "Right!")

Since Mort Sahl emerged as a star, every one of the other top talents associated with New Comedy—Shelley Berman, Bob Newhart, and Dick Gregory—has taken one route: onward and upward from Chicago. Here's how:

Berman, a West Sider who studied serious acting at Chicago's Goodman Theater, tried his luck elsewhere and found it discouragingly consistent—all bad. During a lean period in Florida, he actually flipped a coin to decide his future: Heads, he and his wife Sarah would hitchhike to Los Angeles; tails, to New York. It was heads. But L.A. offered no acting jobs. Only by selling a few comedy sketches to Steve Allen could Shelley survive until the Compass Players called. I first saw Shelley when he was working as a single at the Gate of Horn in Chicago. His fresh humor brought down the house. George Jessel, with his hilarious telephone calls to his mother, introduced the format used by Berman. But Shelley's refinements—with philosophy and psychology thrown in—entitle him to credit for a complete new style.

Button-down Bob Newhart, of suburban Oak Park, worked in a number of jobs outside of show business. Among other things, he was an accountant for the U.S. Gypsum Company, a cigar-counter salesman, and occupied various desks in advertising agencies and commercial film studios. For diversion he used to phone an advertising copywriter friend, Ed Gallagher, and the two made up comic situations which Gallagher tape-recorded. Credit must go to a Chicago disk jockey, Dan Sorkin (a funny fellow in his own right) for much of the speed of Newhart's rise. Sorkin heard one of Bob's tapes at a party and immediately got him a recording contract. And then, Bob hooked on with Frank ("Tweet") Hogan, at that time Shelley Berman's manager. After hearing Newhart only once, I was convinced he should play at an upcoming local Emmy Awards dinner at which I was to preside. He did (the president has some power), and was off like his submarine *Codfish* which, as his admirers know, shelled Miami Beach—in the off-season. Newhart showed his gratitude to Sorkin by making him a regular on the Bob Newhart NBC-TV show.

So rapid was Newhart's rise that he and State Street merchant Joel Goldblatt, for whom Bob had been a fifty-dollar-a-week cigar salesman two Christmases earlier, couldn't resist indulging in some good-natured badinage at a Loyola University Stritch School of Medicine dinner not long ago. Bob had attended Loyola, but it was the first time the two had met. Reminded of Newhart's cigar-counter experience, Joel quipped: "We can use you again this Christmas—and we'll up the salary to seventy-five."

Dick Gregory, another ex-Chicagoan, was also talent-scouted by a broadcaster, newsman Alex Dreier. Dick has known lean days—times were so hard that his family was on relief. But he ran his way to a track scholarship at Southern Illinois University, and then ran on to comedy stardom with an engagement at Chicago's Playboy Club. After Dick appeared on the Jack Paar show and won nation-wide acclaim, his home town of St. Louis gave him the key to the city. "But," cracked Gregory, who is still snubbed by many there because of his color, "then they changed the locks!"

Why have all these fresh talents received their big break in Chicago? For a reason which many Broadway producers still haven't fathomed because it doesn't fit in with their stereotyped ideas of Chicago. Because our theater audiences are tremendously discriminating. We won't support the hackneyed or the second-rate. We demand what is new, fresh, and first-rate. When we get it, we finance it. We encourage it with our attendance and approval.

"People are always asking where the new comedians are coming from," wrote New York *Herald-Tribune* drama critic Walter Kerr, himself a former Chicago suburbanite who taught at Northwestern University. "They're coming from Chicago. Coming? They're here."

But there is much more to the Chicago entertainment beat. Through the branching out of our home-grown personalities, it stretches to Hollywood, to Broadway, and beyond.

Start in Hollywood, with the first stop the glamour department, where many consider today's number one vamp to be slim Kim Novak, the gorgeous Wright Junior College alumna whose Hollywood career has been nothing short of meteoric. The first time I saw Kim she was a leggy addition to a parade of models in a fashion shop on West Madison. During an intermission I happened to stroll backstage. There was Kim, reading a book, as part of her school homework. Now, long since her "discovery," she still has a scholarly bent—she quietly earned a degree in her spare time at Los Angeles City College. She is also the homebody type (every home should have such a body!). On Chicago visits, she shuns bright lights to stay on the Northwest Side with her parents or in Aurora with her sister, Mrs. Arlene Malmberg. Her attractive aide and traveling companion is her former Farragut High School friend, Barbara Mellon.

Another ex-Chicago favorite is Dorothy Lamour, the sarong girl herself. Dottie preceded such beauties from Chicago as Dolores Hart, Joan Tabor, Pamela Tiffin, ex-WGN "Blue Fairy" Brigid Bazlen, Myrna ("Miss USA") Hansen, Jean Blake (Beacham to "Miss Photoflash" fans), Marsha Hunt, Mercedes McCambridge, and Northwestern University coeds Pat Neal, Ann-Margret, Paula Prentiss, and Jean Hagen. And—oh, yes—Karyn Kupcinet.

In the male ranks, suburban New Trier High School has produced Roy Fitzgerald—somewhat better known as Rock Hudson —Hugh (Wyatt Earp) O'Brian, and Charlton Heston. Warren Beatty, Shirley MacLaine's younger brother, served his apprenticeship at Northwestern. It may be reaching a bit to call Marlon Brando a Chicago product. But he did live in Evanston and Libertyville, where he was an acting enthusiast and trackman (with, we assume, a torn T-shirt). Marlon comes by his acting skill naturally: his mother was once a fine community-theater actress.

Among ex-Chicago box-office bait on Broadway there are Cornelia Otis Skinner, Geraldine Page, Richard Kiley, Tom

Bosley, Bob Fosse, Carol Lawrence, and former Northwestern songwriters Jule (*Gypsy*) Styne and Sheldon (*Fiorello!*) Harnick. Styne has not so far had Harnick's good fortune in sharing a Pulitzer Prize. But his shows—*High Button Shoes, Gentlemen Prefer Blondes, Peter Pan, The Bells Are Ringing,* and others —have won virtually every other award in the field.

Vocalists? Mel Torme, Johnny Desmond, Joni James, and Frankie Laine are only a few of Chicago's graduates. Frankie, who as Frank LoVecchio was a choirboy at Immaculate Conception Church on North Park Avenue, adopted his high school's name, Lane, plus an "i," as his own. He has never forgotten Chicago. At the height of his popularity, when "Lucky Old Sun," "Mule Train," and other Laine recordings were selling to the tune of eight million copies in three years, he came back home to play a special benefit for his old parish church. Among the distinguished Chicago bandsmen are David Rose, Gene Krupa, Muggsy Spanier, and Benny Goodman. Gene, one of nine little Krupas, recalls taking his bride to a honeymoon apartment where they lived in a bedroom while fellow jazzmen Eddie Condon, Red McKenzie, and Pee Wee Russell slept in the living room. Muggsy, whose family bankroll was practically nonexistent, developed his trumpet style at the age of fourteen, sitting on a curb outside the Pekin Café, where such jazz artists as King Oliver and Satchmo Armstrong blew hot. Benny, the eighth of eleven children, took his first lessons in a West Side synagogue which furnished the band instruments. Later he took lessons at Hull House, and from Chicago Symphony clarinetist Franz Schoepp.

A little-known point of jazz history is that Benny Goodman's size determined his future. As Benny recalls it: "When the three of us went to the synagogue classes together for the first time, my brother Harry got a tuba because he was the biggest. Freddie got a trumpet. I was the smallest; I got a clarinet. If I had been twenty pounds heavier and two inches taller, I probably would be playing a tuba in some band today!"

Offstage and backstage, you will find such experts in their fields as producer Hal Wallis and Oscar-winning fashion designer Helen Rose, both ex-Chicagoans. And there, too, you will find Mr. Cartoon himself, Walt Disney. Walt, a native Chicagoan who later spent several years in Missouri, still has a warm feeling for Our Town: He studied here at McKinley High School and took night courses at the Chicago Academy of Fine Arts. And he worked here as a post-office employee and a rush-hour el train conductor. (Never sneer at a motorman—he may be heading for Fame and Fortuneland.)

Nor could this recital end without proper homage to the great Chicago-produced comedians and radio-TV stars.

Ever since the "good old days" of burlesque, Chicago always has been a major springboard for funny men. One of my favorites is my good friend from Waukegan, Jack Benny. (Actually, though he grew up in Waukegan, which named a junior high school for him not long ago, he was born in Chicago itself, where his mother was shopping when the time came to enter a hospital.) For years Jack returned to the city regularly to visit his father, who is now dead. He's still in and out of Chicago more than any other city, largely to visit a sister, Mrs. Leonard Fenchel, who still lives here.

For timing, control, good taste, and generosity in giving laugh lines to others, Jack has no peer in his field. He is also a true gentleman. By now it should be no secret that his favorite comedian is George Burns, who has only to walk on to make Jack break up. And it should be common knowledge that he is not really the skinflint and antique collector of his comedy sketches.

Jack gives lavishly to charity. During World War II, he insisted on paying the line charges for his broadcasts made around the country for War Bond drives and Army recruiting—an expense of one hundred thousand dollars in one year alone. Once, when Eddie Cantor invited him to dinner and began discussing a Bonds for Israel campaign, Benny overwhelmed his old friend by writing a check for $25,000. But Jack observed later: "Don't ever eat at Cantor's house. He serves the most expensive meals in town." The appeal of Jack's benefit violin concerts is well known. To date they have raised more than two million dollars for charity.

Danny Thomas, another good friend and comedy artist with a Chicago pedigree, traveled a rocky road up as a café comic. I remember him well from his days at the 5100 Club on Chicago's far North Side, in the early 1940s. He was just in from Detroit, jobless, with a wife and one child to feed, and another child on the way. Agent Leo Salkin, then of the William Morris Agency, booked him into the 5100 for seventy-five dollars a week. Danny played there for three solid years. That success led to a radio show (WMAQ), the night-club big time (first at La Martinique in New York)—and Danny was up and away.

Chicago also plays an important part in the story of Danny's service to St. Jude Thaddius, the "patron saint of hopeless causes." After being fired from a night club in Detroit, Danny prayed to St. Jude for a sign that he should continue in show business, and he received one; a telegram arrived, inviting him to come to Chicago to do a radio tooth-paste commercial. Later, reflecting on his good fortune and seeking a way to honor St. Jude by helping others, he asked the late Samuel Cardinal Stritch of Chicago for suggestions. "Why not a hospital for children? And why not in a city I've always felt close to—Memphis, where I began my priesthood," said the beloved prelate. Through personal appearances and fund drives, Danny raised $1,500,000 in five years, and in 1961 his six-million-dollar leukemia research hospital, dedicated to St. Jude, was opened in Memphis.

George Gobel, a Roosevelt High graduate and former singer on the WLS National Barn Dance, also calls Chicago home. In 1954, he stole the two-hour, four-network Diamond Jubilee of Light show with his explanation of a complicated electronic calculator:

"The reason I've been asked to explain the workings of this thing is because of my education in the field of elec . . . elec . . . elec . . . well, I know so much about the intric . . . I'm able to put technical terms into the language of the . . . I work cheap, is the reason."

George's break came after years of knocking around the small clubs, capped by a long stay at the North Side's Helsing's Lounge. It was a replay of the familiar Chicago success story. Many others came up the same way—Joey Bishop in the Vine Gardens on North Avenue, Olsen and Johnson in the old North American Restaurant, Shecky Greene at the Old Cuban Village, New

Yorker Alan King at the old Silver Frolics on Madison, and the late Willie Shore at the High-Hat on Rush Street.

Willie, nicknamed "Benefit Willie" (and during the war "Off-Shore Willie") for his willingness to play benefits anywhere, was particularly beloved. As familiar a part of the Near North Side as the Water Tower, he set what must be a record for a single stand—nine consecutive years at the High-Hat.

Then there is Stephen Valentine Patrick William Allen, a show-business kid almost literally born in a trunk (in New York), but most closely associated with Chicago and Hyde Park High School. Steve Allen, whose rise as a comedian began as an ad-libbing Los Angeles wrestling announcer and disk jockey, awes everyone with his versatility—as an author (two volumes of poetry, four other books, including his autobiography *Mark It and Strike It*, and miscellaneous short stories and teleplays); actor (star of *The Benny Goodman Story*); musician (he plays trumpet, tuba, clarinet, and, of course, piano); and composer of two thousand songs, including the title numbers for the movies *Picnic* and *Bell, Book and Candle.*

Once, Frankie Laine bet Allen $1,000 he couldn't compose 50 songs a day for a week. Steve moved a piano into a music-store window in Hollywood and went to work. He not only won the bet but one number, "Let's Go to Church Next Sunday," as recorded by Perry Como and Margaret Whiting, became a record hit, and sold 300,000 sheet-music copies!

Last winter Chicago TV station WBKB (ABC) chose Allen as the first subject for a series called *Back Home*, created by producer Dan Schuffman and his staff. In this program, Steve visited his former neighborhood in Hyde Park on Chicago's South Side and reminisced about the days when, as a boy, he had spent hours thinking and composing poetry in Jackson Park near the Museum of Science and Industry, and how his unhappy childhood was manifest in such actions as his repeatedly playing hooky from school, and running away from the relatives with whom he lived during his mother's long absences. It was a touching narrative which did much to explain the serious, introspective side of this highly talented entertainer.

And there is Julius ("Groucho") Marx and his brothers. They called Chicago their home early in their careers. Recalls Groucho, "We lived in a slum area for many years. It wasn't a slum until we moved in. We . . . that includes my mother and father, grandfather, my four brothers, aunt and uncle, and their child—a total of eleven living in a house with one bath. It was the busiest bathroom in town."

A classic story concerns the Greenebaum banking firm, which held the mortgage on the Marx' house. The payments always worried their mother. In the early days of their act, she would stand in the wings and as soon as the wacky brothers strayed from the script (it was inevitable), she would shout: "Greenebaum!" The word snapped everyone back to reality.

Several years ago, when the Greenebaum firm observed its centennial, Groucho wired: "It amazes me that you stayed in business a hundred years loaning money to people like us." But the bank thinks highly of Groucho. Not only did it never foreclose, it even elected him an honorary board member!

Internationally, however, there is no better known or more beloved comedian than the one who has been the hero of hundreds of such scenes as this:

The time: *Christmas*. The place: *Korea*. "Well, here we are in Korea, the Miami Beach of the Far East," the performer begins. "I won't say it's cold, but when we landed, Betty Furness opened the door of the plane. . . . You know, my grandfather was in the Navy. He was known as Admiral Tuna, the chicken of the sea." Peals of laughter thunder out over Bayonet Bowl, near the 38th parallel that separates South Korea from its hostile neighbor to the North. Men and women in uniform forget the subzero weather, forget that they are eight thousand miles from home and its comforts, forget the blues that envelop a person separated from his loved ones at Christmas. Bob Hope is making it a merry holiday.

It is an everlasting source of pride to us that Chicago gave Hope his start. Born Lester Townes Hope in England, he moved with his family to Cleveland as a youngster. He had a brief career as a boxer, and then came to Chicago in 1928 with dreams of breaking into vaudeville. With the help of a Cleveland school chum, Charles Cooley, he met Charley Hogan, then a prominent vaudeville booker and now one of Chicago's leading talent agents. His first professional assignment was as a Sunday night emcee at the old West Englewood Theater (now the Ogden)—for which he was paid fifteen dollars. Next Hogan booked him into the old Stratford Theater, where he played for six straight months, learning every trick of the trade. Bob Hope was on his way.

I've been watching Bob perform for years. So much has been written about him that it's difficult to talk about him without repeating what has been said. But I'll pass on a few personal observations. Bob is one of the most relaxed persons in show business—the Perry Como of the comics. I've seen him doze off, no matter how great the pressures, at the drop of a quip (his own). I've seen him asleep in planes, tents, igloos, golf locker rooms, and Japanese bathhouses. And then I've watched him bounce up to do a month's quota of shows in a single day—and top it off by visiting all the night spots on Tokyo's Ginza before beginning a new round of appearances the next morning. He is always in excellent physical condition, thanks to golf and an intelligent schedule of planned exertions, including bending exercises twice a day. He never overeats. And he insists on being thoroughly prepared for whatever he is to do. Although he can ad-lib with the best, he appears only after committing a long list of gags to memory. His collection of jokes—reportedly more than three million gags, neatly filed in cabinets—is probably the largest of any comedian's.

Year in, year out, when a charity needs help, Ol' Ski Nose is among the quickest to respond. Tirelessly he plays benefits for hospitals, for the Red Cross, for medical research, for fellow entertainers in need, for underprivileged kids—you name it. No matter that he must pay his staff to help produce a lively routine for each appearance; Bob cheerfully foots the bills. His is one of the biggest hearts in Hollywood. His theme song, "Thanks for the Memory," well expresses the sentiments of anyone who has known him.

Finally, I must stop at a corner of the entertainment beat that will always be special for Chicagoans: Radio-TV. There is something about radio—bigtime radio, as it was in the days before TV —that evokes an irresistible nostalgia. Since Chicago was radio's real home, we feel that nostalgia especially sharply here. The great network radio shows are gone now, and so is much of network TV to which Chicago contributed an incomparable, original, creative spirit. Yet we're still the home of five TV channels, some thirty AM outlets, and nearly two dozen FM stations. And the Chicago broadcasting beat is still packed with famous performers.

One of the most remarkable is the ol' Breakfast Clubber, Don McNeill. "You have no future in radio," he was once told at a station in Milwaukee. Now *The Breakfast Club,* nearing its thirtieth anniversary, is the longest-running show in broadcasting. It even got McNeill "nominated" for President—a 1948 gag. A smiling, personable performer, McNeill has come through the most turbulent period in our entertainment history, merely by being himself. As is proved by the hundreds of letters that flow into his Madison Street office every week, he is not only liked by his audience—he is loved.

So much good old-fashioned corn is featured on the show that one of McNeill's most important attributes is frequently overlooked: He is an astute judge of talent. A partial roll call of those he "discovered" and helped to success includes Fibber McGee and Molly (Jim and Marian Jordan), Sam ("Fiction and Fact") Cowling, Fran Allison, Alice ("Champagne Lady") Lon, Homer and Jethro, Johnny Desmond, and even Jack Paar, a one-time vacation replacement.

A stay-at-homer (he and wife Kay live in suburban Winnetka), Don is the father of three sons, Tom, Don, Jr., and Bob. One of the tribulations of fame to which they all had to adjust was evident when the boys were playing basketball at New Trier High School. Each time one of the young McNeills appeared on the court, the entire crowd would break into the chant, "Good morning, Breakfast Clubbers." Several years ago McNeill built a summer place on a forty-five-acre estate near Barrington, Illinois, "Himself's Hideaway," complete with a lake stocked with fish. But typical of McNeill, it is not for his family alone. In each of ten weeks every summer, ten members of the Chicago Boys Clubs are his guests.

Fran Allison, *The Breakfast Club's* "Aunt Fanny," is another down-to-earth Chicagoan with a delightful sense of humor. It is no exaggeration to say that none of her quips and barbs is prepared—they are all completely ad-lib. That's how she got her first break. One day at WMT in Waterloo, Iowa, when an emcee suddenly ran out of material, he grabbed Fran, who was on the staff of the station, pulled her in front of the microphone, and shouted, "Well, here comes Aunt Fanny! Come on in and say something, Fanny." Fran had to go on cold. As sharp then as she is now, she created her lovable character on the spot. "Aunt Fanny" has been convulsing radio listeners ever since. Fran first met Chicagoan Burr Tillstrom during World War II when they appeared together at bond rallies. Burr is as adroit at improvisation as Fran—all their *Kukla, Fran and Ollie* shows were done without a script. And for years this girl who has won fame for working without prepared material was also one of the best readers of lines in the business—as a Chicago soap-opera actress. Off-mike, Fran is the wife of Archie Levington, a successful music publisher.

Speaking of soapers, Chicago is the home town of the queen of the serial writers, Irna Phillips. In 1930 she became one of the founders of soap opera with *Painted Dreams* on WGN. Since then, she has aired as many as five shows a day as the creator of such sudsy classics as *The Guiding Light*, *Road of Life*, *Today's Children*, *Right to Happiness*, *Lonely Women*, and *Woman in White*. And for all the domestic tribulations she has dramatized, Miss Phillips herself has never married!

Thanks to such talent as Clifton Utley, Paul Harvey, John Harrington, Len O'Connor, Fahey Flynn, and Alex Dreier, Chicago's radio newsrooms are among the most active and respected anywhere. Pound for pound, there is probably not a newshawk anywhere who compares with Dreier. A native of Hawaii, ample Alex has a record as one of broadcasting's most accurate prophets. In one World War II broadcast he predicted the Allied invasion of North Africa—almost to the hour. He missed the date of

Germany's surrender by just four days. He called the turn on the rout of Rommel and the war in Russia. In 1948, when most pollsters predicted Thomas E. Dewey's election as President, Alex rightly named Harry S. Truman. And in 1952 he came within two electoral votes of pegging General Eisenhower's landslide. A "Man on the Go" in fact as well as nickname, Alex is one of Chicago's most popular banquet speakers. (His secret: "I never speak longer than the weakest kidney.")

Other home towners—Mike Wallace, Lowell Thomas, Durward Kirby, and Betsy Palmer (if I may claim East Chicago, Indiana, too) have had distinguished network careers. But of all the prominent Chicagoans in broadcasting, none has acquitted himself with more distinction than Hugh Downs, whose difficult task it was to serve as the balance wheel in a delicate mechanism that was *The Jack Paar Show*. I have known Jack Paar for years. When his show succeeded the old NBC-TV *America After Dark* program (on which I had been one of the participants), I was host at his first press reception in Chicago. After his much-publicized walkout over censorship of the "water closet story," I was one of the two newspaper columnists that Paar wanted to "grill" him on the air (Hy Gardner, of the New York *Herald Tribune*, was the other). A number of Paar fans protested that Hy and I "grilled" Paar too vigorously, but that had been our assignment and Jack had thanked us for it personally. My files, in fact, contain many letters and quotes of endearment and respect from Paar. The outburst against me that he finally made in the aftermath of his "expedition" to West Berlin came as a surprise, and Hugh Downs' response to it, to my mind, shows best what a thorough gentleman Hugh is. Downs, as you'll recall, stood up to his boss and criticized him openly for making a personal attack on me. Poor Hugh was called on to restrain Jack on many other such occasions.

Make no mistake about Paar. He had his "good side": his sharp wit, his unquestioned ability as an interviewer, and his flair for spotting talent and popularizing new stars that made late-night TV viewing so exciting for many months.

Incidentally, in the event that you are still wondering what heinous things I wrote about Paar to occasion his outburst, here is the item in its entirety. Recall, if you will, the spate of headlines about Paar's Berlin show and the fact that this was written with obvious tongue in cheek, and you'll have a better understanding of the incident.

> In Mike Fish's the other night, members of the Damon Runyon set were discussing the refusal of NBC-TV's Meet the Press to schedule Jack Paar for a guest appearance. "I do not think Paar should be angry on account he cannot get on Meet the Press," exclaimed Society Kid Hogan. "He would be much better on a show called To Tell the Truth. I would like to see the real Jack Paar stand up."
>
> "You got the wrong show for Paar," offered Morose Artie. "He should by all means appear on What's My Line? Nobody seems to know the answer to that one."
>
> "I do not wish to argue with my closest chums," cut in High Hat Harry, "but to me the show for Paar is I've Got a Secret. Then he can tell the audience his secret is that it is not so tense in Berlin and what's all the excitement about, anyhow?"
>
> Five-Star Final could hold back no longer. "The trouble with you guys is that you don't understand Paar. If he wants to guest on a show, the one for him is Yout' Wants to Know. He is very good with the youts of our nation on account he has nice, easy answers for everything."

Dave Garroway is another whose professionalism I admire greatly. His old 11:60 *Club* disk-jockey radio show on WMAQ, and *Garroway at Large* on TV, proved him a versatile, mature, and conscientious entertainer long before he left Chicago. On such snafu-prone network shows as *Today* and *Wide Wide World* probably no one except Dave, with his unique, even temperament, could have survived. He still chuckles over such incidents as the one involving a TV producer who almost overslept the morning that *Today* was scheduled to do a remote pickup from the middle of New York's George Washington Bridge. In the early dawn, wild-eyed and still in pajamas, he hailed a cab and said breathlessly, "George Washington Bridge, and stop in the middle." "Oh, no, you don't, buddy," yelled the driver. "Not in my cab!" (After a proper explanation, the producer arrived and the show went on.)

And then there are the all-important men and women behind the scenes in radio and television. Louis G. Cowan, former president of CBS-TV is only one of many Chicagoans who have set the trend in mass communications. His *Quiz Kids* on radio, and *Stop the Music* and $64,000 *Question* on TV, were among the most popular programs of all time. (Cowan is now with Brandeis University, and a book publisher. His successor at CBS Television, James Aubrey, Jr., was also a Chicagoan.) The late H. Leslie Atlass, of WBBM, helped build CBS radio and CBS-TV, and popularized such stars as Gene Autry, Dale Evans, the Andrews Sisters, Ben Bernie, and Janette Davis. Other notable "backstage" personalities include Clark George, Atlass' successor at WBBM, and his opposite numbers, Sterling Quinlan of WBKB-ABC, Lloyd Yoder of WNBQ-NBC, and Ward Quaal of the highly respected independent station, WGN-TV; Rod (*Twilight Zone*) Serling, a former Herrick House instructor who is one of TV's ablest writers; Bernie and Rita Jacobs, who turned a bankrupt FM franchise into a Peabody Award winner and the most successful cultural station in the nation (listeners once kicked in $11,000 in one week to keep their WFMT going); former automobile distributor Pete DeMet, the "Mr. Bowling," "Mr. Golf," and "Mr. Fishing" of TV production; and Bill Morrow, program producer for the Ol' Groaner, Bing Crosby.

Then there is the funniest backstager of them all, the zany king of the comedy writers, Goodman Ace who—with his wife Jane—once broadcast the fondly remembered *Easy Aces* from Chicago. Goody, a former Kansas City columnist, has not only been head gag writer for Milton Berle and Perry Como, for a time he was also supervisor of comedy for CBS radio. The latter assignment didn't last long, however. Explained Goody, who found that few of his ideas were accepted: "If an atom bomb ever fell on New York, I'm sure the safest place to take shelter would be the eighteenth floor of CBS. There's no radioactivity there."

Some say there is no radio activity in Chicago, either. Or TV activity. So far as network-originations are concerned, this is essentially true. But competition on the local scene, with four commercial TV stations, one educational station, and dozens of radio stations, is extremely lively and healthy. Chicago always will be a grooming ground for its hordes of talent, which will find its way to the greener pastures of Broadway and Hollywood.

4. Meet the Press, the Publishers, the Writers

Every newspaper that rolls off the presses in Chicago reflects the special personality that has always distinguished Chicago journalism. You can call it an inheritance from the colorful days immortalized in the Hecht-MacArthur play, *The Front Page*, but it is actually a reflection of the nonconformist spirit that has characterized the city from its beginnings. Either way you look at it, the fact remains that Chicago journalism is steeped in a rich tradition—a tradition that affects every one of us who works in a Chicago city room or covers a beat.

The period between the turn of the century and the late 1930s was a time of some of the wildest literary high-jinks in newspaper history, and the most outrageous ruses and pranks of all were contrived by newspapermen in Chicago. "Every newspaper editor owes tribute to the devil," said the French poet and fabulist La Fontaine. In the case of some Chicago editors, this aphorism seems almost an understatement.

Chicago dailies provided a fairgrounds for the literary antics of such outstanding newspapermen as Ring Lardner, Ben Hecht, Charles MacArthur, John Gunther, and Robert Casey. And also active on Chicago newspapers of the period were a number of major literary figures who are no longer thought of as reporters—

Carl Sandburg, Ernest Hemingway, Sherwood Anderson, and Theodore Dreiser.

Today we have four downtown dailies: the *Sun-Times* and *Daily News* of Marshall Field IV, and the *Tribune* and *Chicago's American* of the McCormick interests. In those early days, there were as many as nine newspapers on the streets at one time, all of them run by hard-drinking, hard-driving, not always ethical staffs who would do anything for a story—including stealing it.

The *Post and Mail*, a short-lived paper owned by the McMullen brothers, did just that—steal stories. Every day, shortly after the *Daily News* hit the streets, some of the *News'* stories would turn up verbatim in the columns of the *Post and Mail*. *Daily News* publisher Melville Stone tried a number of unsuccessful expedients to stop this blatant plagiarism. Then, one day, he had an inspiration: in the middle of a legitimate story, describing a famine in Serbia, he planted this alleged comment from the Mayor of Belgrade:

"Er us siht la etsll iws nel lum cmeht!"

This, translated, was said to mean: "The municipality cannot aid."

Just as Stone expected, the McMullens reprinted the story—word for word. Then Stone phoned the other Chicago papers to let them in on his hoax. Spelled backwards, he explained, the quote actually said:

"The McMullens will steal this sure!"

There were some reporters who captured, single-handed, public enemies and locked them in hotel rooms until their scoops were printed. It didn't matter to these reporters that they were violating the law against harboring lawbreakers. Hecht and MacArthur used such an incident in the plot of *The Front Page*.

Other reporters carried out elaborate masquerades to get their stories. One novel adventure was the inspiration of *Times* managing editor Lou Ruppel; it was carried out by three of his staff photographers, George Emme, Bob Rankin, and Fran Byrne, with the connivance of their photo chief, Mike Fish, shortly after an El train crash. To gain admission to St. Francis Hospital, in Evanston, where the injured conductor was being kept in isolation, they rented priests' cassocks from a costume shop. Then, with cameras and flash bulbs hidden beneath their robes, they strolled casually up to the policeman who was guarding the entrance to the conductor's room.

"Is this the room of the poor, tortured soul who was in the terrible El train wreck?" one asked.

The officer was properly impressed. He assured the "priests" that this was indeed the room they sought, and allowed them to enter. Once inside, they calmly proceeded with their picture-taking—until a flash bulb exploded. The guard, suspicious, opened the door, and soon was struggling with the photographers. He managed to seize their big press camera, but he was not aware of the tiny Leica that Byrne had brought along for just such an emergency. Cassocks flying, the "priests" made their escape and the *Times* scooped every paper in town.

For sanctioning this impersonation, Ruppel was reprimanded by the ranking Roman Catholic prelate in Chicago, the late George Cardinal Mundelein. But in the end, Ruppel was released with only a mild rebuke, largely because of his sincere regret for the escapade, but partly, perhaps, because he had been one of the children baptized by young Father Mundelein when he was a parish priest in Brooklyn.

A few reporters have confessed to even wilder escapades. Ben Hecht, for example, delights to recall the days when, with the aid of photographer Gene Cour, he titillated Chicago *Journal* readers with a succession of downright hoaxes: a series of accounts of piracy along the Chicago River, a major disaster involving a runaway streetcar, and even a description of an earthquake that supposedly shook the North Side.

"That earthquake story," said Hecht later, "wasn't such a good idea. I had to quote every relative I had to make it convincing. And creating a 'fissure' along the Lake Shore took two hours of hard digging!"

Hecht might have continued his "scoops" indefinitely. But to illustrate a story about an exiled "Romanian princess," he selected an unfortunate model for his photographs—one of the vice district's most spectacularly notorious prostitutes. Only Hecht's promise to cease from such shenanigans saved him his job.

Subsequent work for the *Daily News* showed Hecht to be not only a good newspaperman, but a gifted creative writer. A personification of the era, he was at the hub of a group which included Harry Hansen, Charles Collins, Vincent Starrett, John Gunther, and others who frequented the old Covici-McGee Bookstore, and a restaurant called Schlogl's. With the fitful assistance of poet Maxwell Bodenheim, Hecht also published a tabloid journal called *The Chicago Literary Times.*

This paper is a collector's item today, if for no other reason than the pot shots that the two gifted eccentrics took at one another. Hecht's book, *1001 Afternoons in Chicago*, wrote Bodenheim in one issue, was "the vivid etching of a disillusioned mind." Bodenheim's *Blackguard*, according to Hecht, was "as definite an experience as inhaling a quart of chlorine gas." Both agreed, however, that New York City was "the national cemetery of arts and letters"—and, ultimately, both moved there.

It was during this period that Hecht and Bodenheim staged what may still be the world's shortest and screwiest formal debate before a paying audience. They were to discuss the proposition, "Resolved; that people who attend literary lectures are fools." The affair was well publicized, and the house was sold out. Both speakers, meanwhile, had insisted on being paid in advance. When Hecht rose to take the affirmative side, he merely gestured toward the audience, turned to Bodenheim, and said:

"I rest my case."

"You win," said Bodenheim, and the two debaters walked out arm in arm.

We will always remember Hecht, not only for his iconoclasm but for his amazing literary output: at least a dozen books, more than fifty uncollected short stories, and innumerable magazine articles. Working sometimes alone, but more frequently in collaboration with Charles MacArthur (late husband of actress

Helen Hayes), he wrote a number of successful Broadway plays and the scripts for more than sixty movies, including *Spellbound, Notorious, Wuthering Heights,* and *A Farewell to Arms*—a record approached by few others. And as Charles MacArthur's brother, Chicago insurance magnate, Alfred MacArthur, could testify, there probably wasn't a ghost-written piece in the lot.

Alfred once bet Hecht $2,000 that he couldn't write a book in two days that would win critical praise and also sell more than 20,000 copies. Thirty-six hours later Hecht finished dictating a book that won the bet—*The Florentine Dagger.*

There were other well-known writers on the Chicago papers then: Ring Lardner and Westbrook Pegler of the *Tribune* sports staff, Jack Lait, Lowell Thomas, Burton Rascoe, and humorists George Ade, Finley Peter ("Mr. Dooley") Dunne, Bert Leston Taylor ("B. L. T."), and the widely loved Franklin P. Adams ("F. P. A.," as he later signed his column in New York).

There was Robert J. Casey, *Daily News* reporter now retired, who made famous such wry leads as these:

"Anna Marie Hahn's 11 husbands came to court today—10 of them in glass jars and one in a blue serge suit."

And after Richard Loeb was stabbed to death in Statesville Prison, in what was alleged to be a homosexual quarrel:

"Richard Loeb, who graduated from college with honors at the age of 15 and who was a master of the English language, today ended his sentence with a proposition."

And this, some time after Pearl Harbor Day, about his own boss, *Daily News* publisher Frank Knox who was then serving as Franklin Roosevelt's Secretary of the Navy:

"The Navy has just raised the eighth of the two ships which Secretary of the Navy Frank Knox said were sunk on Dec. 7."

Ed Lahey, Casey's former *News* colleague and now chief Washington correspondent for the Knight Newspapers, is one of the few today who still writes in this manner. When "Machine Gun" Jack McGurn, a golfing enthusiast, was slain near Eightieth Street on Chicago's South Side, Lahey's opening sentence read:

"Machine Gun Jack holed out last night. He died in the low Eighties."

There were our noted cartoonists: John T. McCutcheon of the *Tribune* and Vaughn Shoemaker of the *Daily News* (both Pulitzer Prize winners), and Harry Hershfield, also of the *Daily News*. And later there was another *News* "comer," a North Side kid who once chalked drawings on the blackboards at Senn High School—the pixyish, Pulitzer Prize winner Herbert L. ("Herblock") Block, now of the Washington *Post & Times-Herald*.

And there were the distinguished theater critics, including the *Tribune's* Burton Rascoe and Percy Hammond; the *Daily News'* Amy Leslie, who was a friend of Stephen Crane and the wife of Frank ("Bring 'em Back Alive") Buck; and the Hearst Newspapers' Ashton Stevens.

As long as there is an American theater, the beloved Ashton in particular will be remembered. A wiry, debonair man about town who had previously been a reviewer in San Francisco and New York, his carefully phrased opinions were read and respected by every major theatrical figure of the period. "The Mercy Killer," as he was called, was critically uncompromising, and wonderfully good-humored.

Yet this doesn't mean he couldn't be mordant. After one opening night, during which a gangster had been murdered outside the theater, Stevens reported succinctly:

"They shot the wrong man."

William Randolph Hearst wanted Stevens to return to New York. But Stevens found ample challenge in the exciting west-of-Broadway world of those days. Furthermore, he and his attractive wife Kay, a former actress whom he had met in Chicago, were comfortably established in the city. He remained a Chicagoan until his death in 1951.

One reason that Chicago journalism has been so distinctive is that a special pioneering breed of publishers and editors was developed in those early years.

There was S. Emory Thomason. Because of differences with owner-publisher Colonel Robert R. McCormick, Thomason tore up the contract which had provided him with a six-figure salary as vice-president and general manager of the *Tribune*, and thereafter established the *Times*, which he proceeded to build into a literate and liberal tabloid which supported Franklin Delano Roosevelt.

There was Richard J. Finnegan, the great editor whom I remember warmly for the personal help and inspiration he gave me when I first joined the *Times*. No editor pursued stories with greater drive than Finnegan, and few weighed the news value of a story as seriously as he did against the harm it might do. I'll never forget the time a reporter rushed breathlessly into the city room with an interview that would have made lively reading on page one. Finnegan killed that story because it could have done great harm to an innocent person.

Over in the Tribune Tower, the late Colonel McCormick was at the peak of his power. Grandson of the pioneer *Tribune* publisher, Joseph Medill, who had played such an important part in Abraham Lincoln's nomination for President, McCormick was among the last of the publishers who could be considered rugged individualists. Few men were spared his wrath; he was always on the offensive. His targets included Mayor "Big Bill" Thompson; Marshall Field III (to whom he tried to deny Associated Press membership for the *Sun*); Henry Ford (who once emerged from a million-dollar libel suit against the *Tribune* with six cents in damages); all of Great Britain (which he frequently envisioned as "attacking" the United States from Canada, through Detroit!); and even the Colonel's own cousin, Captain Joseph Medill Patterson. Though the two shared control of the *Tribune* when they took over in 1914, they soon agreed to separate. Patterson returned from World War I to establish the *Tribune*'s sister paper, the New York *Daily News*.

The Colonel's diatribes against Franklin D. Roosevelt are still famous. The two men had been schoolmates at Groton School. McCormick delighted in saying of Roosevelt: "He wasn't one of those students regarded as most promising or likely to succeed. In fact, I don't think I would have remembered him if he hadn't become President!"

The Colonel had many eccentricities. His enormous desk was set on a high dais in his tremendous office. He made frequent midnight forays into the city room of the *Tribune*, accompanied by a pair of huge German shepherd dogs. When rock-ribbed Republican Rhode Island ousted several GOP judges from its Supreme Court, he ordered a star to be torn from the Tribune Tower's American flag. And he initiated the phonetic spelling system that often puzzled *Tribune* readers. His pride in his military service was reflected in the annual picnics he sponsored for the World War I Army buddies with whom he served in France. They would meet at his Cantigny Farm estate on the outskirts of Wheaton, Illinois. (Pursuant to the Colonel's bequest, the farm is now an $850,000 military museum.)

As often as many of us disagreed with the Colonel's policies and smiled at his foibles, we had to give him credit for his remarkable courage, daring, and newspaper acumen. These qualities are still reflected in the *Tribune*, under the editorial direction of W. Don Maxwell, who arrived at his present position by way of DePauw University in Greencastle, Indiana, and the *Tribune* sports department.

Although the late Marshall Field III did not enter the newspaper publishing field until he was advanced in years, he, too, must be considered an outstanding individualist and a publishing pioneer. Field, known as the "millionaire with a conscience," made tremendous contributions to Chicago, including one of America's first large-scale, privately financed slum clearance projects, the Marshall Field Garden Apartments. He also built the Field and Pittsfield Buildings in the Loop and helped found Roosevelt University, which he endowed through the $11,000,000 Field Foundation. But we newspapermen remember him best for his determination to establish a strong, liberal newspaper to compete with the conservative *Tribune*, which then held a monopoly in the morning newspaper field. This new paper was the Chicago *Sun*. (Field also helped found *PM*, an ill-fated, adless daily in New York.)

"I happen to have been left a great deal of money," Field once said. "I don't know what is going to happen to it, and I don't give a damn. If I can't make myself worthy of three square meals a day, then I don't deserve them."

The late Lloyd Lewis, author, editor, and critic, was one of the many who could testify as to how worthy Field made himself. During the 1930s, when Lewis invited a group of wealthy Chicagoans to a series of luncheons to help campaign for higher salaries for teachers, Field was the only one to accept.

"In fact," said Lewis, "he was the only one with more than ten bucks who attended those luncheons."

Field expressed his philosophy in his book, *Freedom Is More Than a Word*, in which he wrote: "The spirit of man cannot become satisfied so long as there exists any fellow being in want, any disease uncured, any injustice unquestioned, or any pool of darkness unlit by the lamp of knowledge."

This was the credo by which he lived. No one who knew the man will ever forget him.

Marshall Field III's son and successor, Marshall Field IV, has built on his father's heritage—and he has built handsomely.

The elder Field established the Chicago *Sun* and later purchased the evening tabloid, the *Daily Times*, to form the morning *Sun-Times*. Under the guidance of young Field, the *Sun-Times* has grown into a lively, highly enterprising newspaper that today is giving the *Tribune* a race for morning circulation. And after the *Tribune* acquired *Chicago's American* from Hearst, Field bought the Chicago *Daily News*, the leader in the afternoon field. Now, fortified with these two powerful newspapers, young "Marsh" has become the first publisher to threaten the *Tribune's* long domination of the Chicago newspaper scene.

I have great respect for Marshall Field IV. He has a steel-trap mind that clamps down hard on facts and figures. He keeps abreast of developments in every phase of his publishing empire; yet he believes in delegating authority and letting each executive run his own department. He has wit and charm. And while he takes his work seriously, not so himself. I recall the time several of us were celebrating his birthday in the offices of circulation director Lou Spear. Field had just turned forty. "Here I am, forty years old," he commented sadly, "and what do I have to show for it?" What he had was a multimillion-dollar fortune and a publishing empire, but apparently he did not consider these things worth mentioning.

The elder Field, in the process of founding the Chicago *Sun*, had also established Field Enterprises, which operates the newspapers and which had also acquired other properties, such as *The World Book Encyclopedia* and *Childcraft*, Pocket Books (for a brief period), *Parade* magazine, and a chain of radio stations across the Midwest and Far West. Within a few years, Field Enterprises was a communications empire.

But as is typical of young Field, he soon divested Field Enterprises of its peripheral operations. He considered them too distracting to his main business of publishing newspapers in Chicago. First the radio stations were sold; then *Parade*, with its headquarters in New York. Marshall Field IV is determined to concentrate his efforts in Chicago.

Young Field's attitude toward money differs from that of his late father. Whereas the elder Field practically subsidized his newspapers with his vast fortune, Marsh insists that his publications be financial successes on their own. He wants them to operate in the black—not so that he can make a fortune (most of the profits are plowed back into the operation), but because he prefers to be identified with solid, businesslike publications that require no subsidy for their existence. He is willing to work tirelessly to achieve this financial solidity, as his *Sun-Times* and *Daily News* executives are aware.

The courage and strength of purpose which Marsh demonstrates as a publisher were evident in World War II, when he served with distinction as a Navy officer in the Pacific. For his heroism as a gunnery officer aboard the U.S.S. *Enterprise*, he was awarded the Silver Star, the Presidential Unit Citation, and the Purple Heart.

Of all the newspaper publishers and editors I have known down through the years—and I have known many—only two would qualify for the Hollywood version of the hard-bitten newspaperman. One was the late Walter Howie, a Hearst editor. He was the prototype of the dynamic, fire-snorting, stop-the-press editor in *The Front Page*.

I knew Walter and his wife Gloria only in the final stages of his career, when he had been dispatched back to Chicago by

Hearst to revitalize the fading *American*. Howie tried desperately to save the paper, and frequently showed flashes of his old imaginative, inventive self. But it was too late. Times and conditions had changed. His era had ended.

I've already told a story about my other nominee—the late Louis Ruppel, who was managing editor of the Chicago *Times* when I was hired by sports editor Marvin McCarthy in late 1935. Ruppel was an imposing figure standing six foot three. Our first meeting was extremely informal. Every morning at nine, he would step out of his office, seat himself at the city editor's desk, and scan the first edition of the paper, page by page.

No mistake ever eluded him. And each mistake he found set off a bellow of profanity that would have blistered the mouth of a Civil War mule driver. On this particular day he spotted a mistake in the sports section and blasted out: "Hey you blankety-blank-blank in sports! Change that blankety-blank-blank caption on page forty. How blankety stupid can you blank-blank guys be?" Inasmuch as I was the only member of the sports staff on duty at the moment, I caught the full effects of the Ruppel temper.

A short time later, we met more formally. I was still writing sports. We were seated next to each other, ringside, at the Chicago Stadium, waiting for Heavyweight Champion Joe Louis to flatten another of his "bum of the month" contenders. A politician whom I knew well was Ruppel's guest. He introduced us.

Ruppel didn't recognize me.

"You with the *Times?*" he asked.

I assured him that I was. In sports.

"Who'd you know? How'd you get the job?"

I replied that I didn't "know" anybody, that I had applied and thought that I had been hired on my ability.

He fixed a quizzical eye on me for a few seconds. Then, in his usual lusty manner, he gave me a hearty slap on the back and exclaimed, "Glad to have you aboard, kid."

Any further attempt at conversation was impossible. Joe Louis landed a right and the fight, less than two rounds old, was over.

Years later, when I wrote Ruppel's obituary, I said: "Working under him was like working under a time bomb that could go off at any moment." But despite all his bluster and bluff, Ruppel had an appealing personality, an uncanny sense of news, a keen ability to appraise photographs—and a stubbornness that never allowed anyone to challenge his authority. It was this last characteristic that cost Ruppel some of the best newspaper jobs in the nation.

A classic example of mulishness occurred while Ruppel was editor of what is now *Chicago's American*, a job he held after serving as a Marine in World War II. He was a rare Hearst editor. He was audacious enough to declare that he, not William Randolph Hearst, would decide which of "The Chief's" editorials would run in Chicago. Once, when Ruppel was asked the whereabouts of one of Hearst's "sacred cow" editorials on antivivisection, Ruppel pointed to the wastebasket.

"It's in there," he shouted. "And that's where the goddam thing is staying."

As might be expected, Ruppel's connection with the Hearst organization was severed shortly after.

(It is interesting to note that the *Chicago's American* has enjoyed much more editorial freedom since it has been sold to the McCormick interests. Most observers expected the *Tribune* management to enforce its own rigid policies on the new acquisition. The management has not done so. As a matter of fact, Publisher Stuart List and Editor Lloyd Wendt have often taken positions directly opposed to the *Tribune's*, both in editorials and in news treatment. The *American* continues to support some Democrats on the local scene—a position that would be untenable at the *Tribune*.)

With his razor-sharp intelligence, Ruppel was a masterful headline writer. One headline which created journalistic history was written by Ruppel in 1936, when President Roosevelt was seeking his second term. The *Tribune*, whose Colonel McCormick detested FDR, was running a "box" daily on its front page, in which the days remaining until election were counted off, one by one. These boxes were headed "ONLY—DAYS LEFT TO SAVE YOUR COUNTRY."

The campaign was the prime topic of conversation throughout Chicago. Ruppel was aware of this, and he was also aware that the *Tribune* "box" was a perfect target for a page-one gag head-line on Election Day. But what should it say? For three days he racked his brain for just the right headline. It finally occurred to him during dinner on Election Eve, in the now defunct Chez Paree. His companions were Ray Hahne, production manager of the *Times*, and Mike Fish, then chief photographer of the *Times* and now a thriving Chicago restaurateur.

Ruppel had been pounding the table and tossing out headline after headline. "I know what I want but I can't put my finger on it," he said. Hahne finally exclaimed, "Aw, let's forget the whole thing and go home. We can't stay here until Christmas. That's about fifty days away, you know."

"That's it!" shouted Ruppel.

The next day, when the big story was the fact that the nation was going to the polls to elect either Roosevelt or Landon as President, Ruppel's headline ignored the obvious and struck out at the *Tribune*'s campaign "to save the country." His headline read:

52 DAYS
TO XMAS

The influence of such colorful figures will not soon diminish. But imaginative journalism is only part of the tradition that Chicago has inherited from those early years. The distinction of having nurtured the most extraordinary renaissance in modern literature is another. Not even New York, the present literary capital of the United States, has spawned so many giants in the field of letters in so short a period as did Chicago in the first quarter of this century.

There was Sherwood Anderson, the former Ohio paint factory executive, working in a Chicago advertising agency by day and writing the novel, *Winesburg, Ohio,* by night.

There was Hoosier Theodore Dreiser, who drew on his memories of Chicago reporting days when he used traction magnate Charles Yerkes as the model for Frank Cowperwood, the hero of his novels, *The Financier* and *The Titan.*

There were Hamlin Garland, Willa Cather, and poets Vachel Lindsay, Lew Sarett, and Edgar Lee Masters—a law partner of

Clarence Darrow. And James Gould Cozzens, Edna Ferber, John Dos Passos, and Archibald MacLeish.

And there is the author of the most-quoted description of Chicago ever written:

> Hog Butcher for the World,
> Tool Maker, Stacker of Wheat,
> Player with Railroads and the Nation's Freight Handler;
> Stormy, husky, brawling,
> City of the Big Shoulders . . .

Carl Sandburg was a man who had already been around when he wrote those awe-struck words. A native of downstate Galesburg, he had played semipro baseball, worked on Mississippi River steamboats, soldiered in the Spanish-American War, washed dishes in Kansas City, picked fruit in Colorado, covered a police beat in New York City, served as secretary to Milwaukee's Socialist Mayor—and had even spent two weeks at West Point in the same class with General Douglas MacArthur (where fortunately for American letters, Sandburg had been washed out). But Chicago stirred him as nothing had before.

Chicago was first to honor him for his poems. *Poetry*, the magazine founded here by Chicagoan Harriet Monroe, bought "Chicago," "Fog," and many other famous early poems. It was also here that he learned writing discipline, while pounding out spot news and feature beats on the *Daily News* staff of Henry Justin Smith and Lloyd Lewis. And it was here that he found time for a project that he had dreamed of since his boyhood days in Galesburg, site of the fifth Lincoln-Douglas debate—a biography of the Prairie Years of Abraham Lincoln. His great break came when he became movie critic for the *Daily News:* by working desperately he found that he could complete his week's assignments on Monday, Tuesday, and Wednesday, seeing all the new films and stockpiling his reviews. This left the rest of the week free for his poetry and his Lincoln studies.

As Hecht and quite a few others had demonstrated, however, a creative genius on a Chicago news staff did not always make for editorial tranquillity. In Sandburg's case, nothing demonstrated this more than the way he handled an assignment to cover a bitter national labor convention in Minneapolis. Disorder had been expected at the meeting. And the first day, right on schedule, all the wire stories told of a near-riot on the floor of the convention. Eagerly, *Daily News* editors awaited Sandburg's exclusive firsthand report. None arrived. There were further disorders the second and third days, and on the fourth day several delegates were wounded in a general gun battle on the convention floor. Still no copy from Sandburg. Finally, in desperation, managing editor Henry Justin Smith telegraphed his correspondent:

"Dear Sandburg: Please come home. Smith."

Hours later came Sandburg's reply:

"Dear Smith: Can't leave now. Everything too exciting. Sandburg."

Long one of America's most popular and active senior citizens, Sandburg has only recently begun to curtail (slightly) his travel and lecture schedule. He waited until he had passed his eightieth birthday. He still likes to visit Chicago, and comes here often from the Flat Rock, North Carolina, farm where he lives with his wife, Paula, the sister of photographer Edward Steichen. His stamina never ceases to surprise me.

I remember one night in the Pump Room, after the local première of the play *The World of Carl Sandburg*, when he and Bette Davis and Gary Merrill of the cast sat up with several of us long after midnight. Thinking Sandburg must be tired, the rest of us didn't dance, but remained in the booth talking. This did not last long.

"Maybe nobody else is going to dance," said Carl, "but I am." Whereupon the white-haired poet offered a hand to Chicagoan Donna Workman and took dozens of spirited turns around the floor.

Another time, in New York, Carl was invited out to dinner by ex-Chicago bookman Bill Targ, now editor in chief of The World Publishing Company. Bill expected Sandburg to suggest some small, quiet restaurant. Instead, he was surprised to hear the poet reply, "How about 21?"

Once at the night club, Targ suggested that they occupy an

inconspicuous corner table, which well-known people often prefer in the interest of privacy. But Sandburg shook his head mischievously.

"I'd rather sit up near the entrance," he said. "Then we can watch the celebrities."

Almost every honor Carl Sandburg could wish for has come to him—including the preservation of his birthplace in Galesburg as a shrine. Quite a few schools have been named for him, and he has been awarded two Pulitzer Prizes. Only the Nobel Prize for Literature remains to be captured—and a few years ago when it was awarded to Ernest Hemingway, Hemingway himself said publicly that it should have gone to Sandburg. Someone asked Sandburg how he felt about it. "Shucks," he answered, "it makes no difference."

Then, with humor that has endeared him to all who have known him, Carl added, "Twenty years from now some fellows will be sitting around and one of them will ask, 'Say, did Sandburg ever get the Nobel prize?' And another will answer, 'Sure, he got it in 1954—Hemingway presented it to him.'"

Either way, the Chicago area can still establish its claim to the prize. For "Papa" Hemingway grew up in Oak Park, one of our oldest and largest suburbs. (Oak Park, incidentally, has also been the home of Edgar Rice Burroughs, creator of Tarzan, of Frank Lloyd Wright, and of Robert St. John.)

The son of a doctor, Hemingway had to his credit a long list of accomplishments before leaving Oak Park High School, including co-editorship of the school paper and letters in swimming (he was team captain) and football (he was a tackle). Then he spent six months as a reporter for the Kansas City *Star*. From there, he left for Canada, and thence Europe and the beginning of his extraordinary life of adventure and success.

One of the few times he returned to Oak Park, in 1929, it was partly to investigate a report that his book, *A Farewell to Arms*, had been banned from the Oak Park library. Thus it was that the librarian one day was challenged by a broad-shouldered, barrel-chested young man:

"May I see that book by Hemingway—*A Farewell to Arms?*"

"Well, we have it," she replied, "but it's not on the shelves. Being the sort of book it is, we couldn't possibly display it for general circulation."

Hemingway turned without a word and stalked out of the building, a look of wry amusement on his face.

(Of course, the library now has an extensive selection of Hemingway novels, short stories, and poems, including a fine collection of first editions and galley proofs obtained by Chicago bookseller Ralph Newman from a former head of the Scribner's rare-book shop.)

Hemingway's many brushes with danger and high adventure have been chronicled in detail—as a World War I ambulance driver, as a big-game hunter and fisherman, as a World War II correspondent and soldier of fortune, and as the survivor of two plane crashes in the course of a single journey. But two stories of incidents that resulted from the publicity given to such exploits merit telling here.

The writer, Max Eastman, once openly challenged Hemingway's manliness. He wrote an essay in which he questioned whether there was even any hair on the famous author's chest. Both the wording and implications infuriated Papa—so much so that he cornered Eastman in his publisher's office. Without a word, he tore open his shirt to reveal a small jungle of hair—then swatted the essayist with a copy of his own book!

The other incident occurred at the Stork Club in New York, when a society leader who had spotted Hemingway among the patrons began to disparage him as a "professional he-man." In the best tradition of one of his own movies, Hemingway took one swing and knocked his detractor flat.

Unlike many authors, Hemingway was as forceful in person as in his writing. This fact was well demonstrated once when I met him in prerevolutionary Cuba. It was at the Florida Restaurant, his favorite haunt, and our appointment had to be arranged through the owner of the Hotel Ambos Mundos, the only contact through which Hemingway could be reached when he was "holed up" in his inaccessible home in the suburbs. Papa proved to be a brilliant conversationalist, but that isn't what I remember most.

Rather, it was the way he *listened*. He would rivet his attention so completely even on somebody making mere tourist talk that one might have assumed that he was listening to nothing less important than the Gettysburg Address.

Few men can dominate a group merely by listening. Hemingway could, and perhaps it was this quality that caused so many visitors to describe him as "charming." Another unforgettable trait was his passion for perfection. Once, he told me, he rewrote a single chapter in a book thirty-eight times!

No author since Lord Byron has captured the public's imagination as did Hemingway. With his dynamic personality, his spirit of adventure, and his literary skill, he was the personification of what many of his readers would like to be themselves. Hemingway is one author that they will be writing about for decades to come. (His brother, Leicester, has recently published a biographical study of him.)

Yes, Chicago was the stamping ground of giants in those days. Henry L. Mencken called it, "The literary capital of America." And that it was. What is it today?

Since that time, many other noted authors have been nurtured in Chicago, including Willard Motley, Mary Jane Ward, Meyer Levin, Saul Bellow, Nelson Algren, and the Pulitzer Prize winning poet, Gwendolyn Brooks.

Miss Brooks, who is married to insurance salesman Henry Blakely, writes only at night. A mother of two, she devotes the entire day to being a South Side housewife. The family income has always been modest, but it was even more so in 1950. When a reporter phoned her to ask, "Have you heard that you've won the Pulitzer Prize?" Gwendolyn had to admit that she was literally in the dark about it—because the electric bill was overdue and she had no lights in her apartment.

James T. Farrell, a master of the naturalistic school, supplements his modest royalties with earnings from lectures and magazine articles. Though his three Studs Lonigan novels are classics today and still sell widely as paperback reprints, they sold poorly in their original editions. Ironically, this work of Farrell was never taken by a book club.

For years, Nelson Algren (a Detroiter by birth) was in similar financial straits. He wrote his first novel, *Somebody in Boots,* on a twenty-dollar-a-month advance on royalties from Vanguard Press. When he got married (he's now divorced), he could not even offer his bride Amanda a wedding ring.

"Nobody told me until three years later that you were supposed to have a ring," he explains. "It was lucky I had two dollars for the license!"

A $2,000 fellowship arranged by Carl Sandburg and several postwar awards for short stories finally enabled Nelson to work without interruption on *The Man With the Golden Arm,* the novel that won him the first National Book Award. Though never affluent, he is probably Chicago's most important resident novelist. He has this to say of the city's more glib disparagers:

"Before you earn the right to rap any sort of joint, you have to love it a little while."

As his books reveal, he does love the city and its people. But he is also one of Chicago's severest critics. The lyrical blasts he fired in his prose poem, "Chicago, City on the Make," incensed readers all the way from the Tribune Tower to the Association of Commerce & Industry. But to Nelson's lasting credit, he continues to call 'em as he sees 'em. An interviewer once said of Algren: "He is a man who betrays no inclination whatsover toward politeness, but he has a natural generosity and compassion."

Many writers spend their time in the vicinity of universities, bookstores, and symphony concerts. Not Nelson. You will most probably find him in a rumpled suit and a shirt whose color doesn't harmonize at a Chicago jazz spot, or—in summer—at Comiskey Park. (Like James T. Farrell, he had a boyhood dream of being a big-leaguer.) He also spends a great deal of time among the drug addicts, derelicts, and drifters who inhabit the "neon wilderness" west of State Street between Division Street and Chicago Avenue, north of the Loop. It is there that he still prefers to make his regular home, although he sometimes moves to a secluded Indiana dunes retreat when he is writing.

Nelson is not the only Chicago writer of note who is fascinated by such Skid Row locales. John Bartlow Martin, who lived in suburban Highland Park until President Kennedy appointed him United States Ambassador to the Dominican Republic, also used to haunt those slums, flophouses, police stations, and courtrooms for many of his *Harper's* and *Saturday Evening Post* articles. Before he undertook his ambassadorial post, Martin was considered one of the leading magazine reporters in America. He has tackled almost every type of serious reporting assignment, from mental health to his award-winning story of the Centralia, Illinois, mine disaster. But crime and its sociological implications are the topics which most intrigue him as a reporter.

One assignment he won't soon forget involved the murder of a pretty Chicagoan named Susan Hanson. Gathering material for the story with his customary thoroughness, Martin attended every session of the coroner's inquest and the subsequent trial of Susan's husband, Duncan, who was charged with the killing. At a dramatic moment in the trial, a key witness was asked to select from a group of spectators the person she remembered seeing near the Hanson residence that fateful morning. She looked slowly around the courtroom, and then pointed straight at Martin! (Not long after this startling demonstration of wrong identification, Hanson's attorney, Charles Bellows, won his client an acquittal.)

In magazine editing and publishing, especially in the more specialized fields, Chicago is second in importance only to New York. It was in Chicago that the Smart family originated *Esquire* and its sister publication *Coronet*. (Ultimately both magazines were moved to New York where *Coronet* languished and died.) It was here that a gadget-minded family named Windsor launched that perennial school-library favorite, *Popular Mechanics*, now part of the Hearst Magazine chain and, until this year, when it moved to New York, edited at 200 East Ontario Street. And Chicago today is the headquarters for the most spectacularly successful new magazine of the postwar era—Hugh Hefner's much copied but still inimitable *Playboy*.

A five-dollar difference in salary was the turning point in Hefner's career. It all started when *Esquire* moved to New York. Hefner was on the staff and his employers offered him eighty dollars a week if he made the move from Chicago. Hefner demanded eighty-five. *Esquire* refused. So Hefner stayed in Chicago and put together his own magazine.

For six hundred dollars (which he had to borrow) Hefner bought the rights to the celebrated nude calendar photograph of Marilyn Monroe, and *Playboy* was off and running. Today it is one of the wonders of the magazine field. Successful as it is, however, the bulk of the Hefner fortune now comes from the "Playboy Clubs," a chain of Key Clubs in leading cities across the United States. The four-story Playboy Club in Chicago alone nets Hefner more profit than his magazine.

Hefner recently had a disillusioning experience with another magazine, *Show Business Illustrated*, which he introduced in September of 1961—at the same time that multimillionaire Huntington Hartford, the A & P heir, was launching a rival magazine called *Show*. There was a good bit of speculation about which of the two—if either—would survive, in view of the fact that they were both set up to blanket the same market. Because of Hefner's phenomenal success with *Playboy*, most of the "experts" thought that he would run rings around Hartford.

But *SBI* never got off the ground. Hefner poured more than $1,250,000 into the publication before giving up and selling out to Hartford. He had made the common mistake of trying to handle too many enterprises at one time.

While overseeing his empire, Hefner still manages to live the kind of after-hours life portrayed in his magazine—with money, parties, and girls, girls, girls. There are voluptuous Playboy "Bunnies" in his office, his reception rooms, his swimming pool, and throughout his lavish North State Parkway mansion. And they are the enticing decorations at his famous Friday night parties, which start at midnight and continue until sunup.

But make no mistake—Hefner works hard. Long after the last guest has stumbled his good-by, Hefner will be at his desk, in the private office in his home. He plays hard, but he works hard—and at the most unusual hours.

Three times within a period of a few months in early 1962, Hefner has been honored by brotherhood organizations. These citations have disturbed a considerable number of people, and for a while the newspapers were deluged with angry letters-to-the-editor. The writers could not understand why a man with Hefner's reputation as a playboy should be so honored.

The reason is apparent to all who know Hefner's uncompromising stand on race relations—who know, for example, that he bought back the franchise to the Miami Playboy Key Club when the operators refused to admit Negroes, because such a policy is in direct contradiction to his principles. (And, incidentally, some of the cutest Bunnies in his Chicago Playboy Club happen to be Negro and Japanese girls. How many opportunities are there for such girls, however beautiful they may be?)

Chicago is the publishing center for a very important class of magazines—the nationally distributed, general-interest periodicals edited for a selected audience. Here you will find the editorial offices of the world's largest and most influential chain of Negro magazines, headed by John H. Johnson, the handsome, forty-four-year-old son of a former Arkansas sharecropper who left an insurance company house organ to launch *Ebony*, *Jet*, and the *Negro Digest*. Johnson does not claim to be a civil rights crusader. However, his role as publisher of *Ebony* has enabled him to break down some significant barriers in the path of interracial progress.

It was Johnson who first demonstrated to the advertising executives of major corporations that the economic and educational levels of the American Negro have risen greatly in recent years. By the impressive response that his readers made to *Ebony* advertising, he proved that a new market had developed. And, editorially, *Ebony*'s many articles about leading Negroes have filled a void created by the failure of other publications to give adequate coverage to this important minority group.

On many occasions Johnson's magazines have managed to strike some telling blows for our country in the battle for the minds of men: their South Michigan Avenue office, a handsomely refurbished mansion that had once been used as a funeral home, is a high-priority stop on the itineraries of visiting African and Asian dignitaries. Johnson himself has traveled abroad with former Vice-President Richard M. Nixon, and has dined with Presidents Eisenhower and Kennedy.

Chicago is also the home of such influential select-circulation publications as *Advertising Age, Down Beat, Poetry, Christian Century,* and *Today's Health,* and headquarters for dozens of trade periodicals and professional journals so highly specialized that they are distributed only to readers who can prove that they are qualified to receive them.

But newspapers, not magazines, are the backbone of the press. And what of Chicago newspapering today?

There is still an occasional reminder of the spirit of *The Front Page.* Take the promotion stunt that the *Daily News* almost pulled off a couple of years ago, to advertise its various editions. It was announced that three homing pigeons named "Blue Streak," "Red Streak," and Triple Streak" would race cross country, with the *News* issuing periodic bulletins on their progress. But one pigeon got lost. This prompted the *News'* afternoon competitor, the *American,* to burlesque the whole affair with references to a mythical pigeon named "Losing Streak."

There is the City News Bureau, the co-operative reporting pool maintained by the Chicago press for basic spot-news coverage. It is traditionally the beat on which cub reporters learn their trade. With so many rookies on its staff, the events of any single week at the Bureau are almost enough for a full-length comedy.

A few years ago, for example, a reporter covering his first fire made the mistake of trying to phone his story from a booth inside the burning building itself. Despite the smoke and flames, he kept relaying details to his rewrite man. "It's getting awfully hot," he kept saying. "I may have to quit soon." Suddenly there was a tremendous crash and the line went dead.

From the rewrite man's description of what he had heard, the entire Bureau staff had all but given up the youth for lost. And then the telephone rang again. It was the young reporter. Almost unbelieving, the rewrite man grabbed the phone.

"Bill," he shouted, "tell me—is it very hot where you're calling from now?"

(City News is far from being a mere comic operation, however. Under veteran editor Isaac Gershman, it has trained hundreds of successful "graduates," including Charles MacArthur; NBC-TV sports director Tom S. Gallery; Ernest Leiser; the *Tribune's* City Editor, Thomas Furlong, and its Washington Bureau Chief, Walter Trohan; Hollywood columnist (and my good friend) Mike Connolly; a couple of reporters who drifted into acting, Melvyn Douglas and Bruce Cabot; and even the notorious con man Joseph ("Yellow Kid") Weill. Of the last, Gershman says, "When we train a man, it doesn't matter what field he enters—he goes to the top!"

And, even more like *The Front Page*, there was the courtroom correspondent for one paper who, until quite recently, was operating a bookie joint on the side, for the convenience of the clerks and bailiffs. And, of course, some of the slickest amateur poker in the world is still played in Chicago's City, County, and Federal Building pressrooms.

Probably the best known of the handful of working newspapermen who actually date back to the "good old days" is a reporter from my own paper, Ray Brennan. Widely acclaimed as America's top crime reporter, Ray has won so many honors over the years that everyone stopped counting years ago. He holds a Heywood Broun Award, five Chicago Newspaper Guild Sticks o' Type, a Mystery Writers of America citation, and the Joe Fay Memorial Award, which was established by the *Sun-Times* editorial staff in honor of our late, beloved assistant city editor.

Ray made his first nation-wide scoop in 1933, when he broke the story of the escape of John Dillinger from the jail in Crown Point, Indiana. He just happened to phone the jail at the right time—but he had the perspicacity to keep the line tied up with small talk until his scoop was safe. He has since been the first to disclose major developments in such famous trials as those of Dr. Sam Sheppard, Mickey Jelke, and the Greenlease kidnapers.

He filed the first story on the death of Al Capone. (To get that story, he masqueraded as an oxygen technician to gain admission to Capone's heavily guarded house in Miami Beach.)

He set out to interview Fidel Castro during the Cuban Revolution. Before he got his story, he was nearly killed in a riot in Havana; he was jailed and threatened with death in Santiago; he was thrown from a mule, and contracted dysentery and lost twenty-eight pounds—but, in the end, he got an exclusive series, which he later expanded into a book, *Cuba, Castro, and Justice.*

Daring as these adventures are, however, Ray will probably go down in journalistic history for a reportorial exploit he pulled off in 1950. A few days before the senatorial and county elections that year, the Kefauver Crime Committee, meeting in closed session, had questioned Dan Gilbert, Democratic candidate for Sheriff of Cook County—a man who had been nicknamed the "world's richest cop." At the end of the session Gilbert's testimony was unaccountably suppressed.

Brennan smelled a rat. He flew down to Washington, called the stenographic service which was supposed to be typing up the transcripts, and duped a receptionist into sending him an unedited copy. And then he flew back and plastered the whole ugly story over twenty-five columns of the *Sun-Times.* This scoop not only resulted in Gilbert's immediate defeat (by 270,000 votes)—it changed the entire course of national affairs. In the backlash of the scandal, Illinois Senator Scott W. Lucas, the popular Democratic Majority Leader, was also defeated, and the Republican candidate, former United States Representative Everett M. Dirksen (now the Senate Minority Leader) was swept into office.

For a time the Justice Department threatened to try Brennan on the charge of impersonating a Federal employee. But ultimately the case was dropped.

Ben Hecht and some of the other old-timers have been inclined to disparage our modern newspapers. But a former reporting crony of Hecht's, publicist Julius Klein, is only one of the many people who differ on this point—completely.

According to Klein, "Chicago's newspapers today are doing a better job, with better newspapermen, under much more difficult conditions, than ever before."

There may be fewer poets and novelists in the modern city room, but there are more professional reporters and editors. There is little of the irresponsible sensationalism of Hecht's day. You will find better-balanced coverage of national and international news, tighter editing, and a more thorough reporting of local government and business affairs. The educational level for reporters and editors is higher than ever before. All this has made possible such important exposés as the one with which the *Sun-Times* forced the State Democratic Party to change its 1956 Illinois gubernatorial candidates, and the great *Daily News* disclosures which resulted in the imprisonment of former State Auditor Orville Hodge in a record $2,500,000 misappropriation case. (For that one, reporter George Thiem won a Pulitzer Prize.)

Granted, the Chicago dailies no longer express as wide a diversity of political viewpoint as they did when there were twice as many being published. But this is true of the surviving dailies everywhere.

And of course the big downtown dailies are not the only papers that serve the Chicago area.

There is the Chicago *Daily Defender*, the Negro daily published by John Sengstacke, the descendant of a pioneer newspaper family. The successor of a chain of smaller weeklies, it had a top circulation of 230,000 even before World War I. The *Defender* each year stages one of the largest newspaper-sponsored events anywhere—the annual Bud Billiken Day festival for underprivileged South Side children. More than 250,000 persons take part.

And here you will also find one of the strongest neighborhood newspaper complexes in the country, led by young Bruce Sagan of the South Side's *Hyde Park Herald,* the *South Town,* and the *Southeast Economist,* and Leo Lerner of the North Side Newspapers. Lerner, a noted liberal and author of the recent *The Italics Are Mine* and other books, was a founder of the Independent Voters of Illinois, one of the largest branches of the Americans for Democratic Action.

And besides these giants you will find dozens of weekly suburban papers and seven foreign-language dailies.

But let's get back to the downtown dailies. And, specifically, let's talk about my talented colleagues, the men and women who make up Chicago's working press today.

There is the accomplished *Daily News* contingent, headed by such veterans as editor Tom Collins, managing editor John Stanton, sports editor John P. Carmichael, literary critic Van Allen

Bradley, and columnists Tony Weitzel, Terry (TV) Turner, John Justin Smith, and Sydney J. Harris, whose "Strictly Personal" has, through syndication, become one of the most widely read and quoted columns in America. Harris is also drama critic for the *News*. One of Chicago's most popular lecturers, he delights in choosing such provocative subjects as "Are Women People?" and "Great Books and Small Minds." And movie critic Sam Lesner enjoys an enviable reputation, as does medico-science expert Art Snider.

Another prominent Chicago newspaperman, Herman Kogan, joined the *Daily News* staff just recently, in an executive capacity. Kogan is not only an excellent reporter, he is also an author of considerable repute. His finest works were written in collaboration with Lloyd Wendt, who was once his co-worker on the *Tribune* and is now editor of *Chicago's American*.

On the *Tribune*, redheaded Claudia Cassidy probably wields more power over the cultural life of Chicago than any other individual. Claudia, who formerly worked for the old *Journal of Commerce* and the *Sun*, covers both music and drama for the *Tribune*.

As a critic, her barbs can be devastating. She must be credited or blamed—depending on your point of view—for having provoked the dismissal of two conductors of the Chicago Symphony Orchestra: Desiré Defauw and Rafael Kubelik. She is also one of the severest critics of Carol Fox, general manager of the Lyric Opera. And there are a number of Broadway producers who swear that they will never bring another show into Chicago, for fear of Miss Cassidy's devastating remarks.

But stinging as her scorn can be, Claudia can be generous in her praise when the occasion warrants. Her standards for artistic performances are high. They are so high, indeed, that some of her critics maintain that she has "ruined" the theater in Chicago. But I feel, as do many others, that her insistence on praising only the best has done much to raise the caliber of the shows brought into Chicago. All too often in the past, we have been sent hastily mounted and poorly rehearsed play productions, with the attitude that "anything is good enough for the hick towns." Claudia resents this attitude bitterly, as do our other drama critics—

Glenna Syse of the *Sun-Times,* Sydney Harris of the *Daily News,* and Roger Dettmer of *Chicago's American.*

(And every one of our drama critics, I might add, is as proficient, as painstaking, and as professional as any in New York.)

The Tribune Tower harbors many other eminent holders of press cards. Robert Cromie, author of *The Great Chicago Fire* and *John Dillinger,* edits a lively book section with great personal enthusiasm, supported by the distinguished Fanny Butcher, Literary Editor, and veteran Baker Street Irregular, Vincent Starrett. At the city desk, you will find feature writer Norma Lee Browning and political correspondent George Tagge. The sports section, recognized as one of the finest in the country, is directed by Wilfrid Smith, with the assistance of the dean of professional football writers, George ("Coach") Strickler, and David Condon, who writes the column, "Wake of the News." Tom Morrow's column, "Line o' Type," enlivens the editorial page, and Herb Lyon conducts "Tower Ticker."

And then there is the *Tribune's* Chester Gould, creator of Dick Tracy, who draws his internationally syndicated comic strip in a studio on his farm in nearby Woodstock, Illinois (where the landscaping once included a cemetery with markers for Pruneface, B-B Eyes, The Brow, and other cartoon villains that the indomitable Tracy has laid to rest).

The staff of *Chicago's American,* headed by Publisher Stuart List and Editor Lloyd Wendt, has many distinguished members. Luke Carroll, who was formerly with the New York *Herald Tribune,* is recognized as an expert managing editor. Sports columnist Warren Brown is a master of devastating humor. Veteran sports editor Leo Fischer is the McCormick member of a remarkable newspaper family—his brother Ritz Fischer is city editor of the *Daily News,* and another brother, Jo Fischer, the cartoonist, draws the delightful "9 to 5" strip for the *Sun-Times.* Columnists Jack Mabley (general), Ann Marsters (movies), and Maggie Daly entertain readers with their lively reporting.

Maggie, who succeeded the late Nate Gross, has demonstrated that there is room for beauty on the night-club beat—a quality that Charlie Dawn, Bill Leonard, Herb Lyon, Tony Weitzel, and I cannot pretend to offer. (But we weigh more!) Maggie is one of the well-known Daly sisters—others are Revlon vice-president Kay, and authors Maureen and Sheila John—and the mother of Hollywood starlet Brigid Bazlen. Whenever Maggie and I meet, our first topics of conversation are the latest accomplishments of her actress-daughter Brigid, and my actress-daughter Karyn.

Yes, the competition is brilliant. But I'm sure you will forgive my provincialism when I insist that the greatest pool of newspaper talent in town can be found in my own paper, the *Sun-Times*.

In all probability, there would never have been a "Kup's Column" if it had not been for Russ Stewart. He was managing editor of the old *Times* early in 1943, when he and editor Richard J. Finnegan summoned me into the front office and I emerged with "Kup's Column."

Stewart did much more for me. Because of his show-business background (he had come to the *Times* from the Metro-Goldwyn-Mayer exploitation department in Hollywood), he had many connections in the entertainment field. In the early days, he would make the rounds with me every night. He would lead me from night club to night club, introducing me to celebrities and giving me expert tips on how to handle "items." There were many nights when we both staggered home in the small hours. Russ still makes the rounds with me from time to time, but these occasions have become increasingly rare as he has shouldered more and more responsibility as vice-president of the Field Enterprises' newspaper division. Russ Stewart did more than any other individual to get "Kup's Column" into orbit, and I am eternally grateful.

Editor Milburn ("Pete") Akers is as astute a political writer as you will find in the Midwest. No mere theoretician, he brings a rich background in practical politics to his job as editor and columnist—he served as press officer for Illinois New Deal Governor Henry Horner. Much of the *Sun-Times'* current success must be attributed to executive editor Larry S. Fanning, formerly of *Collier's* magazine and the San Francisco *Chronicle*. At the

Chronicle, incidentally, one of Fanning's reporters was Pierre Salinger, who is now Presidential Press Secretary.

Then there is our managing editor Emmett Dedmon, author of the best-selling *Fabulous Chicago* and other books; sports editor Dick Hackenberg and his stable of fine writers, which includes Edgar Munzel, Jerry Holtzman, Jack Clarke, the beloved Herb Graffis, and Jack Griffin; and city editor Karin Walsh, who—with reporter Jack McPhaul and the late Jim McGuire—won a Heywood Broun Award for the Joe Majeck story, on which the movie, *Call Northside 777*, was based.

There are our Pulitzer Prize-winning political cartoonists, Bill Mauldin, newly arrived from the St. Louis *Post-Dispatch,* and Jacob Burck, both of whom are generally considered to be among the best ten in their field; political editor John Dreiske, whose abilities are highly respected both at City Hall and down at the State capital; and financial editor Ed Darby, who at one time traveled with President Eisenhower as *Time* magazine's White House correspondent. And there is the distinguished Washington staff, headed by handsome Carleton ("Bill") Kent, former president of the White House Correspondents Association, and including Frederick Kuh, *Time* magazine's choice for "Best U. S. Foreign Correspondent of World War II," and young Thomas Ross, whose string of scoops is the talk of the National Press Club.

There is also a distinguished assemblage of critics: Eleanor ("Doris Arden") Keen (movies); Glenna Syse (drama); Niemann Fellow Hoke Norris (books); Robert Marsh (music); Paul Molloy (TV); and Jean Neal (fashion). I'm especially proud of Jean, because she learned the newspaper business as my secretary.

And, as fifty million readers in six countries know, there is a syndicated columnist named "Ann Landers." In private life "Ann" is Mrs. Esther Pauline Lederer. Eppie, as her friends call her, is fully as remarkable as her excellent columns indicate. She never had written a line of copy before she came to Chicago from her home town, Eau Claire, Wisconsin—and that was less than ten years ago! Today she is the most widely read columnist in her field. One of her competitors is a Californian who writes under the pseudonym of "Abigail Van Buren." In private life, "Abigail" is Eppie's (or "Ann's") twin sister.

Ann Landers is pretty, pert, and sparkling. She not only dispenses sound advice—she lives by it herself. Happily married to Chicago businessman Jules Lederer, she is the mother of a twenty-one-year-old daughter, Margo.

"Ask him if he ever tried jumping into a cement mixer."

"You ain't never been a woman at eight o'clock in the morning."

"Turn off the waterworks, Mama, you're wasting your natural resources."

Ben Hecht didn't write those lines. Nor did Charlie MacArthur nor Bob Casey. Ann Landers did. She is living proof that Chicago is still the world's liveliest newspaper town—and always will be, as long as there is a corner newsstand.

5. Politicos

It's a popular pastime, ridiculing Chicago politics. "Like a page out of *The Last Hurrah*," the critics like to sneer. "Shot through with fraud!" "Populated by clowns!"

It is true that a look backward does reveal a political past of which no Chicagoan can be especially proud. Many of our mayors were completely corrupt—not servants of the people but slaves of selfish special interests. City councilmen were for sale to the highest bidder, who usually was a vice lord or an unscrupulous businessman. As Al Capone said of the era of one of our most notorious mayors, Big Bill Thompson, "Nobody was on the legit."

When our combination City Hall-County Building was constructed, the County Building side cost a million dollars more than the City side, although the two sections were identical. When businessmen sought franchises for trolley lines, or for gas and electric utilities, the "Gray Wolves" of the City Council shook them down for huge pay-offs in every ward in which they operated. Chain-balloting, "deadheading," and other fraudulent election practices were commonplace.

Like everything else in Chicago, politics made good copy. Such colorful characters as ("Bathhouse") John Coughlin, who operated a Turkish bath, and Michael ("Hinky Dink") Kenna saw to that.

124

Back at the turn of the century, when each ward had two aldermen, Bathhouse and Hinky Dink ran the notorious First Ward, which included parts of the Loop and the Near South Side.

Hinky Dink, the team's "inside man," supervised police payoffs and other administrative details of their gambling and vice empire. He seldom spoke in public—but when he did, he was always worth quoting. Returning from a trip to Europe, for example, he had this to say for two of the cities he had visited:

"Rome? Most everybody in Rome has been dead for two thousand years. Monte Carlo? Great place! I spent two days there and broke even. I didn't play."

Bathhouse John was the speechmaker and "front man." Passionately fond of loud clothing, he might appear at a City Council meeting in a pearl-gray suit, green-and-white checked waistcoat, and yellow-tan shoes. He was a prolific composer of songs and "poetry." One song to which he claimed authorship had the evocative title, "Dear Midnight of Love." One of his more delicate poems began:

> On with the dance,
> Let the orgy be proper.
> Don't drink, smoke, or spit on the floor,
> And say, keep your eye on the copper.

Of all the activities of Hinky Dink and Bathhouse, their First Ward fund-raising balls are probably the most renowned. At the beginning, these balls were relatively small affairs, but they soon had to be moved to the Seventh Regiment Armory. Finally they got so big that they overflowed even the enormous Chicago Coliseum. More than fifteen hundred people attended the last one, which was held in 1908. And what people! As one reporter noted, any disaster at a First Ward ball would have "wiped out every dip, second-story worker, plug-ugly, porch climber, dope fiend, and scarlet woman in Chicago." The 1908 ball might not have been the last if a few of the merrymakers had not grown overly enthusiastic. But when they began smashing chairs, breaking glasses, and throwing their fellow guests into the alley, a general riot developed, and reform elements in Chicago decided that this was the dramatic issue they had long been waiting for. Led by stationer John Cole, better known as "Citizen Cole," they staged a campaign that ultimately resulted in a cleanup of the notorious Levee district. The Everleigh Club and other fancy brothels were closed down, and the empire of Hinky Dink and Bathhouse fell to pieces.

In recent years, there have been only a few politicians with the boisterous flair Bathhouse had. The late Charlie Weber was one. As alderman of the Forty-fifth Ward, he sponsored the annual Garbagemen's Ball, built a group of public playgrounds at his own expense, and instituted Charlie Weber Kids' Days at Riverview Amusement Park. He also published a chain of newspapers on the Northwest Side.

An even more flamboyant individualist is Mathias ("Paddy") Bauler, the Near North Sider who is known as "the last of the saloonkeeper aldermen." One of thirteen children, Paddy began his career as a singing waiter and master of ceremonies in a saloon owned by his older brother, Herman, who preceded Paddy as alderman. As an entertainer, Paddy always wound up his act by holding a half gallon of beer at arm's length, then draining it in one long, unbroken swallow. As alderman of the Forty-third Ward he used to hold court in a back room of his saloon (now closed), which he had registered in the name of his lawyer because municipal employees are prohibited from selling alcoholic beverages. Paddy, wearing a tall silk hat, would hoist a beer stein, and bellow, "Awright, everybody, come on and have a drink!" He is responsible for such *bon mots* as, "Sit down, you slobs, you look like a federal grand jury!" and the more frequently quoted "Chicago ain't ready for reform!" My favorite story about Paddy is reported by Judge John Gutknecht, who urged the alderman to keep a journal of his travels:

"Paddy, I've been to Europe twenty-five times and around the world three times, and I've always had a diary."

"Judge," replied Paddy, "you can get rid of that with Pepto-Bismol."

All these individuals are part of a colorful, sometimes seamy stage of politics through which every large city has had to pass.

They have left their mark on Chicago—and not always for the better. But anyone who approaches Chicago politics with unqualified condescension is making a mistake. Admittedly, there has been boodle and fraud. But there has also been sound, long-range planning and civic responsibility—as witness our unspoiled lake-front (much of which is set aside for public parks), our Cook County Forest Preserves (nearly fifty thousand acres of woodland stretched in a great, green belt around the city), our parkways, our subways and rapid-transit lines.

Many public figures of national stature have come out of Chicago—Stephen A. Douglas, Charles G. Dawes, Harold Ickes, Frank Knox, Paul Douglas, Adlai Stevenson, to name only a few. And as the leading host to national political conventions for over a century, Chicago has witnessed the nomination of ten Presidents: Abraham Lincoln (1860), U. S. Grant (1868), James Garfield (1880), Grover Cleveland (1884 and 1892), Benjamin Harrison (1888), Theodore Roosevelt (1904), William Howard Taft (1908), Warren G. Harding (1920), Franklin D. Roosevelt (1932, 1940, and 1944), and Dwight D. Eisenhower (1952).

It is true that Chicago is the only American metropolis never to have experienced full-scale governmental reform. And it is also true that Chicago is the last outpost in the United States of the big-city political machine. But in the past few years, this machine, under Mayor Richard J. Daley, has provided government comparable to the best among large cities. And with each recent election, the machine has shown an increasing readiness to put forward fresh new faces, to give us first-rate people—at least in the major offices—instead of the usual party hacks. Cambridge-educated Otto Kerner, Illinois' present governor, is one of its offspring. So are Cook County State's Attorney Daniel Ward, the former dean of De Paul University Law School; Municipal Court Chief Justice Augustine Bowe, once president of the Chicago Bar Association; and former Sheriff and State Treasurer Joseph D. Lohman, now dean of the School of Criminology at the University of California.

Chicago's judicial benches include men from both parties—men of whom any city could be proud. In the Federal Courts, we have such distinguished judges as William Campbell, Michael Igoe, Hugh Will, Walter LaBuy, Julius Miner (originator of Illinois' sixty-day "cooling off" requirement in divorce cases), the controversial Julius ("the Just") Hoffman, and James Parsons, the first Negro appointed to the Federal judiciary. The eminent jurists who sit over our Circuit, Superior, and Municipal courts are men of great probity and lofty erudition—and many of them offer daily proof that a long face does not necessarily have to scowl out from over that long robe. Judge Abraham L. Marovitz, a collector of Lincolniana, is a pillar of Chicago's Anti-Superstition Society. Judge Henry Burman is one of my jolliest golfing partners—who raises few points of order with me except in the sand traps. And Judge Jacob Braude has compiled a number of popular anthologies of very funny after-dinner anecdotes.

The late John Sbarbaro was one Chicago jurist who made major contributions to society both as a public official and as a private citizen. With attorney Arthur Morse, Judge Sbarbaro was instrumental in inaugurating the famous Chicago Stadium Basketball Double-Headers. As a man of law, he is warmly remembered for his many acts of judicial enlightenment and compassion. As a young Assistant State's Attorney, he had helped "break" the celebrated Leopold-Loeb case. Many years later, when Nathan Leopold's record finally came up before the Parole Board, Sbarbaro was one of the first to advocate that Leopold should be set free, on the grounds that he had been completely rehabilitated.

Other splendid jurists in Chicago include Cornelius Harrington, Thomas Kluczynski, Walker Butler, Joseph Drucker, and Hyman Feldman.

In writing of jurists, however, I cannot help but delve into the past to recall the memories of some of Chicago's more colorful judges. One was the late United States District Court Judge John Barnes, known as "The Beard." Judge Barnes had the reputation of being the most able—and most feared—judge on the bench. He was brilliant but bitter. The loss of two sons in World War II had left its mark on him and there was no nonsense in his courtroom. His stern manner caused many a lawyer to fear bidding him even a normal "Hello."

Kup as sportswriter early in career, interviews Woody English of Brooklyn Dodgers

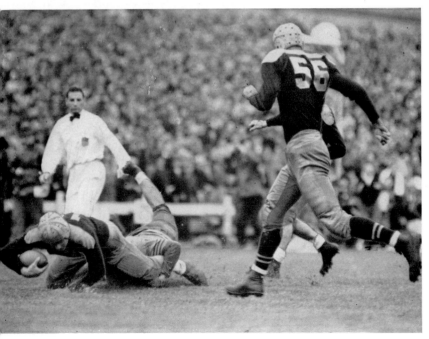

Kup as football official in National Football League
(Associated Press photo)

Kup (a regular Mickey Mantle!) swinging in celebrity softball game

Der Bingle and Kup, at Crosby's Elko, Nev., ranch, choosing up for softball

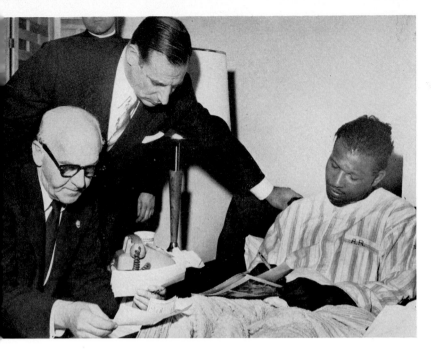

Walter Winchell, Kup, and Sugar Ray Robinson after Robinson
defeated Carmen Basilio, in Chicago (photo by Bill Mark)

Cerebral palsy telethon, Kup emcee; Peggy Lee and Bob Hope, guests
(Sun-Times photo by Dave Mann)

Mrs. Kup and her idol,
Clark Gable, in Chicago

Daughter Karyn,
Kup's favorite actress

Son Jerry with proud father

Kup's mother, Olga, being interviewed by Martha Crane in Chicago

An *At Random* panel: Dick Shawn, Dr. Frank Baxter, George Burns, Jack Benny, and Kup (WBBM-TV photo, CBS Television, Chicago)

Kup receiving Emmy Award as TV's Man of the Year, with Lee Philip,
another Emmy winner (WBBM-TV photo, CBS Television,
Chicago—Peter J. Haas)

Kup and Alfred Hitchcock

Kup and Jerry Colonna on one of Bob Hope's annual Christmas junkets. This one, 1957, was in Far East (NBC photo by Gerald Smith)

Carl Sandburg, Pamela Mason, and Hollywood director George Stevens on one of the *At Random* shows (WBBM-TV photo, CBS Television, Chicago)

Kup waving to his Purple Heart cruise ship, SS *North American*

Kup greets ex-Chicagoan Steve Allen

The Kups visit with Liz Taylor and the late Mike Todd in
Mr. Kelly's, Chicago night club

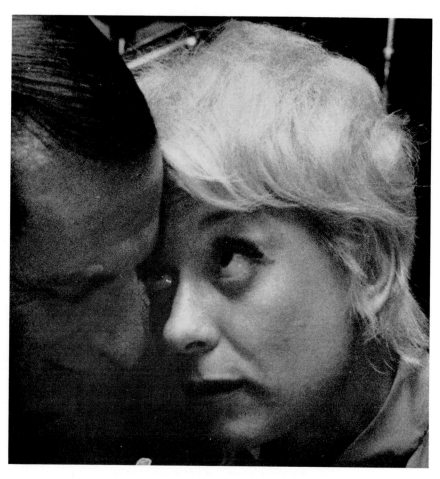

Kup and Carol Channing (photo by Lee Balterman)

Kup and Joe E. Lewis (LOOK Magazine Photo)

The Kups with columnist Art Buchwald in the Pump Room

Kup and Bob Hope exchanging quips at Chicago Airport
(Metro News photo)

The late John Balaban, Chicago theater magnate, speaking, while Kup,
Bob Hope, and Frank Sinatra kibitz (Lawrence-Phillip Studios)

Kup as Man of the Year for the Jewish National Fund, with Jack Arvey, Rabbi William Novick, and Danny Kaye (Sun-Times photo)

Kup and Richard Nixon having coffee before *At Random* show
(WBBM-TV photo, CBS Television, Chicago—Peter J. Haas)

Mahalia Jackson, queen of gospels, being introduced by
Kup at civic affair

Kup interviewing Jayne Mansfield and Jerry Lewis on TV (Fran Byrne)

Kup and Marlon Brando (photo by Phil Stern)

Kup and Dinah Shore

Kup with Frank Sinatra and cast of *Guys and Dolls* during break in filming (photo by Phil Stern)

Kup and the late Alben Barkley, then Vice President, in Chicago

The Kups and Adlai Stevenson visit backstage with Melvyn Douglas,
starring in *Inherit the Wind*

Kup interviewing President Truman following his acceptance
speech in Chicago Stadium

Kup and Jimmy Hoffa

Kup, Kup's actress daughter Karyn, Leslie Caron, Hedda Hopper,
and Joshua Logan

Kup receiving TV Emmy from Dave Garroway, while another Chicago
Emmy winner, Sheldon Cooper, looks on (Sun-Times photo)

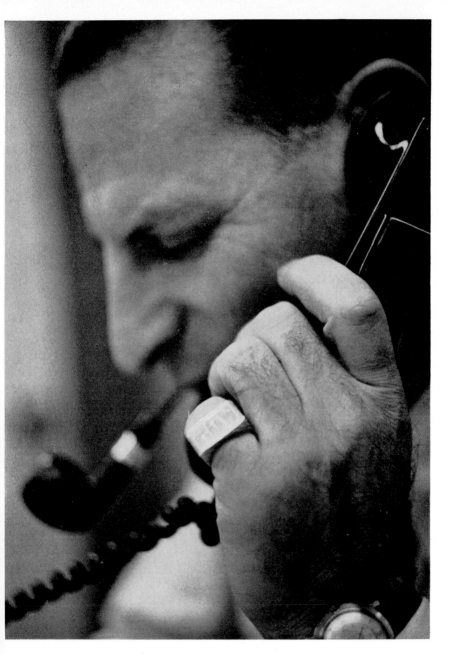

Kup at work (LOOK Magazine Photo)

Kup getting an earful . . .

. . . and making a note (LOOK Magazine Photos)

Chicago's Kup

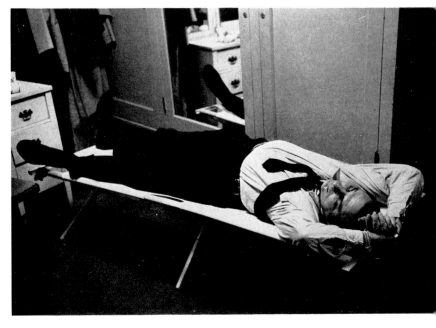
A break during cerebral palsy telethon (photo by Mickey Pallas)

One of the more colorful of the bygone era was Judge Joseph David, who once made headlines by ruling in favor of Sally Rand on a nudity charge by asking, "Would you put pants on a horse?" Lawyers delighted in having a case tried by Judge David. His brilliance as a jurist was matched by his flair for the flamboyant. As one attorney described an experience in the judge's court, "It's a combination legal lesson and vaudeville act."

Another in the same spectrum was the late Judge William Lindsay, a noted and admitted tippler. Lawyers take an oath that Judge Lindsay, after imbibing a few too many, fell asleep on the bench one day—and then fell off!

And there was the time the judge and his good friend, real estate tycoon Paul Caspers, decided to make a night of it. They drank well into the wee hours, when the judge decided it was time to freshen up and head for his court, without benefit of sleep. He reported promptly on time—8:00 A.M.

Caspers, who was due in court at 10:00 A.M. to represent himself in a real estate matter, didn't fare as well. He fell asleep after showering and missed his ten o'clock appearance in court. Judge Lindsay spared no vehemence when his old friend and drinking partner of the night before finally appeared. He delivered a blistering rebuke to a man "who, for ANY reason, could not keep his court appointment."

Then, shaking a shaky finger at Caspers, he exclaimed, "If you must play, then you must pay!"

And then there's the sad story of a jurist who shall remain nameless, except for his nickname, "Cash Register." The reason is obvious. "Cash Register" would take anything, including a hot stove, for favors rendered on the bench. The voters finally caught up with him and he was defeated for re-election. "Cash Register" then returned to his law practice with equally disastrous results. He was disbarred. From Chicago he drifted to California, where a few years later "Cash Register" died. His last known employment was as a milk-wagon driver.

I, personally, arrived on the scene just a bit too late to cover the end of the really outrageous era. But I did get here in plenty of time to know (and appreciate) the last of the old-line Chicago bosses—that much underestimated Democratic king-maker of the thirties and early forties, our late Mayor Edward J. Kelly. A Back-of-the-Stockyards Irishman who had studied engineering in night school to qualify for a job with the Metropolitan Sanitary District, Kelly was an amazing politician. So impressive were his charm, his professionalism, and his showmanship that for many years he even enjoyed the personal approval of the late Colonel Robert R. McCormick, a die-hard champion of the opposite political camp. McCormick had served as president of the Metropolitan Sanitary District, while Kelly was a supervisor on the engineering staff. One day Kelly lost his Irish temper and threw a punch at a laggard subordinate. He was called before the Colonel. Instead of reprimanding the fiery young executive, the Colonel congratulated him warmly on having the courage to assert his authority—and gave him a fifty-dollar-a-month raise!

"You gotta be a boss" was Kelly's motto, and he was seldom outdone at it. During the tense 1940 Democratic convention, he even outbossed Jim Farley, who, as National Committee Chairman, was technically in charge. Farley, working desperately to block Roosevelt's nomination for a third term, had instructed the organist to play a certain sentimental tune at a crucial moment. When the time arrived, instead of Farley's tune out came a song that Kelly preferred: the rousing "Franklin D. Roosevelt Jones." Farley was astounded. I was with Kelly when Farley came steaming up, demanding to know who was running the show and how Ed had managed to outflank him. Kelly only smiled and changed the subject. "I didn't have the heart to tell him," he said later, "but I had Jimmy Petrillo instruct the organist to play that song. I knew Petrillo's word would carry more weight with a musician than Farley's."

Few persons realize it, but Kelly did much to influence Franklin D. Roosevelt's decision to seek an unprecedented third term. As the 1940 convention drew near, even such Roosevelt intimates as Harry Hopkins had been unable to persuade the President to declare for renomination. Fearful of employing too many New Deal amateurs in their efforts, the leaders of the pro-third-term faction of the party summoned Kelly, a stanch Roosevelt supporter but still a wise and objective old pro and a major power in the regular Democratic Party organization. In a long session at the White House, Kelly talked to FDR like a Dutch uncle, pointing out that the nation, the world, and the party needed him. Later Kelly reported back: "He didn't commit himself, but I think I just did my greatest selling job." History soon proved him right.

In 1944, Big Ed also helped plan the strategy that won the Vice-Presidential nomination—and eventually the nation's highest office—for Harry S. Truman.

Kelly enforced an iron discipline within his organization, but he often showed a soft side as well. Through the efforts of Mayor Kelly and his wife, Margaret, Chicago's Servicemen's Centers in World War II won the reputation for being the most fabulous anywhere—regularly mustering two thousand hostesses to distribute millions of free cakes, hot dogs, beverages, and transportation and amusement tickets.

Kelly had a sharp Irish wit. Once, after playing host to General De Gaulle at a civic reception, Kelly was asked whether the Frenchman, as is the custom in his country, had kissed him. "Why, no," replied the mayor. "In fact, I've been with him all day and didn't see him kiss anybody." But, it was objected, hadn't the tall general been photographed embracing the diminutive Fiorello La Guardia, the Mayor of New York? Kelly chuckled. "That wasn't a kiss. De Gaulle merely was taking his bending exercises."

Kelly's successor as Cook County Democratic Chairman, Colonel Jacob M. Arvey, is another who worked his way up through the ranks into national prominence. Now Democratic National Committeeman from Illinois and a law partner in a LaSalle Street firm, Jack Arvey has long ranked as one of the most astute political brains in the nation. Even as a student at John Marshall Law School, his unusual qualities were apparent. Stumped by a difficult question on an examination, he deliberately ignored the specific issue and handed in a twenty-page essay on what he *did* know, in which he expressed some strong and unorthodox personal opinions. When he saw his grade, he found that the professor had written:

"You don't know a damn thing about the case referred to in this examination. For that you flunk. But you show an amazing instinct and feel for the law and its ultimate purpose. For that you would get an A. The two grades average C—so you pass." In further good humor, he had added: "Just between us, Arvey, you're lucky you've got a professor who agrees with you!"

If uncertain health had not prematurely undermined his career, forcing him to vacate the Cook County Chairmanship now held by Mayor Daley, Arvey might today be one of the most powerful men in the regular Democratic Party organization. During his twenty-eight years as alderman of the Twenty-fourth Ward, he built up a model political organization. In the 1936 election, when the Republicans got 700 votes in the ward, Arvey's Democrats got 29,000! "Not a sparrow falls inside the borders of the Twenty-fourth Ward without Arvey's knowing of it," said an admirer. "And then, before it hits the ground there's already a personal history at headquarters, complete to the moment of its tumble."

At the approach of the 1948 elections in Cook County, Arvey, with other ranking Democrats, realized that the slate needed new faces. It was time for a change, he said—a cry that was to be taken up nationally by the Republicans in 1952. And the first change had to be made at the top, where Ed Kelly had reigned so long as Mayor and County Chairman. Boss Kelly's popularity had dipped considerably; it fell to Arvey, as the number two figure in the organization, to convince Kelly that he would wreck the machine if he ran again for mayor. It wasn't easy for Jack to talk his forceful chief into retiring. But after Kelly had listened to all the arguments and studied the results of a poll that Arvey had had taken, he accepted the fact that he faced personal defeat in the coming election. Kelly was too proud and too astute a politician not to realize that it was time for him to retire. As graciously as was possible under the circumstances, he withdrew.

The man that Arvey selected to run for Mayor was Martin H. Kennelly, a successful businessman and a well-known civic leader. He had not previously been active in politics, and his private life had been exemplary. Kennelly, with the backing of the powerful Democratic organization, was an easy victor.

At Arvey's urging, the Democrats introduced other new faces into the political arena in 1948—all highly respected men with unblemished reputations. Paul Douglas, former University of Chicago economics professor and alderman of the famous Fifth Ward, was nominated for United States Senate. Adlai Stevenson was nominated for Governor. By slating candidates of such high caliber, Arvey not only kept his machine's power intact in Chicago, but helped to lay the foundation for the astonishing triumph of his good friend, Harry S. Truman, in the national election. (A fact not generally known is that Stevenson was originally slated to run for United States Senator in 1948, an office he preferred to that of Governor. But because the Republican incumbent, Senator C. Wayland Brooks, owed much of his popularity to his military record in World War I, Arvey decided instead to match Marine combat veteran Douglas against him.)

Arvey also stage-managed the 1952 nomination of Stevenson for President. Overriding Adlai's avowed reluctance, he spread the word in the right places that Stevenson should be the candidate. When the convention finally mounted its "draft" of Adlai, he accepted the nomination—as Arvey had planned all along.

Arvey worked diligently for Harry Truman's renomination at the 1948 convention. But only a short time earlier he had been a key member of the small group of party leaders who maneuvered desperately behind the scenes to sponsor Dwight D. Eisenhower as the Democratic Party's candidate for President.

How Eisenhower almost became the Democratic nominee in 1948 is a footnote to history that I will tell here for the first time.

A group of atomic scientists, headed by Harold Urey, called on Arvey in late 1947. They brought ominous tidings. They described in detail the destructive potentials of the nuclear bomb. They predicted that soon there would be intercontinental ballistic missiles and rockets and, perhaps, a military base on the moon. There was no way, the scientists explained, to prevent Soviet Russia or any other power from making the same scientific strides.

"Our entire civilization will be at stake unless there is strong leadership in the White House—leadership that is beyond partisan politics and that can unite the entire nation," the spokesman for the scientists exclaimed. He turned to Arvey and said: "You, as a powerful political figure, must act in this emergency. *We must all think in terms of a man who is above politics.*"

Arvey was greatly impressed. This was the first time, to his knowledge, that the scientific community had felt so deeply concerned about a political problem that it was willing to send a committee of its most prominent men to deal directly with a party boss.

But where was the country to find a national leader who was not in politics? The one man that all the scientists felt had the necessary qualifications was General Dwight David Eisenhower, who was then president of Columbia University.

Arvey was convinced—and perhaps a bit more readily because relations between the President and himself were strained. He was completely out of contact with the White House, where the "Palace Guard" had rebuffed his every attempt to communicate with Mr. Truman. In addition to this, he knew that Truman's chances of winning in 1948 were considered very remote. The political experts were predicting that *any* Republican candidate could defeat him.

With these factors in mind, Arvey went to work. He flew to Washington to relay the scientists' message to a few leading Democracts, and to sound out their opinion. He also contacted William O'Dwyer, Mayor of New York, and Jimmy Roosevelt, then Democratic National Committeeman from California. Both men heartily endorsed the idea of offering the Democratic Presidential nomination to Eisenhower. Jersey City Boss Frank Hague got wind of the plan and phoned Arvey to say that he, too, was in favor of it.

With all the groundwork laid, a prominent Democrat who was close to Eisenhower was selected to open the actual negotiations. After the first meeting, the spokesman reported that Ike had listened with considerable interest. "His first reaction," this spokesman told Arvey, "was favorable."

Meanwhile, word of what Arvey and his supporters were hoping to accomplish had spread in the inner circles of the party. Marshall Field III invited Arvey to his office and asked for the complete details. Mr. Field grew more and more enthusiastic as Arvey spoke. At the end of their meeting, he offered as much moral and financial assistance as might be needed.

With Eisenhower's interest in the nomination assured, Arvey, O'Dwyer, and James Roosevelt started to map their plan of operation. It was agreed that Ike was, under no circumstances, to be asked to campaign for the nomination. It would have to be offered to him as a draft by the delegates to the National Convention.

The next problem was how the story should be "leaked" to the public.

One of the Democrats said that he could arrange for Arthur Krock of *The New York Times* to interview Eisenhower and, in the course of the interview, establish Ike's intention to accept a draft. Krock could then reveal the news to the public in his column.

Remember that this was 1947. The Democratic Party was splitting into a number of hostile factions. In the next few months, the "Wallaceites" and the "Dixiecrats" were to abandon the party completely.

While Arvey and his friends were planning their Eisenhower draft, another powerful group of party leaders—the "ultraliberals" —was working to swing the nomination to Supreme Court Justice William O. Douglas. Arvey and most of his supporters sent word that under no circumstances would they endorse Justice Douglas. It was their feeling that, if they could not get Eisenhower, the nomination traditionally and rightfully belonged to the incumbent President.

Arvey's hopes collapsed at 8:15 one morning late in 1947. He received a phone call from the spokesman who had first talked to Ike. "It's all off," the spokesman said. "He won't accept under any conditions."

As Arvey now recalls the story, Eisenhower had been visited by a prominent Republican, Thomas Watson, who had learned of the recent developments and rushed to Eisenhower's side to urge him not to identify with the Democrats. According to this version, Watson convinced the General that he was "being used" to pull the Democratic Party's chestnuts out of the fire.

Another theory has it that when Ike learned that Truman was being by-passed for the nomination, he decided not to become part of any move that would be disloyal to his World War II Commander in Chief. (At this time, remember, the admiration that the two men had for each other had not yet dissipated into the bitter feud which was to develop in later years.)

As soon as Arvey received the news that Ike was no longer available, he rushed to New York to meet with Mayor O'Dwyer and Jimmy Roosevelt. Arvey and O'Dwyer issued a public statement, pledging their support to Truman. (Roosevelt declined to sign the statement, because he still doubted Truman's ability to win in 1948, and wanted to further explore the case for Justice Douglas.)

Arvey then returned to Chicago. To avoid the press, which was clamoring for more information on the Eisenhower story, he secluded himself in the Lake Shore Drive Hotel apartment of an old friend, Colonel Charles Baron. No sooner had Jack climbed into bed for some much-needed sleep than the telephone rang.

"The White House calling," announced the operator. As no one except Baron knew where he was, Arvey suspected a rib. He was about to hang up, but there was something in the operator's voice that prompted him to hold the wire.

A moment later, President Truman was on the phone.

"I just read the statement you issued in my behalf, Jack," said the President. "I want you to know I'm very grateful, and that you never will have any cause to regret your support."

From that time on, the Truman-Arvey relationship, which had for a time been so cool, ripened into a deep friendship that has grown with the years.

Arvey is in semiretirement now, and Mayor Dick Daley is Chicago's "Mister Democrat" and the most powerful leader of the party in Illinois. As mayor he wields all the power that goes with being chief executive of the nation's second-largest city, and this position is strengthened immeasurably by the fact that of

Chicago's fifty aldermen, at least forty-five are not only of his party but are also solidly in his corner. Alderman Thomas Keane, of the West Side's Thirty-first Ward, who is City Council Finance Chairman and number two man in the organization, works as closely and harmoniously with Daley as any administration floor leader ever has with his mayor. Because of this, and because he is also Cook County Democratic Chairman, Daley is the dominant figure behind the scenes in the great complex of municipal and county functions, which includes the Cook County Board of Supervisors; the Circuit, Superior, and Criminal Courts; the Metropolitan Sanitary District of Greater Chicago; the Chicago Park District; the Municipal Court; and such important county administrative offices as those of the County Clerk, the County Treasurer, the State's Attorney, and the Coroner. His commanding presence is also felt in the Illinois State House of Representatives, and in all but one of the major State administrative offices in Springfield—starting with the governorship. (Charles E. Carpentier, the Secretary of State, is a Republican.)

Daley has more power than any of his predecessors ever enjoyed. Were he other than the responsible public official that he has proved himself to be thus far, this fact might be cause for genuine alarm. But on the whole, Daley has used his position wisely, helping Chicago to achieve more efficient municipal management than ever before. Among the accomplishments to which he can point with pride are Chicago-O'Hare International Airport, the McCormick Place Convention Hall, the Hyde Park-Kenwood Renewal Program (in the area around the University of Chicago), and such public relations coups as the visit of Britain's Queen Elizabeth II and Prince Philip for the opening of the St. Lawrence Seaway.

"Good politics is good government, and vice versa," says Daley.

In many important ways, he has proved that he lives by this motto. It was both good politics and good government to bring Orlando W. Wilson to Chicago as Police Superintendent, and to back him in his program to clean up certain unsavory elements not only on the police force, but at the root, in the party machine itself. Under Daley, as under no other administration in the history of Chicago, the Democratic organization derives its power from service to the community. Daley may be the last of the big-city bosses, but he is also the first of a new type of political leader—the boss who knows how to use the machinery of government and politics to get positive results, who has the power to do things and who does them.

Probably no other big-city mayor has the political savvy, experience, and drive of Daley. He is not only a former city precinct captain and holder of several county offices, but also is a veteran of administrative and legislative offices in the State government. He served as Director of Finance during Adlai Stevenson's administration as governor. Before that, in the days of the Kelly-Nash machine, he had been State Senator and floor leader of the Upper House. An encyclopedic memory has enabled him to take advantage of all this experience. As one assistant after another has said in awe, "There's nothing Dick doesn't know about government."

The mayor is the most energetic man in his office. He is usually the first to arrive in the morning, after walking the last few blocks for exercise. And when he leaves at night, he almost always takes along a document-filled brief case. And he's a determined boss when it comes to carrying out his programs. One day, for instance, he saw his press chief, Earl Bush, unthinkingly drop a cigar butt on the sidewalk. A strong believer in clean streets, the mayor immediately pounced on him.

"My own staff members littering the streets!" he shouted, in a voice that caused passers-by for half a block to turn and stare.

Bush meekly removed the butt to a trash can.

There were times in his early years when Daley showed frequent signs of an old-fashioned Irish temper, but since becoming mayor, he has brought himself under control. He can still get so angry that his face turns red, but he has never flown completely off the handle in public.

Daley is one of the most family-minded of all Chicago's mayors. No matter what his official schedule, he always eats breakfast and an early dinner with his attractive wife, Eleanor, and their seven children. And when he has to attend a banquet later in the evening, as he usually does, the mayor sits at his seat of honor and picks politely at the food. He still lives in a modest brick bungalow on South Lowe Avenue in the Back-of-the-Stockyards district, a neighborhood that has produced many of Chicago's mayors (Kelly and Kennelly also came from there). And he has season box seats for all White Sox games—all the Daleys are avid American League fans.

The power center of Daley's domain is party headquarters in the Morrison Hotel. But except for election nights, when the Democratic Suite is an ocean of bottles, coffee cups, and tally sheets, the atmosphere is invariably calm. To the dismay of most reporters, the important stories break quietly. Policy decisions for the organization may be hammered out in stormy caucus among such powerful leaders as Daley, Congressman William Dawson, County Board President John J. Duffy (successor to the late Dan Ryan), and County Clerk Edward J. Barrett—but these sessions have always been held behind closed doors. Once, as the entire Cook County Democratic Central Committee was filing into a meeting room, an enterprising reporter did break the monotony by slipping in with them. Not long afterward he was spotted and evicted. (He wasn't even a Democrat.)

Chicago has many other outstanding public officials. Behind the biggest executive desks in the County Building you will find such men as County Clerk Eddie Barrett, who once was elected Illinois Secretary of State without making a single campaign speech (he was a Marine in World War II, and could not get home for the campaign); County Board President Seymour Simon; Welfare Commissioner Raymond Hilliard, whose program for restoring welfare recipients to productive lives has won national attention; and Public Administrator James J. O'Keefe, invariably an important figure in Democratic National Convention arrangements.

And in city government there are such distinguished leaders as Ira J. Bach, Mayor Daley's chief of city planning; ex-newspaperman Alvin E. Rose, Executive Director of the Chicago Housing Authority; Charles R. Swibel, builder of Chicago's Marina City and Vice-Chairman of the Chicago Housing Authority; penologist Fred Hoehler; and Alderman Ralph Metcalfe, former Olympic sprint champion.

And then there are the distinguished Chicagoans on the national scene. Paul Douglas, the Senior Senator from Illinois, is among the most prominent. A former professor of economics at the University of Chicago, Douglas cut his political teeth as alderman from Chicago's Fifth Ward, that traditional stronghold of the independent Democrats. Now one of the most powerful leaders on Capitol Hill, Douglas is still an independent. He has twice been voted "Best Senator." His wife, the former Emily Taft, is a daughter of the famous sculptor, Lorado Taft, and served one term in the House of Representatives.

The Fifth Ward, which includes the campus of the University of Chicago, has also produced such leaders as State Senator Marshall Korshak, one of Illinois' officials-on-the-way-up; former corporation counsel Barnet Hodes; Robert Merriam; and present alderman Leon Despres—a thorn in the side of the Daley administration (as was Douglas to the Kelly-Nash machine).

The Chicagoan presently considered as the most likely prospect to follow in Douglas's footsteps is United States Representative Sidney R. Yates, a former All-Big-Ten basketball player. Yates was slated by the Democratic organization last winter to oppose the Republican incumbent, Senator Everett Dirksen, in the 1962 senatorial elections. (The Hyde Park area from which Douglas comes is on the South Side; Yates represents a North Side district.) A liberal and a Navy veteran of World War II, Congressman Yates played a prominent role in the drive to keep Admiral Hyman G. Rickover in the Navy, and because Yates and his colleagues were successful, America today holds a clear lead in nuclear-powered submarines. In his seven terms in Congress Yates has earned the respect of veteran Washington newsmen as well as that of his own constituents.

Also serving the national government are such former Chicagoans as the brilliant Secretary of Labor Arthur J. Goldberg (who attended Harrison High with my brother Joe); the sophisticated R. Sargent Shriver, Jr., President Kennedy's brother-in-law, who organized the Peace Corps; United States Representative Roman Pucinski, a former *Sun-Times* reporter, who is one of the outstanding young congressmen in Washington; and—from Adlai Stevenson's law office—Federal Communications Chairman Newton Minow, Undersecretary of Labor W. Willard Wirtz, and Ambassador to Denmark William McCormick Blair, Jr.

Of all the emissaries from Chicago, however, probably none inspires greater respect and affection among reporters than Adlai E. Stevenson, United States Ambassador to the United Nations. I've come to know Adlai well, both in victory and in defeat. He is a remarkable man. So highly developed and well balanced are his qualities of intellect, idealism, and humility that he has actually grown in stature under adversities that would have crushed the spirit of a lesser human being.

To many people, Stevenson appeared to have come "out of the blue" to win the 1952 Democratic Presidential nomination. Actually, as this columnist can testify, his name as the possible candidate had been appearing in various columns for years. Long before he entered politics, he was prominent in public affairs and government. A former three-term president of the Chicago Council on Foreign Relations, he served as special counsel to the Agricultural Adjustment Administration, under the first New Deal Administration in 1933. He held a number of responsible governmental jobs, including that of assistant to fellow Chicagoan Frank Knox, Secretary of the Navy during World War II. After several wartime missions to Europe he became one of the architects of the United Nations in London and San Francisco. (One of the many historical ironies which have peppered Stevenson's career occurred during World War II, when the North African villa formerly used by his sister, Mrs. Ernest ("Buffie") Ives, was occupied for a time by General Dwight Eisenhower—the man who was later to take over a much more important house that Stevenson had his eye on in Washington!)

One interesting fact about Adlai which most people don't know is that, somehow, he had never come to the attention of our local political leaders until Jack Arvey "discovered" him in 1947. At that time, Arvey was seeking "blue-ribbon" nominees for the Illinois State ticket in the crucial 1948 election. At a Washington luncheon arranged for him by former Senator Scott W. Lucas, Arvey talked with James Byrnes, then Secretary of State, who said, "You people in Illinois know you've got a gold nugget out there, don't you?" "Who do you mean?" asked Arvey. When Byrnes answered, "Adlai Stevenson," Arvey had to confess, "I don't know him." Back in Chicago, Arvey quickly made it his business to get acquainted. The late Judge Harry M. Fisher, arranged the introductions. Attorneys Louis Kohn and Stephen Mitchell (later Democratic National Chairman), and businessman Hermon Dunlap Smith quickly formed a committee to promote Stevenson for public office. His 1948 election plurality of 572,000 for governor was the largest in Illinois history.

Stevenson's eloquence and wit are comparable to that of Illinois' greatest statesman, Abraham Lincoln. (Stevenson's great-grandfather, Jesse W. Fell, was an intimate friend of Lincoln's. It was he who first proposed the Lincoln-Douglas debates.) Adlai is one of the few politicians who has no need for a ghost writer. As a writer, I admire his prose style. And as a newspaperman, I am even more impressed by his ability to write under the pressure of a deadline. When he boarded the train that was to take him Downstate to accept endorsement of the Central Committee of the Illinois Democratic Party for the nomination for governor, he had not finished his acceptance speech. He did so on the train, in less than an hour. And when he handed it to Jack Arvey, who was traveling with him, Jack was moved to exclaim, "Don't change a word of it! Don't let anyone ever change a word of anything you write."

To me, the mark of Adlai's character is that he can maintain his sense of humor in bad times as well as good—not only in the face of bitter political reversals, but also in moments of purely personal loss. Shortly after he moved to the Libertyville farm, the house was destroyed by fire. A friend recalls Adlai's refusal to become perturbed: Picking up a still glowing piece of wood from the wreckage, he nonchalantly lit a cigarette with it, then confided: "As you can see, we are still using the house." It is also a tribute to the man that his divorce from his wife, Ellen, in

1949 (an amicable one resulting from the conflict of his interest in public service with his wife's preference for a quieter life centering around art and the theater), left no appreciable scar on his relationship with his three sons, and seemed to be no impediment to his ascendancy in public life.

As a Chicago newspaperman, it has been my good fortune to meet every President who has occupied the White House in the past twenty years, starting with the great man who remembered Chicago as the site of his three renominations to the nation's highest office. From our very first personal contact, Franklin Delano Roosevelt made an unforgettable impression on me— as he did on almost everyone he met. It was in 1944, at a press conference in his office at the White House. In those intimate surroundings, the President could establish a personal rapport with each member of the press that is mechanically impossible in the huge State Department auditorium where President Kennedy must hold his news conferences today. And FDR charmed his visitors with no difficulty. Despite the pressure of his wartime duties, he was warm, unhurried, and witty. It is as much for his wit, in fact, as for his wisdom and humanitarian ideals that I remember him.

Few people realize, for example, that it was Roosevelt, and not Harry Truman, who first took note of the great number of White House matches that were carried off daily as souvenirs, and originated the now-famous imprint (which Truman also utilized on matchbooks): "Stolen from the White House."

It also was Roosevelt who handed down this bit of sage advice to his son, Franklin D. Roosevelt, Jr., on the problem of how to smile spontaneously for the cameras:

"It's easy," said FDR. "Whenever you are about to be photographed by somebody, just imagine you see a chicken on his nose."

No matter how heavy the pressure, Roosevelt never lost his capacity to joke with members of his staff. One man whom he took particular delight in teasing was Mike Reilly, a Secret Service agent. Once, in Chicago, FDR told how a certain scene in the movie, *Wilson*, had made him think of Reilly. It was the scene in which Woodrow Wilson proposed to Mrs. Galt on the White House patio, against a cluttered background of trees and plants. "I couldn't help thinking," said FDR, as he winked at Reilly, "that there was a Secret Service agent behind every one of those trees."

I first met Dwight D. Eisenhower when he was still a general. It was at an Army Day reception in Chicago shortly after World War II, and Ike and President Harry S. Truman were the guests of honor. Realizing that most of his friends hadn't met America's number one soldier, the President personally introduced the General to each guest. The man in front of me in the reception line remarked that he had met Ike a few years earlier. "I'll never forget that day," the man said. But if Ike was expecting to hear the usual compliment, he was as surprised as I was. Explained the man: "Yes, sir, the day we met I had four winners at the race track!"

I have many memories of Ike. One incident that I will not easily forget occurred just after his nomination at the 1952 Republican convention. The last volley had been fired in the complicated and sometimes bitter struggle between his backers and those of the late Senator Robert A. Taft. Ike had just received news of his victory in his suite at the Sheraton-Blackstone Hotel. Contrary to all protocol, Ike didn't wait for Taft to make the traditional call on him. He picked up a phone and called Taft at the Conrad Hilton, "I want to come over and see you, Bob," he said. And Ike and his bodyguard, Chicago policeman Lou Swee, pushed their way laboriously through the mob in the lobbies and on the street outside so that the General could publicly pay his respects to a gallant campaigner who was heartbroken at having lost his last chance to follow in the footsteps of his father, President William Howard Taft.

But the President I came to know best was the Man from Missouri who showed *them*, Harry S. Truman. We were first introduced by Russ Stewart, then managing editor of the old Chicago *Times*, in the days when Truman was still a leader in the United States Senate. Senator Truman's office was a friendly spot that I visited often in Washington. During the 1944 convention he and I spent more time together. And when he was President the White House was always open sesame to me.

His modesty about his success is matched only by that of his family. One of his favorite stories is of the time when, immediately after his inauguration as Vice-President, he telephoned his mother and said, "You're now talking to the Vice-President." "I know," she said, "I heard it on the radio." And then, before hanging up, she scolded the nation's number two public official, "Now, Harry, you behave yourself down there!"

His daughter Margaret, as unassuming as her father and far more charming than strangers realize, still chuckles over this Chicago phenomenon. When she was merely the daughter of the President of the United States, she was always seated at the second-ranking booth in the Pump Room: Number Eleven. But after she starred on TV with Jimmy Durante, she was accorded the Glory Seat: Booth Number One!

Truman's knowledge of American history is as thorough as that of any President, with the possible exception of Wilson. My family will never forget a tour he personally conducted through the White House near the end of his administration. His commentary was an amazing recap of much of the history of the building, its furnishings, and its famous inhabitants. It was a tour similar to the now-famous one conducted by Jackie Kennedy, without TV cameras.

One of my biggest scoops came from Harry Truman. I was the first to report his decision not to run for re-election in 1952, although he was eligible to seek another term, under the Twenty-second Amendment. I've often been asked how I got that story. The answer is simple. The President told me what he intended to do and when, in answer to a direct question I had put to him in the course of our conversation. A big Democratic fund-raising dinner was coming up shortly, but no one knew what Mr. Truman planned to say at the dinner. I merely put the question to him and he replied that he would make it official, at the dinner, that he would not run for re-election and that he would name Adlai

Stevenson, then Governor of Illinois, as his candidate for President. Mr. Truman made no request that this information be kept off the record. Naturally, I didn't ask!

How will history rate Truman? Much higher, I think, than do most of his contemporaries. Harry's greatest hero is Andrew Jackson, and I believe that it is beside Jackson that this forceful, forthright Man of Independence will ultimately be ranked. History faced him with harder decisions than any President since Lincoln—the use of the A-bomb, the launching of the Marshall Plan, recognizing the State of Israel in defiance of his own State Department, dispatching the Army to run the railroads during a nation-wide strike, ordering intervention when the Reds invaded South Korea, firing General Douglas MacArthur. There were those who despised him because he never "looked like a President"—but he never tried to. He is certain to be ranked among the great Chief Executives in our history.

Before we leave the political beat, let's have a look at the one subject that no Chicago reporter can afford to omit: the national political convention. Chicago held its first one in 1860, when the fledgling Republican Party assembled in the old Wigwam at Wacker and Lake to nominate Abraham Lincoln for President. Since then, there have been many memorable moments in Chicago conventions, ranging from the resounding "voice from the sewer" arranged by Mayor Ed Kelly and which mysteriously repeated Franklin D. Roosevelt's name over hidden loudspeakers at the 1940 Democratic convention, to the touching reception given the venerable Herbert Hoover as he entered the Republican national convention in 1960.

As an old sports reporter, I'll have to admit that not even a world series or a heavyweight championship fight can set the entire city aquiver quite like a national political convention can. There is the constant turmoil in the hotel lobbies and banquet halls, and the tense hush in the smoke-filled rooms. There is the scream of sirens as motorcycle police escort Presidents, former Presidents, and would-be Presidents from place to place. There is the unparalleled influx of the working press—the biggest names in newspaper, magazine, and radio-TV reporting and commentary.

Tables in the private clubs and booths in the Pump Room are filled with Governors, Senators, wealthy and influential individual party members, and such pundits of the press as Stewart and Joseph Alsop, Bob Considine, William Randolph Hearst, Jr., Drew Pearson, Leonard Lyons, Earl Wilson, Walter Winchell, Walter Cronkite, Marquis Childs, Roscoe Drummond, John Daly, Doris Fleeson, William Lawrence, David Lawrence, and James ("Scotty") Reston. Telephone company technicians string miles of wire and install hundreds of special telephones. Radio-TV mobile units cluster about the convention building and the major hotels. The major news media set up special news and city desks at the convention site. Wives of delegates and visitors fan out through the Loop and Michigan Avenue shopping area. Bars, restaurants, and theaters are jammed. For the duration of the convention, thousands of us strike one word from our vocabulary— *sleep*. Even were time for sleep available, there would be no need for it. You can't sleep. You run on and on, on nervous energy and excitement.

And then, when it's all over, the whole city heaves a huge sigh of relief—and continues to talk about the convention for weeks.

During the 1960 Presidential campaign, however, the excitement in Chicago didn't end when the Republican convention closed. Our Town was selected as the site of the first televised debate between the candidates. It took place in the CBS WBBM-TV studios, in what was formerly the Arena, at the corner of Erie and McClurg Streets on the Near North Side. The room in which the candidates debated is one which I know well. It is from that studio that my program *At Random* has been telecast since its inception.

Only a handful of political reporters, chosen on a "pool" basis, was allowed in the room with the candidates during the program itself, but I was able to see both of the principals before the debate began. I witnessed Dick Nixon's arrival at the building's front entrance, and I saw him enter the studio after leaving the make-up room. There is no question about his being the victim of a poor make-up job. I remarked at the time that he had looked much better before the make-up had been applied. Others noticed it, too.

During the "debate"—which was really not much more than a joint press conference or question-and-answer session—I sat with other reporters in a viewing room adjacent to the studio and followed the proceedings on a monitor. It was the consensus of those with whom I talked that both men had been well prepared for the program, as one would expect of professionals, but that Mr. Kennedy had been just a little bit better prepared than Mr. Nixon.

After the telecast, I joined Nixon in the dressing room, where he was changing clothes. He was completely relaxed. At that time, I invited him to appear on *At Random*.

"I promise you I'll do that," he said. "*After* the election."

"Win or lose?" I asked.

"Please," he said, feigning seriousness. "Don't mention that word *lose*."

When I saw him again, later in the campaign, Nixon looked even more tired than on the night of the debate. He was visibly wan.

"Oh, what I wouldn't give for twenty-four hours' sleep!" he said.

John F. Kennedy, of course, looked the same way at several stages of the race. Campaigning for the Presidency is a terrible ordeal. If you doubt it, ask any reporter who has covered a campaign. The reporters generally end up more exhausted than the candidates themselves.

Incidentally, I feel that there is no question that television was a decisive influence in that campaign, and that, in ensuing years, it will prove even more important. On the other hand, I doubt that President Kennedy will engage in similar debates with his Republican opponent in 1964. After the election, I put this question to Robert Kennedy, the President's brother and campaign manager. He shook his head and said:

"There will be no Presidential debates in 1964."

He pointed out a significant fact: in 1960, neither candidate was the President, and therein lies the difference from 1964.

When you consider it, Bobby Kennedy's statement seems reasonable. Any incumbent President would have to enter the campaign with one arm tied behind him, because his main job would necessarily be to defend the record of his administration, and to justify its existing policies—a position which is automatically a handicap in any debate. Then, too, the President might be challenged on questions that he could not answer candidly without endangering our national security. But if he were to plead executive privilege, or give an unsatisfactory partial answer, that, too, would put him at a disadvantage.

The Great Debates of 1960 will be remembered for a long time to come, however. To me, it seems highly fitting that the first of them occurred in Chicago, a city with a turbulent political past and what I feel confident will be a brilliant political future.

6. And in This Corner . . .

Mention Green Bay to any sports fan and the chances are that he will think of the Packers. Mention Milwaukee, and he will probably think of the Braves (or maybe of beer). It is the same with Cincinnati (the Redlegs) or Boston (the Red Sox), or Brooklyn (Los Angeles notwithstanding, the Dodgers). But mention Chicago to a fan, and his associations are likely to run away with him. Our Town's appetite for sports knows almost no bounds. Others may be satisfied with one "dish." We prefer a smorgasbord.

We don't stop with supporting such obvious big-time enterprises as major-league baseball (the Cubs and the White Sox), professional ice hockey (the Black Hawks), thoroughbred racing (at Arlington, Washington, Hawthorne and Sportsman's Parks), college and pro football, boxing, and championship golf. We are also devotees of the offbeat—including the peculiar brand of basketball perfected by the Harlem Globetrotters, harness racing, professional wrestling, and just about any other sporting activity that a State commission will grant a license for.

In fact, the Harlem Globetrotters originated in Chicago. It was thirty-four years ago when Abe Saperstein, who loved basketball but was too small to play, first organized the team with no assets but a basketball and a Model T Ford. Since then the Globetrotters have played in Quonset huts, canebrakes, drained

150

swimming pools—any place where they could exchange their street clothes for uniforms and hang up a pair of baskets. They have had a player temporarily incapacitated by landing on a hot cast-iron stove after making a lay-up shot in a barn, and another who was bumped through a barn door and into a manure pile. There were times in the early days when the team was so broke that it was willing to work for coffee and sandwiches, and there have been recent years when it grossed as much as three million dollars. They have played before the Pope, the King of Greece, and an assortment of sultans, sheiks, and potentates. They have provided the sports world with some of its zaniest moments. They were also witnesses to one of the most moving scenes ever to unfold in a sports arena.

It happened in 1951. The place was Olympic Stadium in Berlin, where the Globetrotters were appearing. Their guest was Jesse Owens, whom Adolf Hitler had snubbed after his unforgettable triumphs in the 1936 Olympics. Ludwig Shreiber, West Berlin's acting mayor, greeted the great track star.

"Jesse," he said, "fifteen years ago this month Adolf Hitler refused to give you his hand. I'm proud to give you both of mine."

Chicago is the capital of professional wrestling. Haystacks Calhoon, Buddy ("Nature Boy") Rogers, Verne Gagne, Pat O'Connor, and other mimes of the mat operate out of Chicago, where they are booked from the office of a Lane Technical High School alumnus, Fred Kohler. An ex-wrestler who once took on a 450-pound bear, and won, Kohler is incontestably the sport's number one coach, innovator, promoter, and casting director.

Mention the sporting event, and we'll back it—from a peanut-pushing contest down State Street, starring a sports columnist who made a wrong guess, to an exploit that exhausts me even to think of—the thirty-four-mile swim across Lake Michigan made last year by a young Illinois Tech instructor. If we can't find anything around to support, it doesn't matter: We'll originate something.

When the 1933 Century of Progress Exposition was in full swing, complete with Sally Rand and cable-car rides, to outsiders it looked like an overwhelming success. Not to Chicagoans. It lacked a feature sports event. The Chicago *Tribune*'s sports editor, the late Arch Ward, came up with an idea. Why not promote a super baseball game between the leagues, right in the middle of the pennant race, with each league's teams made up of the best players at each position! The first All-Star Baseball Game was won by the American League on a line-drive home run by Babe Ruth in Comiskey Park. And the next year, just to keep things from getting dull, Arch originated the All-Star Football Game at Soldier Field, one of our outstanding summertime athletic events. In addition to these events, Chicago also created the Golden Gloves Boxing Tournament, the late George S. May's memorable All-American and World Golf Tournaments at Tam O' Shanter Country Club, and the American Bowling Congress Tournament.

Chicago was the site of the first automobile race on the American continent, held on Thanksgiving Day, 1895—a 54.36-mile run won by Frank Duryea at the unheard-of average speed of 7.5 miles per hour. Chicago inaugurated the five-figure purse in horse racing, at Washington Park's noted American Derby. Chicago built the first eighteen-hole golf course, at the Chicago Golf Club in Belmont, Illinois.

This city witnessed the founding of both the National and the American Leagues in baseball, and it was here that the formidable Big Ten Conference in collegiate football was first organized. (And where the Big Ten commissioners—the late Maj. John Griffith, Tug Wilson, and the current Bill Reed—always have maintained headquarters.)

Chicago is where boxing's biggest gate ($2,600,000) and second-largest crowd (104,943) were recorded for the second Dempsey-Tunney fight at Soldier Field, in 1927; where Joe Louis turned pro for fifty dollars, and where he later won the heavyweight title from Jimmy Braddock in Comiskey Park; where Red Grange joined the Chicago Bears to put professional football among "respectable" sports; and where such star basketball players as bespectacled George Mikan have been groomed.

"I'm sorry, Mikan," Notre Dame's basketball coach, George Keogan, had told the awkward, un-co-ordinated youth, "but basketball just isn't your game. You've got a good future in your studies. Keep at them." But at De Paul University, Coach Ray

Meyer saw promise in the young man. He put him on a stiff regimen, which included rope-skipping, trying five hundred shots a day with each hand, and learning balance by shooting while holding a towel under his right arm. Under Meyer's guidance, Mikan developed rapidly into the basketball player voted "Greatest of the Half-Century."

And speaking of basketball, the sport took on new importance in Chicago thanks to the college doubleheader program, originated by the late Judge John Sbarbaro and attorney Arthur Morse a quarter-century ago. The first doubleheaders were played in the Madison Avenue Armory on the West Side. From there they were shifted to the Coliseum, and finally to the Chicago Stadium, which has been their home for the past twenty years.

And for years, Chicago was the home of a man who was in on the very beginnings of basketball. Amos Alonzo Stagg, the "Grand Old Man of Football," was a classmate of James Naismith, the young physical education student who, in 1891, was asked to think up a competitive sport that his class could play indoors.

Coach Stagg was seven years old in 1869, when the first intercollegiate football game was played. In his long, brilliant coaching career at the University of Chicago, Stagg revolutionized the game with such innovations as the lateral pass and line and backfield shifts. Under his enlightened reign University of Chicago elevens were perennial Conference and national champions or—at worst— contenders. (Today, of course, the Maroon stars play their most exciting football in the intramurals.)

It was also in Chicago that Charles ("Chick") Evans, Jr., the "Grand Old Man of Golf," won his first tournament as a teenager. Since then, he has played in more meets, and won more championships—including the first sweep of both the National Amateur and the United States Open crowns in 1916—than any other American. His Evans Foundation, organized to help caddies through college, has given more than one thousand scholarships thus far.

It was here, too, that Andy Frain launched the famous ushering service that has become a fixture at ball games, fights, political conventions, and other events where large crowds gather. By personally crashing the Kentucky Derby and then bluffing his way into the executive offices of Colonel Matt Winn, Frain demonstrated to Winn and others how gate-crashers could substantially cut into gate receipts. Frain's personal counseling of the hundreds of youths he employs each year ranks him as "headmaster" of one of the largest "prep schools" in the nation. Doctors, lawyers, priests, scientists, public officials—all are among the alumni of "Frain Tech."

On a given night, Frain may have as many as seven thousand men on duty in two dozen cities, all of whom receive their instructions from his headquarters on West Madison Street across from the Chicago Stadium. By now, there are few gate-crashing alibis they haven't heard. Some gate-crashers have carried ladders and posed as maintenance men. Others have brought such props as ice buckets and press cameras. One even arrived at a sports event carrying a clock and claiming to be the timekeeper. But Andy has stopped them all. All, that is, but one—his nemesis, the late James "One-Eye" Connelly, king of the gate-crashers.

Over the years, there was almost no event Connelly did not try to crash. With One-Eye, it was more than a sport, it was a code of honor. Once, before a political convention, Frain had given his ushers a detailed description of One-Eye, had briefed them on all the wily free-loader's standard dodges, and had threatened vague horrors that would dog the life of any man who let him past. No sooner did Andy enter the hall, however, than he saw One-Eye in the middle of the convention floor—selling ice water to the delegates, at fifty cents a glass. Every time that Andy caught One-Eye, he would have him thrown out. And almost invariably, a few minutes later—by means known only to the elusive Connelly—Andy would hear a familiar voice shouting, with a grin, "Hi, Andy." Shortly before One-Eye's death in 1953, Andy visited him for a sad good-by.

"I'm sure he crashed the Pearly Gates," says Andy. "I'd like to have seen St. Peter keep him out."

For those who like their sports at home, Chicago offers some of the best sports broadcasters in the business, including Cubs-

White Sox telecaster Jack Brickhouse, with whom I broadcast the Chicago Bears' games; Bob Elson, a former Paulist choirboy who broadcasts the White Sox games on radio; WBBM's John Harrington, a football specialist with a quarterback's savvy and a lineman's girth; and Jack Drees, the former U. of Iowa basketball star who is adept in every field.

As his winter afternoon radio programs with disk jockey Eddie Hubbard demonstrate, Jack Brickhouse is quite a guy. Just when listeners expect him to discuss baseball, football, wrestling, or one of his other sports specialties, he'll launch into an informed discourse on something like the price of tea in Tahiti. Particularly amusing are his stories of his early radio experiences—such as this one, of his first football broadcast, in Peoria, Illinois.

"I lost track of the score in the first quarter," says Jack, "and I never again got it straight. I incorrectly identified almost every player on the field. After I completely missed a touchdown and called the try for the extra point a field goal attempt, the studio sent another announcer to take over!"

As a baseball town, Chicago really has no equal. Birthplace of both major leagues, ours was the only city that was supporting two ball clubs at the time of the recent expansions. Baseball history has been made here, not only by the players on the field, but by the less conspicuous—though no less colorful—front-office men.

The late Charles A. Comiskey, "The Old Roman," was both a great player and a great executive. A native Chicagoan, he dedicated fifty years of his life to baseball. As a player, he is recognized in the Baseball Hall of Fame as the man who set the pattern for all modern-day first-base play. Later, as White Sox owner, he put together four strong pennant winners, including the magnificent 1906 "hitless wonders," who upset the powerful Cubs of Tinker-to-Evers-to-Chance fame in one of the most dramatic intra-city World Series ever played. He also is locally credited with originating Ladies Day, which is ironic in its way, since it was a lady—his granddaughter Dorothy Comiskey Rigney—who helped bring on the end of the Comiskey dynasty in Chicago baseball.

As all White Sox fans know, Dorothy had a falling-out with her brother Chuck. The disagreement developed when young Chuck announced that he was ready to take over the presidency of the club, and Dorothy felt that he lacked sufficient experience. Dorothy finally concluded the matter by selling majority control of the team to Bill Veeck and Hank Greenberg in 1959. Then, in late 1961, Chuck himself closed the Comiskey-White Sox saga by selling his minority interest to a syndicate of young Chicago businessmen.

And now Bill Veeck, too, is no longer with the White Sox. As any American League fan in Chicago will testify—and the fans in Cleveland, St. Louis, and other cities where Bill has operated will corroborate it—there isn't another baseball executive like him in the game today. Certainly his tenure as president was unforgettable.

Before Bill's arrival here, former General Manager Frank Lane and his "Go-Go Sox" had pulled the club out of a long stretch of the doldrums. But the tempo whipped up by Frantic Frank seemed almost leisurely when compared to the gallop that Veeck sustained throughout his exciting administration.

Bill, the son of former Cubs president Bill Veeck, Sr., had cut his teeth in baseball. Nothing even remotely connected with the game was too trivial for his personal attention—and no tradition was too sacred to escape his shrewd appraisal. The neighborhood around Comiskey Park had grown increasingly shabby over the years, and the ball park itself was in disrepair. Bill cleaned up the park—even to painting the walls a sparkling white—and launched a campaign to renovate the nearby slums. He modernized box-office policy and revolutionized promotion methods. He and his lovely wife, Mary Frances, appeared frequently on television, and Bill hit the speech-making trail oftener than any other top executive in the game. He even took to sitting in different parts of Comiskey Park's bleachers and grandstands to get acquainted with the fans. They loved it.

And the daffy stunts!

One afternoon, for example, Veeck decided that the White Sox should observe "Dairy Farm Day." Before he was finished, the stadium looked more like the ark than a park—with cows, pigs, ducks, geese, and three tiny burros cavorting about the infield, while chickens scattered in all directions with ushers in hot pursuit.

Then there was the time three White Sox players were matched against three members of the Boston Red Sox in a cow-milking contest at home plate. Boston won—the cow being milked by Sox second-baseman Nellie Fox kept kicking over the pail.

Veeck promoted a series of the most improbable giveaways ever perpetrated. One day the prizes were two thousand pizza pies, delivered steaming hot to the fans with the winning numbers. Another time it was free rental of five hundred tuxedos—all for one man. And on still another occasion, the prize was something that no city-dweller should be without—fifty thousand nuts and bolts.

And there is Veeck's famous "Cape Canaveral Scoreboard." If you haven't heard, the scoreboard to all outward appearances looks like a normal one—until a White Sox player hits a home run! And then *boom!*—the whole South Side of Chicago begins to shake. Rocketing into the air go some fifty dollars' worth of colored fireworks. Smoke erupts and aerial torpedoes whistle and explode. Colored lights play up and down the edges of the scoreboard, while horns honk, whistles hoot, and sirens scream. It is like V-J Day and an old-fashioned Fourth of July being celebrated simultaneously.

All this, of course, happens only when a *White Sox* player hits a home run. Four-baggers hit by the visiting team are met with crashing silence. When Casey Stengel was still managing the New York Yankees, this "discrimination" slowly got under his skin. Reverting to the zany days when he once tipped his hat and a bird flew out, Stengel plotted his retaliation. Finally, during a night game, Casey struck back. One of the Yankees hit a home run. The scoreboard recorded it silently. Stengel nodded grimly, and the Yankee bench marched into position in front of their dugout. There was another signal from Stengel, and every man pulled out a sparkler, lighted it, and waved it frantically at the stands.

But the loudest fireworks associated with Veeck's tenure as Sox President weren't set off at his instigation at all. It occurred on

September 22, 1959, the night the White Sox clinched the American League pennant. The game, played in Cleveland, had ended shortly before 10:00 P.M., Chicago time. Suddenly, about 10:30, the eerie whine of air-raid sirens pierced the night air. Every air-raid warning signal in Chicago and in several suburbs sounded for five minutes.

For all that most Chicagoans knew, this was *it*, the general alert that an air-raid might occur at any time. The *Sun-Times'* switchboard, and those of the other papers and the radio stations, were swamped with frantic calls. The police and fire departments were also deluged with inquiries. Panic-stricken apartment-dwellers poured into the streets. A number of home-owners took shelter in their basements. Other Chicagoans took such drastic and dangerous action as leaping into automobiles and heading for the nearest expressway out of town.

It was a frightening moment that could have ended in disaster, had the panic spread further. What had happened, we know now, is that someone had taken too literally a City Council resolution that if the Sox should win the pennant "bells should ring, whistles blow, bands play, and general joy be unconfined." Insiders say that the person who issued the spurious alert was Mayor Daley himself, a dedicated Sox fan. In any event, Fire Commissioner Robert Quinn, like a good Irishman, publicly took the blame for the incident in a handsome statement of apology. Thousands of Chicagoans learned the hard way the necessity of observing one of the first rules of Civil Defense—when the sirens sound, *don't panic!* Tune to the Conelrad radio frequencies for news and instructions!

Bill Veeck's promotional shenanigans and, to a certain extent, his well-publicized practice of wearing an open-neck sport shirt on all occasions have led some people to draw mistaken conclusions about him. As he has proved time and again, he is not just a boisterous circus-lover who should have won the bid he once made for Ringling Brothers' Barnum & Bailey. He's a first-class businessman, extremely articulate and well informed, who could have succeeded in almost any field. He regularly reads three or four good books a week, plows through stacks of daily newspapers, and pursues outside interests ranging from architecture to law.

Arthur C. Allyn, Jr., Veeck's successor, is almost his complete opposite in everything except business acumen. He is relatively quiet and conservative. He knew very little about baseball until he became one of Veeck's financial backers. "Years ago, when I had a box seat for a World Series game," says Allyn, "confidentially, I was bored stiff." But that happened back in 1929, and the game was the grim pitchers' duel in which the Phillies' Howard Ehmke struck out thirteen men to humble the Cubs' Charley Root, and in which neither team scored until the seventh inning— one of the great afternoons in baseball, but understandably bewildering to a non-fan who had come looking for excitement. Allyn is a baseball fan now, all right, and a smart front-office man with many intelligent decisions already behind him—including the selection of veteran Sox publicist Ed Short as General Manager, and the decision to retain Al Lopez as Field Manager.

With Casey Stengel's retirement from the Yankees, Alfonso Ramon Lopez became the dean of American League managers. During Stengel's long and prosperous Yankee reign, Lopez was the only pilot in the league who could beat the Bombers in a pennant race—and he did it twice: in 1954, with the Indians, and in 1959, with the Go-Go Sox.

One of the game's authentic gentlemen, Lopez is exceptional in that he prefers one-year contracts to longer ones, and refuses to jump a contract or even to consider another offer while an agreement remains in force. He is also remarkable in that he is followed to each new managerial assignment by a loyal coaching staff, led by ex-Dodger teammate Tony Cuccinello, who has been one of his closest associates for thirty years.

But the South Side holds no monopoly on front-office individualists. The Cubs of Wrigley Field can also claim one in their owner, chewing-gum tycoon Philip K. Wrigley. The Cubs' president for more than a quarter-century, Phil is one of the most unusual men ever to head a big-league team. Although he enjoys owning his club, he very seldom watches its games. When he does, it is from a back row of the grandstand, instead of from his

private box. He answers his own telephone in his Wrigley Building office, replies to all mail personally, and enjoys no spare-time
activity more than tinkering with greasy engine parts in his private
machine shop. The guest house and servants' quarters at his summer place in Lake Geneva, Wisconsin, are larger than many a
millionaire's year-round mansion.

His father, William Wrigley, conceived the advertising axiom,
"Tell 'em quick, and tell 'em often." By following this rule, and
a few of his own, P. K. Wrigley has tripled the market value of
the Wrigley firm's stock since taking over the reins. Other thriving
family interests include the Wrigley Building and Wrigley Restaurant, a chain of hotels and resorts, mining enterprises—and the
development of California's Catalina Island, which he owns.

Die-hard Cub fans, steeped in the tradition of Grover Cleveland
Alexander, Rogers Hornsby, Gabby Hartnett, Stan Hack, Phil
Cavarretta, and other Cub stars, write Wrigley even more scathing
letters than I get as a columnist. The fans have attacked such
ideas of his as replacing the field manager with a committee of
coaches. But many of Wrigley's innovations have been more
sensible than the fans realize. His coach plan, for example, has
the laudable objective of improving instruction in the minor
leagues and adding incentive both for players and coaches who
otherwise would have no direct contact with the majors.

The great attractiveness of Wrigley Field is also due in large
part to him. It is the only park in the major leagues that has
never installed lighting for night games. Wrigley has refused to
do so, out of deference to residents near the stadium, and
because he believes baseball "should be played in God's warm
sunshine." Advertising signs are standard in other parks. Wrigley
won't allow one, even on his scoreboard. And when the major
leagues moved to the Pacific Coast, he could have held out for a
huge windfall. Instead, to aid in the realignment, he quietly
switched his Los Angeles minor-league franchise and gave up his
West Coast Wrigley Field. Not many owners would have been
so accommodating.

In spite of all the owner's good intentions, however, the Cubs
have undeniably suffered from several traits of the Wrigley per-

sonality. One is his intense personal loyalty, best exemplified in the managerial cliff-hangers known as "The Return of Charley Grimm," "The Second Return of Charley Grimm," and "The Third Return of Charley Grimm." In some cases this loyalty has helped the team—but in others, it has stubbornly kept unproductive staff people in positions of power. It is also regrettable that Wrigley has never managed to delegate full authority, even to such astute aides as former General Manager James Gallagher, one of my ex-newspaperman friends. But Wrigley explains it this way: "If I'm getting the blame, I might as well have the responsibility."

One of the many occasions on which the quipsters have had a field day over Cub affairs was in 1960, when Wrigley made the celebrated exchange of Lou Boudreau for Charley Grimm. Boudreau, then broadcasting the Cubs games, became manager, and Grimm, then manager, took over Boudreau's broadcasting job. Eying Bob Elson, who broadcasts the White Sox games, they asked:

"Does this mean that Al Lopez is up for Elson's job?"

But let's not forget that a ball club is more than a business office. Who can begin to recount all the wonderful stories about the Cubs themselves—the players and managers, past and present.

One story concerns big Lewis ("Hack") Wilson, the barrel-shaped home-run champion of the National League in the late 1920s. Although Wilson's power hitting won many games for the Cubs, when it came to fielding, he was no gazelle. In the bottom of the seventh inning of the fourth game of the 1929 World Series, when the Philadelphia Athletics broke loose for a ten-run rally that erased Chicago's eight-run lead, and won the game, it was Wilson's misplay of an easy fly ball that led to the disaster— and that was not his only error of the afternoon. After the game, as Joe McCarthy, who then was managing the Cubs, was stamping angrily back to the clubhouse, a small boy ran up to him.

"Mr. McCarthy," said the boy, "do you think I could have a baseball for a souvenir? Do you, please?"

McCarthy burned silently for a few moments, then snapped:

"Come back tomorrow, Sonny, and stand out there in center

field with that big fellow, Wilson—you'll find plenty of baseballs!"

Charley Grimm, known as "Jolly Cholly" because of his mischievous wit, is also the subject of many stories. To me, one of the most memorable occurred back in the era of such Cub heroes as Phil Cavarretta and Stan Hack. Charley was contesting an umpire's decision, and getting no place. Finally, in exasperation, he marched back to his third-base coaching box. The next man up to bat was Stan Hack, whom Grimm always referred to by the nickname "Stanislaus." Jolly Cholly tried to forget the disputed decision and get on with his ball game. He started "talking it up," shouting encouragement down to his batter. "Come on, Stanislaus, baby, come on, big Stanislaus," he chanted. But it didn't work—he was too angry, and the temptation was too great. Slowly he began to raise his voice on the last syllable, and then to turn his head from the batter to the umpire as he shouted, louder and louder.

"Come on, Stanis-LOUSE! Come on, Stanis-LOUSE!"

It took the umpire only a moment or two to catch on. Then he stalked over to Grimm, raised an arm, and majestically thumbed the manager out of the game.

There have been many funny moments on both Chicago teams. With uninhibited extroverts such as the Cubs' diminuitive "Dim Dom" Dominic Dallesandro, who always seemed to be standing in a hole, or "Mad Russian" Lou Novikoff, or the White Sox' redoubtable Luke Appling, who could hit intentional foul balls until a pitcher's arm dropped off, how could it be otherwise? And then there was the extravagant character who was a Chicagoan for four unforgettable seasons in the sudden twilight of his brief, brilliant career—my old sparring partner from the Gashouse Gang, the great Dizzy Dean.

When Diz joined the Cubs in 1938 his playing days were numbered. One of his toes had been broken by a line drive back to the mound in the All-Star Game of 1937. He had stayed with the team, and returned to the pitching rotation too early. To favor the painful toe, he had lost the splendid rhythm of his delivery—and this, in turn, had caused a kink in his arm which never again quite left him. As a result of this, his screaming fast ball was gone.

But not his sense of humor, nor his drawling command of his personal version of the English language.

Although it was a bitter accident which cut short his career, Dizzy can still laugh about his frequent injuries. There was the time, for example, when he really used his head to break up a double play. It was the fourth game of the 1934 Series and Dean was on base as a pinch runner. The batter behind him hit into a classical double play, but the hard-thrown relay of Pirate shortstop Billy Rogell somehow hit Dizzy full in the head, knocking him unconscious, but saving the out. His many fans were apprehensive. But later, from the hospital, Dean reassured them.

"I'm okay," he said. "They took pictures of my haid, and the X rays showed absolutely nothin'."

(So he stayed in the hospital overnight and came back to pitch the next day.)

And there was still another time, while Dizzy and his brother Paul were still pitching partners with the Cardinals, that Diz was struck in the head—this time by a murderous line drive. Again, everyone was worried, except the Dean brothers. When his brother Paul came rushing out to pick him up, Dean asked, "Ain't gonna be no lump on my haid, is they, Paul?"

"Shucks, no, Diz," said Paul. "It warn't but a glancing blow."

And at the end of a session of reminiscences, Diz loves to sum up his career in the words he used in acknowledgment on the day when he was enrolled in the Baseball Hall of Fame:

"I want to thank the good Lord for giving me a good right arm, a strong back, and a weak mind."

Where the Sport of Kings is concerned, there has never been a more enthusiastic booster of honest thoroughbred racing in pleasant surroundings than the late Ben Lindheimer of the Arlington and Washington Park race tracks. "Our greatest advertisement," he used to say, "is a satisfied customer." Lindheimer probably produced more walking advertisements over a shorter period of time than any other race-track owner in the nation.

He bought control of Arlington Park in 1940. Immediately, he set about to prove his theory by satisfying the customers. He established record-breaking purses to attract the best stables and

the leading jockeys. He beautified the grounds. He installed esca-
lators and other conveniences in the clubhouse; and kept the
jockeys and stablehands happy with such comforts as swimming
pools and such services as professional tutoring for their young-
sters. And to assure the honesty of betting and riding, he built up
the Thoroughbred Racing Protective Association, and also established a private supervisory agency of his own. The customers
were more than satisfied, and Ben was voted turfdom's "Man of
the Year." The consensus among racing professionals, as well as
among the fans, was that "Arlington is the finest track in the
world," in the words of Calumet Farms' famous trainer, Jimmy
Jones. Since Ben's death, his daughter, Mrs. Marjorie Everett, has
continued the vigilance (and the heavy financial investment) required to keep the track in excellent condition.

Some of the greatest races in turf history have been run at
Arlington. It was there that the famed Citation made his last
public appearance. Native Dancer ran one of his finest races there.
And such outstanding jockeys as Willie Shoemaker, Johnny Long-
den, and Eddie Arcaro have done some of their most skillful
riding at Arlington.

In one race at Arlington, however, Arcaro was notably unsuccessful. The owner of a one-horse stable, to his good fortune, had
somehow managed to sign Eddie to ride the stable's entry in a
stakes race. Before the horses went to the post, the owner gave
the jockey detailed instructions.

"Break fast," he said. "Get into fourth position at the first turn.
Hang there until the clubhouse turn. Then make your move as
you head into the stretch, and you'll win going away."

Arcaro nodded confidently—and proceeded to finish dead last.

The owner was hopping mad by the time the horse finally
came in. He came storming up to the little man with his finger
pointed.

"I told you exactly what to do!" he spluttered. "You were supposed to stay in fourth position until the clubhouse turn, and then
take the lead as you came into the stretch."

"What?" demanded Arcaro. "And leave the horse?"

Chicago's reputation as a prize-fight town is peculiar. I can't decide whether "illustrious" or "notorious" is the word I want to describe it. Either way, "Chicago" is firmly established as one of the prominent place names in the annals of boxing.

On the credit side, it was here that some of the best fights in modern ring history were staged—brilliant matches that did much to elevate boxing to its present position among legitimate sports. Championship bouts promoted here have drawn some of boxing's biggest gates (including Dempsey-Tunney in 1927, Louis-Braddock in 1937, and Graziano-Zale in 1947). Chicago boxing clubs made possible the development of such champions as Battling Nelson, Jackie Fields, Barney Ross, Johnny Bratton, and Tony Zale.

Because Chicago is a boxing center second only to New York, fight fans have been able to follow such great champions as Joe Louis, Sugar Ray Robinson, and Rocky Marciano at their best. As a sportswriter and columnist, I have come to know these three men personally, and to admire each of them for special qualities: Louis, for his superb confidence and calm before a contest in which his whole reputation was at stake; Robinson, for his flawless timing and his ability to emerge from many of his toughest fights almost unmarked and barely winded; and Marciano, for his almost unbelievable modesty. The heavyweight championship is boxing's biggest prize and one of the most coveted and remunerative sports titles in the world—and the Rock won it and retired with it without a defeat on his professional record. He was one of the foremost celebrities of his day, but fame never spoiled his simplicity. When I introduced him to such fans of his as Ralph Edwards, Tony Martin, or Bob Hope, Rocky was as overwhelmed as any wide-eyed boy from the country. It was boxing's loss that no contenders had been produced who could have given Rocky an incentive to remain active as champion.

One of the most rewarding aspects of covering boxing in Chicago has been the opportunity to follow the development of potential champions. I'll never forget the night a young kid from Detroit was appearing professionally for the first time at Marigold Gardens, on Chicago's North Side. He had speed. He had power. He had everything.

"Here is a boy who can't miss becoming a champion," everybody agreed.

He didn't miss. His name was Joe Louis.

The redoubtable Tony Zale also fought some of his earliest matches at Marigold. I'll always remember one of them. Tony, who had been boxing since he was fourteen years old, in Gary, Indiana, was knocked out by a right to the jaw in the first round. He later flattened his opponent and went on to win the first unambiguous middleweight championship of the world in ten years. (This is the simplest way I know to describe a complicated situation that has confused the record books. In the period from 1931 until 1941, the National Boxing Association and the New York State Athletic Commission refused to recognize each other's titles in this division. Zale was the first champion acceptable to both organizations.) At the peak of his career, and just as his title was nationally recognized, Tony spent three years and five months in the Navy in World War II. And in 1946, when he was thirty-two, Tony fought the first of three of the most fiercely contested championship fights in history, against Rocky Graziano.

The most exciting of the three Zale-Graziano bouts was the second, which took place indoors at the Chicago Stadium, on one of the hottest July nights I remember. It was 98 degrees at ringside and 110 under the lights. A capacity crowd packed the enormous building. (The gate receipts still hold the record for an indoor bout.) Graziano, who had lost the first fight, in New York, came out punching. So did Zale. Toe to toe, they never stopped hammering each other until the sixth round, when Graziano won on a technical knockout. The next year Zale regained his title in Newark. He held it until Marcel Cerdan knocked him out of the ring for good.

There have been many luckless boxers on my beat. Most of them never made it at all. A few battled their way to the top, but ended up hooked on narcotics—including welterweight champion Johnny Bratton. And although Tony Zale is one of the cleanest-living fighters I have ever known, I'll have to class him as luckless too. Through no fault of his own, Tony never managed to capitalize on his championship. Military service kept him from the ring in his fighting prime. Because he didn't think it would be fair to other servicemen, he turned down at least one offer to make upward of $25,000 in a hastily arranged exhibition match. Because Graziano was more articulate than Zale, it was Rocky who cashed in on the fame that resulted from the Zale-Graziano fights. And then Zale's wife, from whom he now is divorced, took a huge bite out of what remained of his bankroll. And a Rush Street restaurant which he operated lasted only a short time. When last heard of, Tony was selling insurance for a living, and coaching boxing in his spare time at a Catholic Youth Organization gym in Chicago. The last time I saw him, he was still the "Man of Steel" who thrilled the nation as a boxer, and brought nothing but credit to his sport.

So much for the credit side.

The role of the International Boxing Club, often referred to as "Octopus, Inc.," is less definitely defined in the minds of many fight enthusiasts. None can deny that the IBC, created by multimillionaire Jim Norris and a brilliant Negro attorney, Truman Gibson, Jr., and headquartered in Chicago, brought boxing to new heights of popularity. For a number of years, the IBC was responsible for two network TV boxing shows every week, on Wednesdays and Saturdays. Countless millions were glued to their "watching machines" during this period. Millions of dollars also were involved in the staging of 104 fights each year.

With such stakes, there is little wonder that the underworld muscled into the boxing game. Frankie Carbo, the notorious hoodlum, reportedly had a hand in the affairs of many fighters and managers. Whether Norris, with his personal fortune and power, could have forced Carbo out of the game; or whether Norris, with his 104 matches per year to make for TV, needed Carbo's cooperation to assure fighters, is a moot question that may never be resolved.

Uncle Sam finally entered the fight game and ordered the IBC dissolved in an antitrust suit. The IBC was charged with controlling (1) arenas, (2) fighters, and (3) television contracts. Except for television, then not a factor, both Tex Rickard and Mike Jacobs operated in much the same way. And with the government-ordered dissolution of the IBC, boxing fell on evil days, with more evil characters moving to the fore.

There can be no doubt about Norris' role in building the Chicago Black Hawks into a championship club. He and his partner, Arthur Wirtz, doled out a tidy fortune to rebuild a team that had sunk to the depths and lost its box-office appeal. Now the Hawks are riding high again and their reign, either as challenger or champion, appears secure for years to come because of the "farm system" that assures promising young players.

I covered hockey for the old *Times* for five years, but it took at least two seasons for me to get the feel of the game. I didn't "dig" a sport whose players moved so fast that there seemed to be no co-ordinated effort, no "set" plays, such as in football. But under the guidance of one of the most beloved figures in hockey, Joe ("Chesterfield") Farrell, I gradually learned to appreciate the game. Joe was publicity director for the Hawks and every morning during the season, en route to my office, I'd stop for coffee with Joe, whose offices at that time were in the McLaughlin Manor House Coffee plant. Major Frederic McLaughlin was the first owner of the team and the Black Hawk headquarters were in his North LaSalle Street building. (Our morning coffee was always piping hot and on the house.)

When Norris eventually purchased control of the Hawks, then at low ebb, he was not content to let his team's reputation stand on the memories of past stars, such as Chuck Gardiner, Mush March, Bill Mosienko, and Doug and Max Bentley.

Instead, he has financed a ten-team farm system that provides General Manager Tommy Ivan and Coach Rudy Pilous with a constant stream of young talent—featuring such outstanding players as Murray Balfour, Red Hay, and Bobby Hull. In the 1934 and 1938 championship years, the Stanley Cup was usually displayed on a shelf in the Billy Goat Tavern, across Madison Street from the Chicago Stadium. But when the Cup came back to Chicago in 1961, there was a special niche waiting for it in the Stadium itself—a symbol of our determination to keep it here for many championship years to come.

I cannot close this little love song to the Black Hawks without telling the story of a player who became a legendary figure in the history of the team, in spite of the fact that he played only one game in a Black Hawk uniform and never played in Chicago at all. His name was "English Alfie" Moore. It all happened in the 1938 Stanley Cup play-offs, which I covered as a sportswriter.

The 1938 Hawks had fought an uphill battle all season, just to stay in contention. They finished sixth in the regular-season standings. But by playing their hearts out—and with a little bit of luck—they had managed to advance to the finals in the competition for the cup that is emblematic of world professional championship. Their opponents in the final series were the Toronto Maple Leafs, who then had the most feared line in the game.

The series opened in Toronto. And it was not until the opening day that the Hawks suddenly learned what it had cost them to get there. Their goalie, Mike Karakas, had broken his toe in the last game of the semifinals against New York, but the extent of his injury had not become apparent until the morning of the opener in Toronto. Mike could not possibly play that night. And they had no other goalie!

What could they do?

Hawk Manager Bill Stewart (also a well-known major-league baseball umpire) was willing to use minor-league goalie Paul Goodman, of the Wichita team in the American Association. But Goodman couldn't get to Toronto until the following day. So Stewart petitioned National Hockey League President Frank Calder for special permission to use New York Ranger goalie Dave Kerr in the opening game. With this, Stewart thought that everything was settled. It was almost gametime when he learned that his request for Kerr had been denied, apparently after pressure had been brought by Connie Smythe of the Maple Leafs, and that another man had been assigned to tend goal for the Hawks that night—a member of the minor-league Pittsburgh Hornets, who had played higher-level hockey only as a substitute for the New York Americans. That man was "English Alfie" Moore. And Alfie, in town only to attend the game as a spectator, had spent most of the afternoon in a Toronto tavern! In his own words, he was in "no condition to play hockey" by the time he was notified of his unsolicited appointment.

About two hours before gametime, Moore was rushed from his bar stool to the stadium to dress and sober up. But he wasn't taken to the Hawks' dressing room. Instead he was led to a separate room, where trainers provided by the Leafs zealously gave him rubdowns and otherwise tried to restore his equilibrium, while Moore protested that he wouldn't play because it wasn't fair to the Black Hawks. Not unexpectedly, when Hawk Manager Stewart learned what was going on, he and Smythe began throwing punches—and only the intervention of players and the police prevented a possible double knockout.

"It's not fair to the Hawks," Moore kept mumbling as the teams warmed up. "They wanted Kerr. I was picked because I'm a bum."

As the game started, it appeared that Moore's self-appraisal might be all too correct. Before two minutes had elapsed, Toronto's Syl Apps, Bob Davidson, and Gordon Drillon descended on him with the puck. Apps loosed a shot. Moore was barely able to stretch and make a save. Before he could regain his position, Drillon took the rebound and fired the puck past Moore into the corner of the net.

With that beginning, Toronto well might have gone on to stage a rout. But this was the spirited Black Hawk team of Doc Romnes, Johnny Gottselig, Mush March, Art Wiebe, Alex Levinsky, Jack Shill, and other rugged stars. They refused to be routed. By now they were exploding with anger. And, by now English Alfie Moore was beginning to pull himself together. Considering the circumstances, you almost would have had to see it to believe it (I saw it, and it's still incredible), but from then on the tide shifted. Gottselig scored a goal for the Hawks. Paul Thompson clicked with another. Then Gottselig swooped back with a third. English Alfie, meanwhile, performed like an all-star. Toronto couldn't get the puck past him again that night. The Hawks won, 3 to 1, and English Alfie was carried from the rink on their shoulders, a hero.

The next night, when the rookie substitute arrived from Wichita, the Hawks wanted to use Moore as their goalie again. "Nothing doing," said the Maple Leafs. "Moore is ineligible." So it was that young Paul Goodman, who never had seen a major-league hockey game and hadn't practiced for three weeks, tended goal for the Hawks. They lost, 5 to 1.

But the saga of English Alfie Moore was not quite ended. When the Hawks returned to Chicago for the third game of the series, English Alfie traveled with them, as the guest of the team. Chicago gave the team a hero's welcome, and excited fans packed the Stadium on the night of the game. By that time, regular goalie Mike Karakas, his toe splinted and guarded by a special shoe, was back in the nets. But the biggest ovation of the evening was not for him, or for any other member of the team. It was for English Alfie Moore. When he was introduced to the crowd and presented with a watch, the walls of the Chicago Stadium shook with applause. When the demonstration was finally stilled, the Hawks swarmed out to win the game, 2 to 1. From there, they went on to win the final series and become the professional hockey champions of the world—thanks to a substitute goalie they didn't want and one who didn't believe he should play for them in the first place. And that was the last I ever heard of English Alfie Moore.

To all these regular sports attractions, add such major special events as the 1960 Pan-American Games, and you will have a list of activities that would do any city proud. And I have not even started to talk about football. As I've already confessed, to me all else pales beside the excitement of a football game—which is another reason why I'm a confirmed, contented, card-carrying Chicagoan. There is no livelier football town anywhere.

Metropolitan Chicago high schools, which have produced Otto Graham, Terry Brennan, Buddy Young, Leo Nomellini, and Red Grange, play America's toughest schoolboy football. Chicago's public and Catholic high schools, whose league champions play each fall for the city title in 100,000-seat Soldier Field, have produced more All-American and professional stars than the secondary schools of any other city. My former Harrison High coach, Bob Daugherty, in a career stretching over thirty-eight years, himself produced enough greats of the gridiron to give any major team a long afternoon—including Andy Puplis, Hank Pojman, Andy Pilney, Dr. Wally Phillips, Frank Leonetti, Al Brosky, Frank Kopczak, Nap Hearn, and Walt Kudzik.

For Chicago fans of big-time college football, there is Northwestern, of the Big Ten, and—in the extreme environs of our metropolitan area—Notre Dame. For a more intimate game, there is the ring of suburban colleges that includes Wheaton and Lake Forest. And, of course, for pro football fans we have the Bears. (To complete the record, add two names of fond memory: the Chicago Cardinals, now in St. Louis, and the University of Chicago Maroons, now in class.) The football fan in Chicago doesn't need that hip flask to get his kicks on a crisp autumn afternoon.

To me the biggest kick comes from the fast, wide-open pro football played today. And as most fans realize, much credit for the development of the modern professional game rightfully belongs to George S. Halas, the Papa Bear.

One of Chicago's most colorful personalities, George was in on the pro game from the start—but literally by accident. As one of the University of Illinois' outstanding athletes of the World War I era, he not only was a star end on a great eleven, but a superlative baseball outfielder as well. After the war, when the New York Yankees signed him to play right field, he appeared destined for a career in baseball. But a hip injury soon slowed him down so much that he returned to football.

"I felt so sorry for the Yankees," says George. "They had to replace me with a reconditioned pitcher from Boston named Babe Ruth."

A statement of the late Illinois coach, Bob Zuppke, kept echoing in George's mind: "It's a pity that just when my players get to know something about football, I lose 'em."

George turned the coach's statement around to read from the player's point of view, and an idea blossomed. He got in touch with a number of recent college stars who regretted having been forced to quit the game at the peak of their powers, and in 1920 George sold officials of the Staley Starch Works, in Decatur, Illinois, on the idea of sponsoring a team, with himself as player-coach. The next year, when he moved to Wrigley Field in Chicago and adopted the name "Bears" to indicate these were the Cubs' big brothers, the team with the proudest tradition in the game was launched.

Since then, Halas' contributions to pro football have far outnumbered those of any other man. It was he who, in 1920, suggested forming a league—and proposed, furthermore, that it be called the National Professional Football League. And when he signed Red Grange and barnstormed the Bears across the country with the Wheaton Iceman, George lifted the postgraduate sport from sandlot status to front-page respectability. Today, George is the only coach from that period who is still active in the game.

He can remember a time when fans in Rock Island, Illinois, chased center George Trafton and other early Bears off the gridiron and out of town for roughing one of their players. It wasn't only Trafton's neck that was at stake. The team's share of the gate receipts were also threatened. In those days, you took it with you or it didn't go. To the astonishment of many, George tossed the heavy moneybag to Trafton as the center raced toward the exit with the ugly mob at his heels.

Explained Halas later: "I would have been running only to save seven thousand dollars—but Trafton was running for his life."

Halas had an even narrower squeak at Comiskey Park during a Bear-Cardinal game in 1923—or at least to hear him tell it he did. (The only detail I care to vouch for is the fierce partisanship of the fans. No other city supported two National Football League teams for so many years as Chicago, and no intra-city rivalry was ever more bitter.) According to George, this game was unusually hard fought and the fans were even more rambunctious than usual. On one play, when Halas, playing end, was tackled hard and high, he dragged his tackler down with him and locked the man in a wrestling hold. A near riot ensued. Players from both benches rushed onto the field, but before they could reach the scene of the fight, a policeman—a Cardinal partisan—raced over to the embattled Halas and placed a gun squarely against his head. "Let go of that Cardinal!" he shouted. (At least, that is what

Halas told me he shouted. I have not been able to get the policeman's version.)

Now, in those days, as in these days, George asked for no quarter, and gave none. I thought of that as I asked him what he did next.

"Discretion is the better part of valor," he said. "Especially when you have no choice. I released my grip on the player. Both he and the cop walked away. Fortunately, nobody has put a gun to my head since—though I'm sure a few would have liked to."

As former chairman of the NFL Rules Committee, Halas was also largely responsible for three key changes which have done much to make the professional game the exciting, unpredictable spectator sport it is today. He advocated cutting down the range for field goals by moving the goal posts from back of the end zones to the goal lines; streamlining the ball to make it easier to pass; and permitting a forward pass from any point behind the line of scrimmage instead of from five yards back. Because of these innovations, there is little chance for a dull moment in the game today.

As a coach, George also has pioneered changes in game technique. It was the Bears who were first to hold daily practice sessions, first to use movies in scouting, first to exploit the potential of the T formation, and first to station an assistant coach in the upper deck with a telephone line to the bench. The telephone, however, was an afterthought. At first, George merely posted Assistant Coach Luke Johnsos up there with a pad of paper. When Luke saw something from his aerie that he thought might not be visible from the field, he would jot notes and float them down. But partisan out-of-town fans quickly put a stop to that: They began intercepting this air mail and tipping the contents to Bear opponents.

George's tirades from the side lines are deservedly notorious. (I have been on the receiving end of several of his tongue-lashings myself, in my NFL officiating days.) But it is all due to momentary emotion and after the game, he is friendly and calm as if nothing had happened. He is one of the most considerate men I know in dealing with players. No Bear ever is dismissed until George has discussed his situation with him, tried to effect a trade, or helped him into a job outside football. And each year, he foots the bills for a huge reunion of former players. These proceedings carry the formidable title of "Annual Meeting of the Bears Alumni Association," although traditionally the alumni accomplish nothing more momentous than to have themselves a ball and re-elect Red Grange president.

For his loyalty to friends and associates, George has few equals. In at least one instance, this loyalty has transcended even his devotion to the Bears as a team: For several years, offensive coach Luke Johnsos and Clark Shaughnessy of the defense have spoken to one another only when necessary. This situation, according to the critics, can have nothing but an adverse effect on the spirit of the team. Yet out of personal regard for the two men, and respect for their individual coaching skills, George has refused to dismiss either of them.

Should everything else about the Bears be forgotten, however, one event will always stand out—their 73-0 victory over the Washington Redskins in the 1940 NFL championship game. (A game, incidentally, at which I had the privilege of officiating.) It is true that the Bears had outstanding personnel in Sid Luckman, George McAfee, Scooter McLean, Bill Osmanski, Bulldog Turner, Ken Kavanaugh, Joe Stydahar, Danny Fortmann, and the rest. Yet the Redskins, led by Sammy Baugh, were the NFL offensive leaders who only two weeks previously had defeated the Bears, 7-3. In practice, Halas, a master psychologist, played on this fact and also on the much-resented accusation that his players were "quitters" and "crybabies," as George Preston Marshall, owner of the Redskins, had called them in the press.

On the train heading East, the Bears did not relax as teams on the road generally do. Instead of playing cards and swapping lies, they silently pored intently over notebooks. The results were fantastic. On the third play of the game Bill Osmanski burst through the line for a 68-yard touchdown run. This was followed by ten other Bear touchdowns, scored by nine other players. By the fourth period, when the Bears were leading 67-0, we officials finally had to ask them to consider passing instead of kicking for any future conversions. We were running out of footballs!

Halas' comment after the game was typical:

"I guess my team deserved to win today!"

I could fill volumes with stories of the famous players of the Chicago area, but I have space here to mention only a few of the greatest, headed by the most spectacular football player of all time, the Galloping Ghost of Illinois, Red Grange.

In 1925, when Red turned pro, a crowd of thirty-six thousand fans (an unprecedented gate for professional football then) came to witness his debut against the Cardinals at Wrigley Field. And the SRO signs were left out for most of the ten exhibitions that he and the Bears played in the next seventeen days.

So talented was Red that, in later years, when Jack Manders, Beattie Feathers, Bronko Nagurski, and other stars were in their offensive prime, Red moved onto the defense squad and played championship ball there as well. In 1934, he finally hung up his cleats for good, and went into insurance, public relations, and broadcasting work. Once something of a man-about-town, he has been quiet and subdued since a heart attack of several years ago. Though he lives in Florida now, he is still active in football as a telecaster.

Bronko Nagurski, one of the few who rank alongside Grange in the Bears' Hall of Fame, is another who has made a lasting impression on me. As a matter of fact, in my playing days with the College All-Stars and the Philadelphia Eagles, he left several impressions on me. The 230-pound Bronk, the strongest, hardest-hitting runner in the game, could rumble downfield so fast and so low that no one he hit is ever likely to forget it. As nobody since, Bronko mastered the trick of getting a shoulder underneath part of a tackler's body, and then upending him with one enormous shrug. And he was as formidable on the defense as the offense. One of the marks of Nagurski's greatness was that he played both ways with equal aplomb.

"There is only one possible defense against him," Steve Owen of the Giants used to say. "Shoot him before he leaves the dressing room!"

But in this game of constant surprises, there are times when all the strength and skill in the world are helpless against the whimsical workings of pure, blind luck. I still remember one game I covered at Wrigley Field when Nagurski faced his number one rival, fullback Clark Hinkle of the Green Bay Packers. Hinkle was almost Bronko's size, and he had more speed. When those two giants came together, it sounded like two trucks colliding.

It was a tight game, and Green Bay was marching. When they reached the Bears' 30-yard line, the Packers sent Hinkle into the melee. He found an opening, buttonholed through it, and was just getting under way when Nagurski, who was backing up the Bears' line, saw him coming. It wasn't Bronko's custom to tackle ball carriers: he just charged into them like a tank, and his block put them down. In this instance, he threw about the hardest block I have seen. I'll swear the press box shook. Hinkle, who had been driving forward at full speed, was suddenly flying through the air in the direction of his own goal line. He was knocked at least five yards backward across the line of scrimmage.

At the sight of this, the Bears relaxed, as they knew they could whenever Nagurski hit someone. But to everyone's astonishment, including his own, Hinkle managed to land on his feet with the ball still in his possession. The Bears were too amazed to react. Hinkle just went through the line—for the second time on one play—and rambled thirty yards for a touchdown.

Legend has it that there is still a crack in the Wrigley Field wall where Bronk smashed into it a quarter of a century ago. Yet in spite of the fear he instilled in opponents—and Bronk was a tremendous psychological weapon—he remains a soft-voiced, mild-mannered man who blushes today when his feats are recalled. After retiring from football, he was a pro wrestler for a while. He now operates a service station in his home town of International Falls, Minnesota.

And how many former athletes have made new reputations in Chicago business and professional life? The sketchiest list will have to include ex-tackle Fred ("Duke") Slater, of Iowa, now a Chicago judge; track immortal Jesse Owens, now a youth board official; former Black Hawk defenseman Thomas Coulter, chief of the Chicago Association of Commerce & Industry; ex-Michigan player and coach Harry Kipke, president of the Coca-Cola Bottling Company of Chicago; ex-Notre Dame coach Terry Brennan, a

steel executive; and former Bear Hugh Gallerneau, a Hart Schaffner & Marx executive. But none has enjoyed a more meteoric
business success than football's "Mr. Quarterback," Sid Luckman,
who is now a cellophane products magnate with an income of six
figures a year.

I first met the brilliant Luckman when Halas asked me to take
him under my wing in my sportswriting days. Sid was then a
young All-American fresh out of Columbia University, who had
never been west of the Hudson River and contended that he never
wanted to. Today, the former pride of Brooklyn is one of Chicago's foremost citizens. Like many another footballer, he chose
to make his home in the city where he gained professional stardom. And he has more than duplicated his gridiron success in the
business world. Sid is one of Chicago's nicest millionaires, thanks
to his adroit management of his cellophane packaging firm.

Calling Luckman "nice" is not loose use of the adjective. His
efforts to please everybody led him into this trap, involving the
football used in the game in which the Bears defeated the New
York Giants, 24–14, for the National Football League championship.

A few days after the game, in which Luckman had performed
brilliantly, he presented a football to Charlie Baron, with this
inscription: "To the dearest friend I have in the world—this is
the ball used by the Bears in winning the 1946 championship."
For weeks Baron displayed this trophy on the mantel of his Lake
Shore Drive Hotel apartment. No visitor could depart without
first paying homage to the Luckman football and its endearing
inscription.

Then, by chance, Baron visited the home of another Luckman
friend, John McGuire. There, on the mantel, Baron saw another
football presented by Sid—with the same affectionate inscription,
word for word! And slowly it developed that Luckman had presented "the championship football" to no fewer than a dozen of
his dearest friends, including Joe DiMaggio, Lou and Cecil Wolf-
son, Leonard Schaller, and Lou Zahn.

7. Night Life, Anyone?

Nightfall in some cities means it's time to roll up the sidewalks. Not in Chicago. It is rather the signal to the Prairie Giant that it is time to turn off his blowtorch and get ready to play. And when he does, as in everything else, he insists on two things: quality and variety. There is plenty of both to be found in the night life of Chicago, which has long held the reputation of being one of the liveliest after-dark towns in the nation.

There is the Near North Side night-club district, second only in size to that of Las Vegas. As twilight descends, walk along Rush Street, the heart of the district. A carnival of light and color will come to life before your eyes.

Or take a late-evening stroll in the fluorescent daylight of the Loop theater district, "The Little White Way," centered about Randolph and State. Broadway after-theater crowds may be larger, but the enthusiasm and excitement of our theatergoers are just as intense.

Night life even has come to the Chicago suburbs. A new "strip," along Mannheim Road and adjacent to O'Hare International Airport, now houses the Sahara Inn, which has taken up the slack created by the demise of the Chez Paree. Here the biggest names on the cafe circuit appear—and, surprisingly enough, lure huge crowds. A few years ago, a big-name night club on the outskirts of the city would have been folly. Today, with expressways that merge urban with suburban, the distance is no drawback. Other cafes are springing up along the Mannheim strip and may indicate the trend of tomorrow.

Right here I'd like to correct a couple of widespread misconceptions among visitors regarding Chicago's reputation as a leading convention center in the nation. Contrary to popular belief, what makes Chicago a convention capital is not the availability of wine, women, and song. It is the city's central geographical location and its vast number of hotel facilities that are responsible for Chicago's popularity with conventioneers. And as for our reputation as a wide-open town, statistics of the Chicago Convention Bureau show that the number of conventions and visitors a city attracts is a direct measure of the actual efficiency of its police protection.

Where do you begin a night-life tour?

With entertainment, like everything else, it is each to his own taste and pocketbook. Nobody could pretend to formulate an all-purpose list. But based on more than a thousand and one nights on the beat, my list may well suggest a preliminary guide. Let me call your attention to some of my favorites.

For anyone who is passing through Chicago for the first time— or for the fifth or the one hundredth—one stop is mandatory: the famous Pump Room of the Ambassador East Hotel.

It is a matter of opinion, of course, but to me this is the most satisfying, the most exquisite room in Chicago, and one of the great rooms of the world. Its crystal chandeliers, deep-blue walls, table-top lights, and white leather booths provide a rich backdrop for the dinners served either spectacularly on a flaming sword or intimately from an individual serving cart by elegant waiters dressed in English Regency costumes. The constant stream of celebrities makes it the most exciting center of night life you will find anywhere.

The atmosphere and that indefinable flair which belongs to the Pump Room alone was nurtured and developed by its founder, the late Ernest Byfield. Ernie, co-owner of the Sherman and Ambassador Hotels with Frank Bering, was one of the most astute, inventive hotelmen who ever lived. Personable and witty, he was also one of the most popular.

As his many friends remember, Byfield had a prankish streak in his nature. He might send you a luncheon invitation by carrier pigeon. Once he staged a breakfast-in-bed party for a celebrity. Because of his wit, he was sought as a guest columnist by newspapermen in various cities. One time, when Robert Benchley and playwright S. N. Behrman were guests at one of his hotels, he not only refused to let them pay for their meals, he gave orders that no bill was to be presented when they checked out, and each received a prime beefsteak and a bottle of whisky as farewell presents.

"You don't suppose that cheap sonuvabitch will forget to pay our cab fare to the station, do you?" asked Benchley with a wink as they left.

Byfield didn't forget. Nor did he let them depart by taxi. He sent them off in style—in the Ambassador East station wagon. He was that type of meticulous, convivial host.

And he was well aware of the drawing power of his celebrity diners, as well as the showmanship of serving his exotic cuisine on flaming swords.

"The customers love it," he would say. "And it doesn't hurt the food much!"

Nothing in the Pump Room is left to chance, down to such points as conversation-amplifying acoustics, which my wife, Essee, and others say makes every night seem like New Year's Eve. The grin of orchestra leader David LeWinter, who is kind enough to send over a cigar on a tray every time I visit, and the warm welcome invariably extended by Wally Babych, successor to long-time manager Phil Boddy, add to the atmosphere of cordiality. LeWinter, incidentally, originally was hired for six months. He is now in his sixteenth year as the Pump Room maestro.

All this made the Pump Room a Chicago institution during the Byfield-Bering reign, which was followed with continued success by Pat Hoy, a protégé of Byfield's, and James A. ("Jimmy") Hart, one of the nation's best-known hotelmen. But with the death of Hart and departure of Hoy, the once-elegant Ambassadors went into a decline. The new ownership was so confused that the quip around town was, "Who owns the hotels today?" Lack of authority stemming from absentee ownership took its toll, as did a policy of cutting expenses and personnel to the bone, hardly the way to operate a luxurious hostelry.

The present owner of the Ambassadors, Louis H. Silver, currently is in the process of restoring the previous stature. He is a connoisseur of quality and a veteran hotelman. Silver is an outstanding rare-book collector and has one of the five finest private book collections in the world in the fireproof, burglarproof air-conditioned library of his Wilmette home. One of his first moves as owner was to inaugurate a multimillion-dollar renovation and expansion program.

No sampling of night life would be complete without a visit to a Rush Street night club. One of the most popular is Mister Kelly's.

This Chicago showcase for comedians Mort Sahl, Shelley Berman, Bob Newhart, Shecky Greene, and other leading entertainers, is nearing its tenth anniversary as a small but outstanding center of good food, good music, and good entertainment. Owners George and Oscar Marienthal, the city's (and probably the nation's) foremost team of café operators, also own three other places: the London House, famous for its fine steaks and jazz; the Happy Medium, an upstairs-downstairs theater night club; and the Brief Encounter, a daytime coffee shop.

Then there is Al Segal's Living Room (which was formerly The Tradewinds); Easy Street, a "hole-in-the-wall" club in an alley, presided over by the jovial "mayor" of Rush Street, Johnny Jonassen; The Gate of Horn, a leading folk-music cabaret; Bourbon Street, featuring Dixieland music by such groups as Bob Scobey's band; and two places which feature the Twist—the Scene and Rumpus Room—where the customers, flinging themselves in wild abandon, provide a floor show that few professional entertainers can match.

There is also The French Village, a picturesque complex of clubs in Tooker Alley just off Rush, complete with iron grillwork and other French touches. The Village includes Le Bistro, which features an intimate combo, Basin Street, where the music is jazz, and Kismet, which offers Egyptian belly-dancers in an *Arabian Nights* setting. On South Michigan Avenue ("Boul Mich") there is The Blue Angel, which was first to introduce calypso to this country.

No recitation of Chicago night life would be complete without special mention of the Club Alabam, on Rush Street near Chicago Avenue. This is the nation's oldest night club continuously operated under one management. Owner Gene Harris recently observed his thirty-sixth year of doing business at the same stand. The Club Alabam hasn't changed in decor in all those thirty-six years. And Harris deadpans that his floor shows are the "world's worst." There is a reason behind his derogation.

"We always have catered to a fun-loving group," he says. "In the early days, it was millionaires who wanted to get out "on the town." The millionaires are gone today, but we still have many of our old-time customers. And they like to get rowdy, sing out loud, walk across the stage during the floor show, and call out to one another. You can't do that with high-priced talent. Some of them won't even let you serve during a performance. So our policy is to hire the kind of entertainers who don't mind these little interferences. And what kind of acts permit this? That's why I say, and say it proudly, we have the world's worst floor show. My customers come first, the entertainers second."

The Club Alabam floor shows aren't that bad, of course. But the customer and his shenanigans do come first with Gene Harris and woe to any performer who insists on "quiet" while working.

Something old and something new help make the Alabam one of Chicago's more popular joints. The "old" is a private upstairs room that seldom closes. Here the most prominent persons in town "relax" in comfort and privacy. The "new" is an upgrading of the food, supervised by *maître d'* Art Carter. The Alabam's floor show may be the "world's worst," but its food ranks with the finest.

Along with at least one Rush Street club you will also want to visit a cabaret featuring the improvisational satire for which Chicago has become famous. Best known is The Second City, located in a renovated building on North Wells near Lincoln Park. New revues are introduced here several times a year, and it was one of these, *From the Second City*, that moved on to New York and, after a brief run on Broadway, settled in an off-Broadway house for a longer period.

Equally successful has been the Marienthal brothers' Happy Medium on Rush. Its first revue, *Medium Rare*, played 101 weeks, thus beating the previous Chicago record of 100 weeks set by *Good Night Ladies*.

The Chez Paree, victim of a high-priced talent squeeze, is no more. But you will find many acts which formerly played there at the Palmer House, the Drake, and other leading hotels.

At the Empire Room of the Palmer House, former Chez favorites Carol Channing, Joey Bishop, Buddy Hackett, Sophie Tucker, and Joe E. Lewis now appear. This room has had a long tradition of fine entertainment, thanks to Hilton Hotels' talent-booker Merriel Abbott, the Chicagoan who first introduced Hildegarde, Liberace, Veloz and Yolanda, Dorothy Shay, and others.

The Camellia House at the Drake, formerly associated almost exclusively with chanteuses, has broadened its booking policy to bring regular appearances by such comedians as Henny Youngman, George Jessel, and Myron Cohen. Here, too, there is excellent food, dance music provided by Jimmy Blade's orchestra, and a sumptuous atmosphere enhanced by the continental manner of manager Frank Amstadt.

There is an air of almost regal dignity in the Sheraton-Blackstone's Café Bonaparte, another favorite society and celebrity room. The Boulevard Room of the Conrad Hilton features a glittering ice revue. There is also the exotic Polynesian Village of the Edgewater Beach and the Pompeian Room of the Pick-Congress—in fact, the variety of hotel attractions is almost endless.

Jazz?

Since Chicago is the city where jazz came of age, there is a special thrill in a visit to one of our jazz clubs. Jazz Ltd., is a thriving Near North Side mecca operated by the husband-wife team of Bill and Ruth Reinhardt. Any of at least a dozen others also present authentic jazz, including the Marienthal brothers' London House on Wacker; Bronzeville's Sutherland Lounge and the Roberts' Show Club; and The Red Arrow in suburban Stickney, where the highly respected Franz Jackson is chief resident practitioner of *Le Jazz Hot*.

Something off-beat?

Try the Near North Side's Gitano's if you like Spanish flamenco rhythms, or catch the Greek-Oriental show at the Athens. For Hungarian, the Budapest. If you're in a sophisticated beatnik mood, make an after-show visit to one of the Near North Side espresso houses—the Café Bellini or the Fickle Pickle.

Favorites of the conventioneers are the strip-tease clubs. You'll find them on North Clark, in suburban Cicero, and in Calumet City (in subdued form following a federally inspired housecleaning). Now, mostly syndicate-controlled, they are mere shadows of their former selves, with watered drinks and less than interesting entertainment.

Burton Browne's original Gaslight Club and Hugh Hefner's Playboy Club, a four-floor extravaganza with a different act on each floor, also draw heavily. But, unfortunately for nonmembers, as with other key clubs, you're up a tree if you lack a key.

There is no need to feel rejected, however. As I hope is apparent by now, key or no key there is ample after-dark activity in Chicago for everyone. Just pick your spot and hail a cab. Your own Thousand and One Nights—Chicago style—will have begun.

8. Where Do We Eat?

It is roughly twenty-five thousand miles around the world—unless you go through Los Angeles, where a wrong turn on the freeways can double the mileage. To enjoy almost any nation's culinary arts, however, you needn't travel all that distance. Just come to Chicago. Among our hundreds of restaurants you can sample the cuisine, color, customs, and culture of every corner of the globe.

Here, the many first-rate establishments can satisfy the palates of even the most demanding gourmets.

Start with the Pump Room of the Ambassador East Hotel, where the flaming entrees are as memorable as the sumptuous atmosphere. The much-traveled John Cameron Swayze aptly says of the Pump Room, "It isn't a place—it's an experience."

The same might be said of other dining rooms in the Ambassador hotels, including the elegant Buttery and Beau Nash rooms in the Ambassador West. It was also Ernest Byfield who created the College Inn Porterhouse, recently renamed The Fountain Room, and The Well of the Sea, its sister room specializing in seafood, both to be found in the Sherman House. Succulent dishes served with stylized pageantry are the keynotes in all of these dining places.

Then there is Fritzel's, a Loop restaurant with an attraction for celebrities exceeded only by the Pump Room. Owned by Joe Jacobson, who was the late Mike Fritzel's partner in operating the Chez Paree for eighteen years, it has a variety of superb dishes, plus excellent service. Jacobson's professionalism and ability to operate on a small profit margin have made it possible for him to offer one of the outstanding bargains among quality American restaurants. Complete luncheons, excluding drinks, cost only two dollars.

This and its central location make Fritzel's the Midwest equivalent of New York's Toots Shor's. At midday it is the main congregating point for journalists, sports figures, radio-TV stars, judges, and other public officials. I'm usually there, too, interviewing the owner, if nobody else.

On the Near North Side, there are a number of restaurants offering fine food, elegance of service, and pleasing decor. Six in particular are my favorites.

Three are in the Drake Hotel: the Camellia House, decorated by the famous Dorothy Draper, is also a leading night spot; the Cape Cod Room, possibly Chicago's leading seafood restaurant; and the International Room, which is restricted to Club International Members only.

Nearby on East Walton Place there is the Imperial House, one of the most exquisite continental restaurants in this hemisphere, presided over by the ebullient world traveler Max Guggiari.

Among smaller establishments in this class, I never tire of The Red Carpet, where both French and Caribbean dishes are the specialties, and Maison Lafite, whose roast duckling cooked the French way is the best I've ever tasted.

For superb food in surroundings almost as lavish as these, there is a long list of outstanding establishments.

Phil Wrigley has had established in the building which bears his name a first-class dining room. He also ordered that the prices be kept moderate and the martinis potent, which make both its bar and dining room a magnet for Chicago and New York advertising men. Phil himself, incidentally, is one of the restaurant's best customers. You can often find him dining with friends at a large round table just inside the lobby entrance.

Other prominent restaurants associated with Chicago landmarks include the President's Walk in McCormick Place, beside the immense convention hall with its incomparable view of the lake shore; the Oval Room of Executive House; the French Room of the new Hartford Insurance Building; and the Water Tower Inn, which offers a view of the old Water Tower and a photo gallery of famous former and present-day Chicagoans.

Due to changes in transportation and marketing patterns, Chicago's stockyards have declined in recent years. But their pens still cover a greater total area than those of any other city and Our Town remains one of the chief beefsteak bastions of the world. Anyone who appreciates good steak will want to dine at one of our restaurants famous for this specialty.

Al Farber's Steak House in the Loop and the Belden Stratford Hotel are two of my favorites. Along with excellent steak, the London House offers excellent jazz. Don Roth's Blackhawk Restaurant, another first-rate steak and chop house, retains the aura of once having been one of the city's most prominent night clubs. The Sirloin Room of the Stock Yard Inn attracts diners to the fascinating neighborhood where the leading cattle marketers of America gather. Here you are invited to select your own cut and initial it with a branding iron.

For barbecued spareribs, few restaurants anywhere enjoy the popularity of The Singapore on Rush Street, established by a little Irishman, Tommy McDonnell, who blew a bosun's pipe whenever a celebrity approached, and Frank Howard, a veteran café owner. Tommy's base is now the Stardust Hotel in Las Vegas, and his half-ownership now belongs to Tom Downes, a former police officer. But the restaurant still uses the slogan he originated: "From a rib to a national institution." The stream of distinguished diners includes many who purchase ribs to take along on trains or planes—testimony to the success of McDonnell's slogan.

Befitting Chicago's role as a Great Lakes and St. Lawrence Seaway port, there are plenty of restaurants where you can enjoy fine fish and seafood. Besides the Cape Cod Room, among those for which I have a special liking are the Marine Room of the

Edgewater Beach Hotel and Ireland's Oyster House on North Clark Street.

If you are feeling adventurous, try Barney's Market Club at Randolph and Halsted. On the edge of a dilapidated neighborhood, it is noisy, informal, and justly proud of its live Maine lobsters.

For off-beat fare, there is the wild-game center of Chicago, the Café Bohemia across from Union Station. Ever tried a buffaloburger? The Bohemia has them—and dozens of equally intriguing menu surprises.

Gastronomic adventures await those who will sample the international flavor of Chicago cuisine.

For Italian food, try Armando's, Adolph's, Mike Fish's, Club El Bianco, the Italian Village, or Riccardo's on Rush Street. Riccardo's, whose sidewalk café is one of the Near North Side's most popular summer gathering places, also qualifies as the most "arty" restaurant in town. Reflecting the taste of both its late founder Ric Riccardo, and his son Ric, Jr., the present owner, there is a row of striking murals behind its Palette Bar, executed by such illustrious artists as Ivan Albright and Aaron Bohrod. The main dining room is a gallery for the work of young Midwest artists.

For German cuisine, there is the noted Red Star Inn (one of the city's oldest), Allgauer's Old Heidelberg, Math Igler's, the Black Forest, the Swiss Chalet of the Bismarck Hotel, and Henrici's on Randolph.

It was a sad day when the lights went out at Henrici's, the Randolph Street landmark where nineteenth-century atmosphere predominated. After 93 years on the same site, Henrici's closed to make way for progress in the form of a mammoth Civic Center. The restaurant dated back to 1868, three years before the Chicago Fire, and was held in the same warm regard as the Morning Call in New Orleans or Durgin Park in Boston. Let's hope that Henrici's will rise again within the new Civic Center. Another popular noontime rendezvous room is the Walnut of the Bismarck Hotel, where many political figures and public servants congregate.

For French cooking, there are not only the three I mentioned earlier as my prime favorites, the Imperial House, The Red Carpet, and Maison Lafite, but also Jacques and Café de Paris. All are on the Near North Side.

For Far Eastern dishes, try the Shangri-La, Jimmy Wong's, Don the Beachcomber, Trader Vic's in the Palmer House, the Polynesian Village of the Edgewater Beach Hotel, or Chiam's in Chinatown or the Hung Fa Village in the Loop.

You will enjoy excellent Russian specialties at Sasha's, Greek ones at the Athens, Polish at Lenard's Little Poland, Romanian at Joe Stein's across from the Edgewater Beach Hotel, Japanese at the Naka No-Ya or Azuma House on the North Side, and Scandinavian at the Bit of Sweden or the Kungsholm.

Along with beautiful appointments and one of the Midwest's most elaborate smorgasbord buffets, the Kungsholm also continues to offer its unique miniature puppet operas. Staged in a two-hundred-seat replica of the Royal Opera House in Copenhagen, this fascinating little production plays to some one hundred thousand people a year. It is an after-lunch or dinner bonus that no diner should miss.

Keep in mind that many leading night spots offer excellent food as well as celebrity entertainers, including Mister Kelly's, the Empire Room of the Palmer House, and the Café Bonaparte of the Sheraton-Blackstone.

Fine eating places are not restricted to the heart of Chicago. You'll find many in the city's fringe and suburban areas. Fanny's, in Evanston, offers spaghetti and chicken; Mathon's, in Waukegan, has seafood. In nearby Skokie there is the Crabapple, in the Old Orchard Shopping Center. In addition to fine food Mangam's Château, in Lyons, offers fine entertainment, and suburban Evergreen Park has The Martinique, a fine restaurant operated in conjunction with its famous year-round theater, Drury Lane.

Lucius Beebe said it:

"When one considers the over-all opportunities Chicago offers a person in search of good food, it is obvious that a visitor who fails to find what he wants should have stayed at home."

Anyone who knows Chicago restaurants will second this. At least I will. Try us.

9. What's To See?

A city is like a Rorschach inkblot test: you see what you look for; you take out only what you put in. Chicago is no exception. To some it appears dirty, sprawling, muscle-bound, and crude. To others it is beautiful and well-planned, friendly and exciting.

So the "real Chicago" is an elusive term. It is what you yourself seek out and what conclusions you draw from your discoveries. Exploring Chicago can be a never-ending delight with its scenic, cultural, historical, and architectural treasures, and its recreational and commercial resources.

It's all there waiting for you.

There is, first of all, Scenic Chicago. Ours is a city which for beauty rivals San Francisco, New Orleans, and Washington, D. C. To savor this, begin with our incomparable front yard: The Outer Drive, and the parks and beaches of our Lake Michigan shore line.

Just as State Street is the point from which east-west street numbering is figured, Madison is the north-south dividing line. I suggest that you begin your tour on the closest lakefront feeder street to it—Monroe.

From Monroe, you can view the lake, the Chicago Yacht Club, and a portion of the city's enormous fleet of pleasure craft. Looking to the west and north, you can see a forest of concrete and

stone highlighted by the graceful spire of the Methodist Chicago
Temple, the dominolike mass of the Prudential Building, the
antiseptic white of the Wrigley Building (which really is two
buildings connected by a façade), the flag-topped peak of the
Tribune Tower, and the Palmolive Building, at the head of Michigan Avenue. From its summit the Lindbergh Beacon sends out
a piercing beam at night.

Driving north you pass the Chicago River, "the river that flows
backward." Years ago, engineers reversed its course in order to
provide lake water for the city's sanitary drainage. Beyond the
busy port buildings of Navy Pier open the Gold Coast and
Northwestern University's downtown Chicago campus, then Lincoln Park, Belmont Harbor, and mile after mile of luxury apartments and spacious parkland.

Driving south, against a backdrop of buildings dominated by
the world's largest hotel, the Conrad Hilton, you will find yourself in the most attractive, best-planned park and museum center
west of Washington. Located here are The Art Institute of
Chicago, the Buckingham Fountain (the largest in the world),
the Chicago Natural History Museum, Shedd Aquarium, and
Soldier Field (capacity, 100,000 seats). The depressed roadbed of
the Illinois Central Railroad keeps the skyline intact as you con-
tine southward past the Meigs Field airport and McCormick
Place convention hall. Then, along a scenic, winding roadway
you will pass more luxury apartments and hotels, and the Museum
of Science and Industry.

But an automobile drive cannot do justice to our lakefront.
Plan to make several stops, including one on the man-made
finger of land on which the Adler Planetarium is located, a favored
place from which to photograph the shore and skyline. You will
also enjoy a walk along any of our fifteen major public beaches,
especially those at Oak Street or North Avenue on the Near
North Side.

Scenic Chicago doesn't end with the lake shore, however. You
will want to visit other portions of our municipal park system, in
which we take great pride.

The Lincoln Park Zoo has become familiar to millions of TV

viewers through Marlin Perkins' program *Zoo Parade*. Also in Lincoln Park is one of the city's chief cultural centers, the Chicago Historical Society. For recreation, the park has two Lake Michigan beaches, three yacht harbors, and baseball and softball diamonds. There are also facilities for horseback riding, rowboating, and golf.

In Garfield Park, plan to see the world's largest conservatory under one roof, where as many as fifty thousand persons a day have viewed the spectacular floral displays. Notable for its gently rolling prairie terrain is Columbus Park, planned by the famed Chicago landscape architect Jens Jensen. An authentic Indian Council Ring is just one of the unusual sights to be found here.

Ringing the city is a unique, fifty-thousand-acre, wooded green belt: the Cook County Forest Preserves. Beyond this, in suburban Wilmette, be sure to visit the "Taj Mahal of the Western Hemisphere," the delicately beautiful Baha'i Temple situated near the lake.

Take a stroll along some of our fine streets of apartment houses —Goethe, North Astor, or North State Street, tree-lined from Dearborn to Lincoln Park.

For an aerial view of the city by day go to the observation floor of the Board of Trade; or see an exciting panorama at night from atop the Prudential Building.

Since the past helps explain the present, before exploring very far, you will also want to become familiar with another significant facet of the city, Historical Chicago.

What could be a better place to begin than the Chicago Historical Society? Its multimillion-dollar archives and exhibits include not only such Chicagoana as old-time handbills and posters, and relics of the Great Fire of 1871, but also material of much broader historical interest.

Among the treasures on view are the anchor of Christopher Columbus' ship, the *Santa Maria*, the weapons used by John Brown in his raid at Harpers Ferry in 1859, and a large collection of priceless Lincolniana. The Society has the table on which Lincoln drafted the Emancipation Proclamation and such important historical items as his personal carriage and the bed on which he died. Twenty stunning dioramas depict various stages of his life. There is also a directory to guide you to other points of interest in Chicago with strong Lincoln associations. One of these is the site of the old Wigwam at Lake Street and Wacker, where he won the 1860 Republican Presidential nomination.

At Michigan and Wacker a plaque and metal strips in the sidewalk mark the former location of Fort Dearborn, around which the city's earliest Chicagoans settled. Elsewhere, plaques call attention to such sites as Haymarket Square at Desplaines Street near Randolph, where the famous anarchist riot of 1886 occurred; Mrs. O'Leary's Barn at 558 West De Koven, where the Great Fire originated under circumstances still disputed (appropriately, today, the property is the location for a two-million-dollar Fire Department Training Academy); and the West Stands (now razed) of the University of Chicago's Stagg Field, where Enrico Fermi's scientific team achieved the first controlled nuclear reaction in history.

Some of our historic structures have been preserved: the venerable brownstone Water Tower, our most cherished surviving landmark of the Great Fire, at Chicago Avenue and Michigan; Hull House, the "cathedral of compassion" founded by Jane Addams at Halsted and Polk Streets, around which the new Chicago branch of the University of Illinois is being built; the old Cook County Court Building—now the Chicago Board of Health—at 54 West Hubbard, where Clarence Darrow masterfully defended Nathan Leopold and Richard Loeb in the celebrated "thrill-killing" trial; and the Sheraton-Blackstone Hotel, where the term "smoke-filled room" became standard political parlance after hours of maneuvering in suites 408 and 410 on behalf of 1920 Presidential nominee Warren G. Harding.

Dignified nineteenth-century town houses, conjuring a nostalgic aura of yesterday, are to be seen in the vicinity of the University of Chicago in Hyde Park, the South Side's intellectual center. Still other handsome town houses remain in the Old Town Triangle, bounded by Lincoln, North, and Ogden Avenues on the North Side.

Crilly Court and other picturesque streets in Old Town, and

the atmosphere of Bohemianism to be found in its coffeehouses, art fairs, and folk-song gatherings, compel many people to call it the Greenwich Village of the Midwest.

To appreciate the charm of Old Town, stroll in the vicinity of its social center, which is North Avenue and Wells Street. You will find poetry-reading and folk-singing at such colorful spots as Oxford's Dram Shop and Coffee House. Or you can look in on art classes at the Old Town Art Center. The Old Town Art Fair, held here each year, is one of the Midwest's leading outdoor art exhibits. More than forty thousand persons attend annually. At the same time various Old Town residents' homes and gardens are open to the public.

For a contrasting view of Chicago's past, seek out a few of the places associated with its earlier immaturity and shame: 2131-33 South Dearborn, for example, where the most sophisticated bordello in America, the Everleigh Club, once stood; the Biograph Theater on North Lincoln Avenue, under whose marquee notorious John Dillinger was fatally shot in an FBI trap in 1934; and North State Street at Superior, where the chipped stone in one wall of Holy Name Cathedral is a reminder of the Prohibition era gang war that broke out when florist-hoodlum Dion O'Banion was gunned down among the lilies in his North Side flower store.

O'Banion, as students of Chicago crime will remember, not only had a thriving floral shop, but also a lucrative North Side trade in homemade alcohol at five dollars a gallon. One day in 1924, as he was arranging bouquets and wreaths for the funeral of Mike Merle, deceased leader of the Sicilian Union, three men strolled into the shop. They greeted O'Banion as if he were an old friend. As O'Banion extended his hand, he was shot three times. His funeral, featuring a ten-thousand-dollar silver-trimmed coffin and flowers by the truckload, was probably the gaudiest in Chicago history. The procession to the cemetery, in which thousands took part, included several brass bands. It was the social event of the year.

But Scenic and Historical Chicago are far from being the city's only absorbing aspects. There is also a part of our civic personality which many outsiders do not realize exists, yet it reaches deep into the heart of the city—Cultural Chicago.

Of its many embodiments, the Art Institute is among the most famous. One of the great art institutions, it is noted for many priceless collections, especially its French, Spanish, early Dutch, and American paintings. Included are twenty-nine Monets, eight Gauguins, and one of the most celebrated single canvases in existence, El Greco's *The Assumption of the Virgin*. But the Institute is more than an outstanding repository for art treasures. It also houses two specialized libraries, the novel Thorne Miniature Rooms, the largest private professional art school in the nation—its enrollment is over 5,000—and a widely respected drama school whose Goodman Theater numbers among its alumni José Quintero, Geraldine Page, Karl Malden, and other well-known theatrical personalities.

Then there is the Chicago Natural History Museum, one of the four most prominent in its field, with its prehistoric dinosaurs, Races of Mankind display, a five-thousand-year-old chariot which is the oldest wheeled vehicle in existence, and other rare items depicting the story of civilization. The stuffed figure of Bushman, the Lincoln Park Zoo's famous gorilla, is also exhibited here.

There are the Shedd Aquarium, with ten thousand fish and reptile specimens; the Adler Planetarium, first of America's "Theaters of the Sky"; and the most entertaining of all American museums, the Museum of Science and Industry, founded by Julius Rosenwald. A full-scale, "working" Illinois coal mine, the captured Nazi submarine U-505, historic airplanes, a Santa Fe steam locomotive, the fabulous Colleen Moore dollhouse—these and hundreds of unique "do-it-yourself" exhibits attract 2,500,000 persons annually to this incomparable institution, making it one of the most popular museums in the world.

The Museum of Science and Industry, incidentally, almost occasioned a minor international crisis in 1955. The story is not generally known, but Major Lenox Lohr, the former NBC president who is chairman of the museum, has told it to friends. It seems that while V. M. Molotov, at that time Russian Foreign Minister to the United States, was on a brief stopover in Chicago en route to San Francisco for the tenth-anniversary observance of the founding of the United Nations, he and his party suddenly decided to inspect the submarine U-505, which is displayed behind the museum. They did not notify the museum in advance, nor did they visit the museum itself. They simply hired a limousine, drove out to the old Midway, and stood for quite a while around the submarine, talking excitedly in Russian. This puzzled Lohr, until he remembered that the Allies had agreed to divide the submarines surrendered to them at the *end* of World War II, and to destroy them all within two years. Molotov, apparently, was getting ready to point an accusing finger at the United States by saying, 'I saw with my own eyes the German submarine you were pledged to sink and did not—visible evidence that you do not keep your international agreements." Lohr, however, was aware that the submarine, which had been captured by a Navy task force under Admiral Dan Gallery in 1944, was not included in this agreement. He immediately alerted the State Department to be prepared for anything Molotov might say. But at San Francisco, Molotov decided to keep silent. On his return trip, he made a formal visit to the museum, but declined an invitation to tour the inside of the sub—and never mentioned that he already had seen it from the outside.

Less publicized, but equally noteworthy are the University of Chicago's Oriental Institute, whose collection of ancient Near Eastern art and artifacts includes a forty-ton Assyrian sculpture dating to the eighth century B.C., and the nearby George F. Harding Museum, with one of the most comprehensive collections of knights' armor outside of Europe.

An indication of Chicago's prominence in education is the fact that its institutions of higher learning also attract thousands of visitors a year. Of special interest are the University of Chicago, with its Rockefeller Memorial Chapel, the International House (center for eight hundred students from foreign countries), the Oriental Institute, and Argonne National Laboratory in suburban Lemont; and Northwestern University, which has lakefront campuses both in Chicago and suburban Evanston.

Three distinguished halls provide outstanding programs of

music and ballet: the new Arie Crown Theater in McCormick Place; Orchestra Hall, home of the nation's third oldest symphony, led by Fritz Reiner, and concert hall for touring recitalists; and the magnificent Civic Opera House (now the Kemper Insurance Building), tycoon Samuel Insull's gift to Chicago opera. Each season the Lyric Opera of Chicago performs here and in the few short years since its founding this American company has gained an enviable reputation. By many it is considered second only to the Metropolitan. It is with Lyric that tempestuous diva Maria Callas made her American professional debut—and, backstage, loosed one of her most publicized tantrums over the serving of a court summons.

General Manager Carol Fox, who in private life is the wife of Dr. C. Larkin Flanagan, started Lyric almost literally on a prayer in 1954. She and other young opera enthusiasts signed a cast of prominent singers for a single "Calling Card Performance." They then set up a desk in the Opera Building offices of the makers of Dr. West's toothbrushes, so that they could use the building's address. From that modest beginning grew the company which is a favorite with Renata Tebaldi, Joan Sutherland, Boris Christoff, Tito Gobbi, and other reigning opera stars. It presented Joan Sutherland in *Lucia di Lammermoor* before she sang the role at New York's Metropolitan Opera. It also is the only American opera company to have received a subsidy from the Italian government in recognition of its achievements. In 1960 it set what must be a west-of-New York record by playing to 96.3 per cent of capacity (3,600) of the huge Civic Opera House for its entire seven-week season.

In summer, as elsewhere, concerts move outdoors. There is wooded Ravinia Park in suburban Highland Park, and the Grant Park Bandshell on the lakefront where free concerts are given, thanks to James Petrillo and the Chicago Musicians' Union.

A dozen major libraries also are part of Cultural Chicago, ranging from the huge Chicago Public Library, which circulates some twelve million volumes a year, to the John Crerar Library, a specialized institution devoted to technology and medicine.

Newberry Library, one of the world's outstanding rare-book

repositories, surpasses the Library of Congress and great European centers in some of its collections. Particularly noteworthy are its collections on the Renaissance, the French Revolution, the history of printing, the American Indian, and classical music. The library also has the complete works of Brahms, Beethoven, and Bach, and nearly two thousand incunabula, books printed before the year 1500.

(Incidentally, it is across Walton Street from the library, in Newberry Square, or as it is sometimes affectionately called, "Bughouse Square," that soap-box orators congregate almost nightly to argue their opinions with whoever will listen.)

The president of the Board of Trustees of the Newberry Library is Everett D. Graff, retired president of Joseph T. Ryerson, Inc., who owns what is probably the world's finest private collection of Western Americana.

And speaking of private collections, Chicago has long been a major capital in the fascinating world of bibliophilism. Many of our great collectors have died in the past few years, but many of the greatest are still among us.

Morton Bodfish, former president of the First Federal Savings & Loan Association of Chicago, has one of the finest collections of material relating to Benjamin Franklin, both books and manuscripts. Philip D. Sang, executive vice-president of Goldenrod Ice Cream Company, is one of the country's leading manuscript collectors—and maybe the greatest private collector of documentary material relating to American history: he was given an honorary degree by Rutgers recently in recognition of his collecting achievement. Fred C. Evers, a retired printing executive, owns what is probably the greatest private collection of material relating to Chicago and Illinois history. He also has fine collections of Sandburg, general Americana, and books about books. Louis H. Silver, president of the Gold Coast Hotels, is truly a giant among modern bibliophiles, as mentioned previously. His collection of English books, incunabula, Elizabethan material, and other treasures rivals the "greats" of past generations. David Borowitz has a magnificent collection of illustrated books. E. B. ("Pete") Long, chief of research for Bruce Catton's *Centennial History of the*

Civil War, has built up what some experts consider to be the great private working collection of material on the Civil War. Joseph L. Eisendrath, Jr., president of Banthrico, Inc. (which manufactures metal plaques, coin banks, etc.), owns one of the best collections of books, pamphlets, and manuscripts on the Lincoln period, and is himself one of the great authorities on the Official Records of the Civil War. And Ralph G. Newman, owner of the Abraham Lincoln Book Shop, has the greatest collection of Sandburgiana extant.

Since Chicago is where modern architecture took root, you will also want to visit several landmarks connected with this heritage.

Unfortunately, the first skyscraper and other classic buildings designed by Chicagoan Louis Sullivan, the "father of modern architecture," have been demolished. And his Auditorium Theater, owned by Roosevelt University, cannot be used until a fund drive for its restoration is completed. But the Sullivan-designed Carson Pirie Scott & Company store remains, and ornamental arches and columns from his recently razed Garrick Theater grace the front of the Second City-Playwrights Theater on North Wells.

For a sampling of the work of Sullivan's one-time Chicago student, Frank Lloyd Wright, visit the Robie House at 5132 South Woodlawn, and the Unitarian Universalist Church in Oak Park. Among the more recent works of Chicago architects, there are the Illinois Institute of Technology and the twin "Glass House" apartments on Lake Shore Drive which represent some of the finest work of Ludwig Mies van der Rohe. Alfred Shaw's work can be seen in the Merchandise Mart, the New Post Office, and McCormick Place. And the new Marina City, designed by trend-setting Bertrand Goldberg, has received world-wide attention. Its twin cylindrical towers are the world's tallest reinforced concrete structures. They not only house apartments for 2,500 persons, but also include a marina, a bowling alley with fifty-four lanes, a swimming pool, a health club and gymnasium, an ice-skating rink, and a 1,200-seat theater.

All along the Loop portion of the Chicago River, in fact, modern buildings and plazas are being erected. The Sun-Times

Daily News Building was among the earliest and most striking of these. Soon to be built along the river west of the Loop is a one-hundred-million-dollar Gateway Center. It will include an airlines terminal, a heliport, a new building over Union Station, and a plaza similar to that of Rockefeller Center. When completed it will give Chicago one of the most beautiful intra-city waterways in the world.

This is only part of a skyscraper building boom now going on in Chicago. A $76,000,000 Civic Center Building, which at 631 feet in height will be among the city's tallest, is being built east of the present City Hall-County Building. A thirty-story Federal Building is going up east of the Old Post Office-Federal Building. Developers John Mack and Raymond Sher (owners of the Sherman House) have announced plans for sixty-five-story and thirty-eight-story apartment buildings along Michigan Avenue between the Chicago River and Chicago Avenue. And a billion-dollar "city-within-a-city" is being built by three developers on air rights over railroad tracks east of the Prudential Building. As part of this Mayor Daley's City Planning Department has suggested a hundred-story skyscraper bordering Lake Michigan, a building which would be second in height only to New York's Empire State Building.

Sculpture depicting Abraham Lincoln is, of course, prevalent in Chicago. You will want to see Augustus Saint-Gaudens' *Standing Lincoln* near the Chicago Historical Society in Lincoln Park, his *Seated Lincoln* in Grant Park, and Charles Mulligan's *The Railsplitter* in Garfield Park. Chicagoan Lorado Taft is represented by the huge *Fountain of Time* on the University of Chicago Midway, *Spirit of the Great Lakes* in the south garden of the Art Institute, and *Idyll and Pastoral* outside the Garfield Park Observatory.

After leisurely contemplation of Cultural Chicago, next consider Commercial Chicago, which contains the sinews of the city. Commerce is one of Chicago's dominant reasons for being, and constitutes an attraction in itself.

Visitors to Chicago are understandably impressed by State Street, the most concentrated retail-shopping area in the nation.

Women in particular find it easy to spend a day in the Midwest's most renowned store, Marshall Field & Company. When they tire of shopping, there are fashion shows on view and five tea-room-restaurants within the store.

And even lacking the necessary bankroll, the fine shops of North Michigan Avenue, the "Fifth Avenue of Chicago," offer inviting opportunities for window-shopping. It is here that Bonwit Teller, Saks Fifth Avenue, and other prestige specialty firms are concentrated, amid the spaciousness and greenery of the "Magnificent Mile."

This section, where each year the Easter Parade is held in the vicinity of the Fourth Presbyterian Church, is a monument to still another Chicagoan of vision, realtor Arthur Rubloff. A former galley boy on a Great Lakes freighter, Rubloff unveiled plans for his "Magnificent Mile" at a luncheon for 250 businessmen in 1947. At that time he had in his hands contracts for thirty-five-million dollars' worth of buildings between the Chicago River and Oak Street. Other new structures, plus improvements such as trees along Michigan Boulevard, soon followed.

The financial district of LaSalle Street, the Wall Street of the Midwest, is another throbbing center of Commercial Chicago. A beehive of daytime activity it is practically a ghost street at night. There are many banks, brokerages, and stock and commodity exchanges between Monroe and Van Buren, but don't miss visiting the Midwest Stock Exchange or the Chicago Board of Trade.

At the Board, America's largest corn- and wheat-trading center, it is especially exciting to see the 9:30 A.M. opening. At 9:29 its hundreds of gray-jacketed "Pit Men" are quietly milling about. One minute later, at the sound of a gong, they are shouting and gesturing in frenzied activity, which may puzzle the spectators—but the "system" works.

Nearby, at 65 West Jackson, is the Union League Club where Chicago moguls have been hanging up their homburgs since the late nineteenth century. There, too, Queen Marie of Romania once caused a sensation by lighting a cigarette—the first woman guest to do so. And it was there that during the Depression a room was papered with a million dollars in stock and bond certificates. Known as the "Million-Dollar Room," it was later peeled clean, as owners realized their holdings were regaining value.

The two-block-long Merchandise Mart, a treasure house of exhibits by America's leading manufacturers of home equipment and furnishings, also is worth a tour. Owned by President Kennedy's father, Joseph P. Kennedy, it is the world's largest commercial building. If it had been built as a skyscraper it would be sixty-eight stories higher than the Empire State Building.

To further appreciate the scope of Chicago's commercial activities, you should include tours of Calumet Harbor on the Far South Side, where it is possible to get a close look at ocean-going freighters, the vast South Works of the United States Steel Corporation, on Eighty-ninth Street, and the Union Stock Yards.

The Stock Yards is also the site of the International Amphitheater, where one of many Chicago-nominated Presidents, Dwight D. Eisenhower, was selected. The International Livestock Exposition, the World Professional Wrestling Tournament, and other noted events are held here. Of all the events, however, it was a solo performance that caused one of the greatest uproars. When Elvis Presley made his first Chicago appearance in the Amphitheater, Manager Merton Thayer worked out a strategic plan involving two hundred policemen, three hundred firemen, six ambulances, and a "secret" entrance for Elvis. Even with these precautionary measures, 13,500 Presley fans smashed dozens of chairs and collapsed a protective railing around the stage before the evening was over.

A tour of Commercial Chicago should also include the headquarters of Sears, Roebuck and Company, on the West Side, the leading firm in a field in which Chicago is also number one—mail-order merchandising; the still-expanding Chicago-O'Hare International Airport, the world's largest and busiest commercial jet airfield; and the R. R. Donnelley & Sons' Lakeside Press, largest of the city's many major printing and publishing plants.

It is at R. R. Donnelley where *Time*, *Life*, and dozens of other national magazines are printed by the thousands each hour. The

Reuben H. Donnelley Company, a part of the organization but a separate corporation, handles publication of Yellow Pages telephone directories and judges four-fifths of the prize contests in America. Of all the slogans and 25-words-or-less statements and jingles that their judges have handled, they will tell you this is their favorite:

> My favorite brunette is Hedy Lamarr,
> Send her to me, and you keep the car.

And it didn't even win a prize.

For a glimpse into the city's importance in the fields of journalism and communications, visit the Midwest Headquarters of NBC (WMAQ-WNBQ) in the Merchandise Mart, or CBS (WBBM-WBBM-TV) in the former Arena at Erie and McClurg Streets, and tour my office, the Sun-Times Daily News Building, one of the most up-to-date newspaper plants in the country, and the Gothic beauty, the Tribune Tower.

Governmental Chicago cannot be overlooked. To capture its flavor, visit the block-square City Hall-County Building, where of special interest are weekly City Council meetings on the City Hall side, and daily proceedings in the courtrooms of the Circuit and Superior courts on the County side. Or visit the Federal Building (the Old Post Office) a few blocks south, seat of the United States District Court which tried such famous defendants as Samuel Insull, Al Capone, and the Standard Oil Trust. The Criminal Courts Building at Twenty-sixth and California, with its daily parade of murder, assault, and narcotics defendants, is poignant testimony to society's weaknesses and failures. Illinois' "alternate capitol," the State of Illinois Building, is located at LaSalle and Randolph. There it is not uncommon to see the Governor chatting in the lobby as he awaits his private elevator.

And there is Melting-Pot Chicago. Start with the most sobering portion, the "Black Belt" of the South and Near West Sides, which is mute testimony to the mistrust, misunderstanding, and outright bigotry that remain to be swept from the city. But don't fail to notice the heartening aspects, the well-maintained properties of many Negroes who now command decent housing on Far

South Side streets, and Lake Meadows, the Near South Side interracial redevelopment project, which was financed entirely by private capital.

Thanks to the good work of such neighborhood self-help organizations as Joseph Meegan's Back of the Yards Council, most of the past waves of immigrants have been assimilated. But there are still remnants of old-country culture in the shops, churches, and restaurants of several neighborhoods.

There is "Chinatown," for example, around Wentworth south of Cermak; "Little Japan," centered about the shop at 1124-28 North Clark operated by Jun Toguri, father of the girl who to his sorrow became the "Tokyo Rose" of World War II; "Little Poland," beginning at Milwaukee Avenue near Division; "Little Pilsen," the Bohemian settlement in the vicinity of Eighteenth and Loomis; and "Little Greece," near the new University of Chicago campus at Harrison.

Chicago's Jewish population, one of the hemisphere's largest and most distinguished, is widely scattered throughout the city. But you will find clusters of excellent Jewish delicatessens in such neighborhoods as the South Side's Hyde Park and the North Side's Rogers Park and Albany Park.

And no melting-pot tour would be complete without a journey to Maxwell Street, where every day except the Saturday Sabbath, peddlers pull up carts and erect booths to create one of the nearest approximations of an old-world market this side of the Middle East.

And finally, there is Recreational Chicago, the facet of Our Town's personality which has made it equally appealing to residents, tourists, and conventioneers. The Loop theaters, Rush Street night clubs, and Loop and Near North Side restaurants, of course, are among my favorites.

In few other cities, especially in the warm-weather months, are there more varied resources for relaxation and amusement. There is the Brookfield Zoo in the southwestern suburbs, where uncaged animals are exhibited in their natural habitat. Nearer the Loop is Lincoln Park Zoo.

For the sports-minded, there are beaches, golf courses, swimming pools, bridle paths, and boating and water-skiing on Lake Michigan. Or, if you prefer a spectator's role, there are major events at Comiskey Park, Wrigley Field, Arlington, Washington, Sportsman's, and Maywood Parks, Hawthorne Race Track, Chicago Stadium, International Amphitheater, and Soldier Field.

And there is the seventy-seven-acre Riverview Park, one of the world's largest and most popular amusement parks.

This is only a beginning. But once you have sought out these sights and landmarks, and become acquainted with the people you meet along the way, you will have taken a long stride toward learning what this city, the Prairie Giant, is really like.

And perhaps you also will understand why I maintain it is the most misunderstood, underestimated metropolis in the world. And why many of us who live here feel a love for it akin to that of former Mayor Martin H. Kennelly, who once said:

"Why live, if you don't live in Chicago?"

10. The Column Has a Heart

Rodgers and Hammerstein put it so beautifully in their hit musical, *Flower Drum Song*: "A hundred-million miracles are happening every day." There must be at least that many. I have seen thousands in Chicago alone—thousands in the course of an afternoon. Sometimes they just "happen," as the song suggests, and I could fill another book with happy stories about them. But in this chapter I want to talk about another kind of "miracle"—the kind that is *made* to happen when good people respond unselfishly to an appeal for help.

It was always the philosophy of my late editor, Dick Finnegan, that "a column, like a newspaper, must have a heart."

It was his way of saying that it is never enough just to stimulate the minds and tickle the funny bones of the readers—that it is necessary to reach straight into their warm, generous hearts. As a result, "Kup's Column" always has been open to a worthy cause. Because of this, it has been my privilege to share a little in the making of many "miracles" which reveal something especially wonderful about Chicago and Chicagoans.

In 1945, in the last days of World War II, most of us civilians wanted to do something to show our appreciation to the young men who had been wounded in the service of our country. Among other things, I helped to organize a special excursion, which was announced in "Kup's Column" with the following statement:

This is the announcement of a Purple Heart Cruise. Wounded heroes who are convalescing in Army and Navy hospitals in the Chicago area will be the guests of the readers of this column on Saturday, June 16,, aboard the S.S. *North American*, one of two palatial sister cruisers on Lake Michigan . . .

If the heartwarming smiles of guests and sponsors alike were any evidence, the cruise was a complete success. It showed these men that their recent sacrifices had not gone unappreciated, and provided them with a welcome break from the monotony of hospital routine. And it gave those of us who contributed to the occasion a nice opportunity to say, "Thanks." So far just a commonplace story of what it was like at the end of the war.

But here is the point: *There has been a Purple Heart Cruise every summer since!* It is all too easy to forget our hospitalized veterans as the peacetime years go by. Chicago has not forgotten these citizen-soldiers to whom every American owes so much.

And there are so many who deserve credit for the perennial success of the Cruise. First of all, of course, there are the veterans themselves. We have many of them in the Chicago area, at the Great Lakes Naval Hospital, and Veterans Administration institutions at Hines, Downey, and Chicago's North and West Sides.

Erwin Goebel, president of the Georgian Bay Line, annually makes available to us the largest luxury liner sailing the Great Lakes. Chicago City Port Director Jack Manley, who was a Navy lieutenant commander in World War II, serves as my "naval aide." Les Lear, a former "Welcome Travelers" staff member and now one of Chicago's top promotion men, is entertainment director and master of ceremonies.

For companionship and dancing, there are flocks of former hostesses from the Servicemen's Center, YWCA, and USO, and models from the A-Plus, Sabie, Patricia Vance, and Patricia Stevens agencies—all under the supervision of the Board of Education's Helen Yerger. There is a seven-course meal, with a menu printed in Purple Heart motif, thanks to Jack Kallis. Phil Gray of Schak's, Inc., "dresses" the ship, stem to stern, with Purple Heart decorations.

Each veteran receives his photograph in a Purple Heart folder, courtesy of Jules Hirsch and a crew of Polaroid cameramen. Soft drinks by the carload are contributed by Jim Millsaps of Coca-Cola, Al Behrens of Pepsi-Cola, and Jules Klapman of Dad's Root Beer. Beer, the only alcoholic beverage served on the cruise (and that, in limited amounts), is contributed by Harris Perlstein of Pabst, Frank Scoby of Miller's High Life, Harry P. Heuer of Meister Brau, Dan Jaman of Van Merritt and Morgan & Company.

Andy Frain ushers also contribute their services. Record distributor Lennie Garmisa furnishes hundreds of records. Arthur Sideman, of Davidson Bakeries, donates two mammoth cakes with Purple Heart decorations.

Other gifts include hundreds of paperback books from circulator Charles Levy, candy in great quantities from Curtiss Candy and drug magnate Lou Zahn, all the ice cream the vets can eat from Phil ("Goldenrod") Sang and Harry Bresler, and cigars, cigarettes, playing cards, and sunglasses.

There is also an all-star stage show, through the co-operation of the musicians' union and the American Guild of Variety Artists, and dozens of individual entertainers. Over the years, the shows have included stars such as Eartha Kitt, Buddy Hackett, Shecky Greene, Larry Storch, Ronnie Graham, Virginia de Luce, June Carroll, Meg Myles, Forrest Tucker, Al Hirt, David Le-Winter and his Pump Room orchestra, the Dukes of Dixieland, Guy Cherney, Connie Mitchell, and Frank York.

In 1961, Chicago Fire Commissioner Robert Quinn's men participated in the Cruise by giving the S.S. *North American* a hero's salute with streams of colored water shot from the fireboats *Joseph Medill* and *Fred Busse*, while special fire crews demonstrated skin-diving techniques from new jet-propelled speedboats.

Thanks to the readers of "Kup's Column," it is always a glorious day on the water—which makes five hundred wonderful veterans glow inwardly for days afterward.

But this is not the only man-made "miracle" that I am lucky enough to have a part in. Every November, the *Sun-Times* sponsors a combination amateur night and all-star talent show that has become nationally known in the entertainment field as "The

Sun-Times Harvest Moon Festival." To America's largest indoor arena, the Chicago Stadium, this gala event annually attracts the largest theater audience in the nation—as many as twenty-five thousand persons. And it's all for charity.

Besides raising money for the needy and the blind, the Harvest Moon Festival alone has financed the purchase of eight $14,500 special buses for wheel-chair patients at the Hines VA Hospital, a $46,000 picnic-and-recreation pavilion, and a $46,000 therapeutic greenhouse at the Downey VA Hospital, as well as a number of improvements normally not available through government appropriations, such as library furnishings, folding wheel chairs, theater-type TV projectors, new chapel facilities, and an intercom system to carry radio and record broadcasts into the wards.

Because of the Festival's national prestige and the drawing power of the professional headliners who pack each show, its talent contest has become a major springboard to success for many young entertainers. In addition to generous prizes in cash and merchandise, winners in various talent categories are also eligible for bookings ranging from engagements in leading Las Vegas hotels to appearances in prominent Chicago radio-TV shows.

Vocalist Bob Vegas, a 1958 winner, played two weeks at the Dunes Hotel in Las Vegas (and then was signed for twenty more) and won a recording contract and a regular slot on a WBBM radio show in Chicago. Al Baca, a 1960 winner, won a two-week booking at the Flamingo Hotel in Las Vegas, and from there went on to other café and TV appearances. Ron Husmann, former Northwestern University student who was a 1957 winner, won so many plaudits for his leading role in the musical *Tenderloin* that he is now an established Broadway actor.

In 1945, when the Festival was first held, the line-up included George Raft, Danny Thomas, Virginia Mayo, June Havoc, Marie McDonald, Willie Shore, and Olsen & Johnson. In 1946 the billing grew larger, and included Bop Hope, Frank Sinatra, Jane Russell, Lena Horne, Frances Langford, Louis Prima, Peter Lawford, Janis Paige, Don McNeill, and Fran Allison.

Since then, every Festival has featured a parade of stars such as few live shows ever could hope to equal.

Dean Martin, Jerry Lewis, Ava Gardner, Marilyn Maxwell, Marge and Gower Champion, Jerry Lester, Peggy Ann Garner, Lex Barker, and Dave Garroway—with Bob Hope and Jane Russell as bonuses—highlighted one card. Another offered Danny Kaye, Perry Como, Jack Carson, Keenan Wynn, Jackie Cooper, John Garfield, Dorothy Shay, and Celeste Holm.

Picture Jerry Lewis, Eddie Fisher, Louis Armstrong, Charlton Heston, Zsa Zsa Gabor, Jayne Mansfield, Cleo Moore, James Arness, and Archie Moore on one bill, as in the 1956 Festival.

Or Carol Channing, Sammy Davis, Jr., George Gobel, the McGuire Sisters, Patti Page, Bob Mitchum, Andra Martin, and cartoonist Milton Caniff all entertaining from the same stage. That was only part of the 1957 Festival.

And imagine the size of the computer required to figure the payroll for booking comedians Jack Benny, Milton Berle, Jimmy Durante, Red Buttons, Edgar Bergen, George Jessel, Jerry Colonna, Robert Q. Lewis, George DeWitt, and Dick Shawn, and comedienne Phyllis Diller.

And for Dinah Shore, Debbie Reynolds, Eydie Gorme, Betty Hutton, Sarah Vaughn, Lisa Kirk, Mahalia Jackson, Julie Wilson, Ann Miller, Fran Warren, Anna Maria Alberghetti, Elaine Stewart, Dale Evans, Yvonne DeCarlo, Rhonda Fleming, Janet Leigh, Dorothy Lamour, Terry Moore, Jeri Southern, Rita Gam, Marta Toren, Dorothy Provine, Diana Lynn, Betty Garrett, Genevieve, Angie Dickinson, and Ann-Margret.

And for Tony Curtis, Tony Martin, Tony Bennett, Harry Belafonte, Fabian, Nat ("King") Cole, Vic Damone, Van Johnson, Burt Lancaster, George Montgomery, Gordon MacRae, Walter Pidgeon, José Ferrer, Gary Crosby, Dennis Morgan, Harry James, Stan Kenton, Skitch Henderson, Hugh O'Brian, Efrem Zimbalist, Jr., Troy Donahue, Roger Smith, Louis Quinn, Keefe Brasselle, Roy Rogers, and Bobby Van.

And for Rocky Marciano as bodyguard!

All these stars and many others, as the *Sun-Times* gratefully acknowledges in thank-you advertisements each year in *Variety* and the *Hollywood Reporter*, have donated their services at the Harvest Moon Festival. Several, in fact, have performed more than once—and Bob Hope, the benefit champ himself, has appeared more often than anybody. (Imagine the computer you would need just to pay him.)

"Just let me know when you need someone to fill out the cast," says Robert. "I'll be there with jokes on."

In giving away the only thing they have to sell—their ability to entertain—these entertainers have been a credit to themselves and to the profession they represent. And considering the willingness of these performers to sacrifice their time and money, I'm happy to report that special benefits have often accrued to them as a result. (These, too, are "miracles.")

It was at the Harvest Moon Festival that Jerry Lewis made one of his first appearances without his former partner Dean Martin. The enthusiastic response of the capacity crowd, says Jerry, assured him as nothing had before that he could "make it" as a single.

A 1957 Festival appearance marked a similar milestone in the career of Sammy Davis, Jr.

"Working without my father and uncle was still new to me," Sammy told me. "But the way this crowd reacted, that was the boost I needed."

And every entertainer thrills to the experience of working before such a large and appreciative audience.

As George Jessel once put it:

"That crowd—twenty-five thousand at one sitting! When can an entertainer nowadays stare so many people in the face at one time? If I'd had that situation in the old days, I'd never have left vaudeville!"

For this, special praise must go to Russ Stewart, Mel Barker, and the other *Sun-Times* executives who help make the Harvest Moon Festival an event in which all of us who participate take great pride.

In addition to the Festival, Chicago has supported many of those hypnotic "Lost Weekend" affairs, the charity telethon. It has been my privilege to participate in a dozen of the major ones, which have raised enormous sums for various causes—mainly the

United Cerebral Palsy Fund, Chicago Boys Clubs, and the City of Hope.

But again, the "miracles" didn't just happen. It is the generosity of thousands of persons that has made the contributions pile up.

First in line, as always, are the professional entertainers. No matter how late the hour, a galaxy of stars is always on hand to assure the presence of a large enough TV audience to make each telethon a success.

In the 1953 Cerebral Palsy telethon here, the line-up of stars included Bob Hope, Dean Martin, Jerry Lewis, Tony Martin, Dorothy Shay, Frankie Laine, Tony Bennett, Jack E. Leonard, Marilyn Maxwell, Rudy Vallee, Bill Stern, Gabby Hayes, the entire Chicago troupes of *Pal Joey* and Leonard Sillman's *New Faces*, Burr Tillstrom, Fran Allison, Don McNeill, and many others.

Hope, who had moved his TV show from Hollywood to Chicago so that he could participate, not only helped open the show, but returned twenty-nine hours later to help close it!

Total pledges as a result: More than $400,000.

In 1961, to assist in Police Superintendent Orlando W. Wilson's revamping of the Chicago Police Department, WBBM-TV's Clark George asked us to help stage a telethon to provide insurance and retirement benefits for the families of officers killed in the line of duty. These entertainers were only a few of those who answered my call—Phil Ford and Mimi Hines, Patrice Munsel, Mahalia Jackson, Annie Farge, Howard Duff, Pat O'Brien, the Kim Sisters, Richard Boone, Andy Williams, Count Basie, Red Nichols and His Five Pennies, Don Cherry, Julie London, Rowan and Martin, and Bob Scobey.

In other cities, there has frequently been great disparity between the amount pledged during a telethon and the funds which were ultimately collected. Probably no one connected with telethons will forget the 1952 fiasco in which Bob Hope and Bing Crosby headed a network-wide, all-star cast appearing on behalf of the American Olympic Committee. Though a million dollars was pledged by viewers, less than 30 per cent of that sum was actually realized. Some $600,000 that was publicly promised was never paid! Such experiences (and this, unfortunately, is not an isolated case) tend to place all telethons in disrepute.

But this seldom has been the pattern in Chicago. From the beginning, our Cerebral Palsy telethons, which were the largest produced locally, realized a return of better than 85 per cent on on-the-air pledges. Considering the vast area covered and the fact that from $185,000 to $550,000 in pledges was involved in each telethon, this is a record which, to my knowledge, still cannot be challenged by any other metropolis.

A large share of credit for this belongs to our "taxicab pickup" system. Through co-operation of the Balaban & Katz Theater Corporation, various neighborhood movie houses are designated as district headquarters. Chicago taxi firms, in turn, assign cabs to operate from these key theaters. When a pledge is phoned in for more than a given amount, usually twenty-five dollars, word is relayed to the appropriate district headquarters, and—before the donor can forget or lose his enthusiasm of the moment—a cabby is at his door to pick up his contribution.

We also have made it a practice to verify all large contributions before announcing them publicly. Unfortunately there are phonies and pranksters in this world who invariably attempt to intrude on the serious purpose of the telethon. In Chicago, we try to keep the number of those who succeed to a minimum.

Then, too, all of us who normally participate in Chicago telethons have counseled restraint in their use. It is my view that telethons, which can raise startling sums of money overnight, should be reserved exclusively for causes that have maximum immediacy and emotional appeal. Even the best of systems will be effective only if the cause is genuinely crucial. This we knew, and this we feared, when we joined in planning the telethon for the Police Department. Police seldom are popular. There is no "heart-tug." And we add, sorrowfully, the police telethon was the only disappointing telethon with which we ever were associated.

I am asked many questions about telethons. But of all of them, the most frequent one is this:

"Don't you have trouble staying awake after the first ten hours or so?"

I always answer this way:

"It's really not different from my usual schedule—sleep is one thing that columnists are accustomed to doing without. And besides, whatever fatigue effects you feel are more than compensated for by the exciting knowledge that phone operators, cabbies, entertainers, TV crewmen, and others all are working along with you—and that thousands of calls are jamming the switchboard with contributions for a worthy cause. You get the feeling you could continue for days—if the contributions would keep rolling in."

But this feeling is not unique to telethons. It is also present in other activities in which I have regularly been privileged to help, such as the Dr. Jerome D. Solomon Memorial Research Foundation, honoring a brother of my wife who gave his life in World War II; La Rabida Sanitarium; the Off-the-Street Club Christmas Party through which the Chicago Federated Advertising Club raises $20,000 for the underpriviliged in one afternoon; and Israel Bond sales and the Jewish National Fund.

The Jewish National Fund was kind enough to honor me as "Man of the Year" in 1960. It also named one section of its immense U.S.A. Freedom Forest in Israel the Irv Kupcinet Forest. But as my family and I planted some of the first of a hundred thousand trees which will help reclaim unproductive desert land for the benefit of thousands of people, we could not help reflecting that we were not the ones who had made this milestone of progress possible—it was the readers of the column and other generous Chicagoans who were responsible.

And make no mistake about it, beneath Chicago's seemingly tough exterior, there beats a big warm heart. This has been proved so many times. Our famous Hull House was the first privately financed neighborhood settlement house, and the model for many similar social-work centers here. Our Hospitality Center for servicemen in World War II was the finest in America. And Chicago supports one of the largest Community Fund-Red Cross budgets in the nation—now more than fifteen million dollars a year.

Generosity is an integral part of Chicago's civic personality—so much so that it makes any charity-minded columnist's job relatively easy.

Permit me one final story on the subject.

In January 1960, a potentially devastating fire broke out in a building in a congested area on Chicago's Near North Side. Firemen were able to contain the blaze, but nine of them were killed. Nine men—fighting one fire! They left not only their widows, but also a total of twenty children, almost all of school age.

Like many other Chicagoans, I was immensely touched by this tragedy. Bill Veeck, who was then president of the White Sox, was, too. He awakened me by phone the next morning.

"Let's do something to help them," he suggested.

Accordingly, my column of January 30 carried this paragraph:

> The death toll in the Hubbard Street fire has numbed all Chicago. Nine lives snuffed out in the line of duty! But the firemen left behind wives and children. We are sending out a 5-11 alarm to aid the victims, especially the children. If you have been touched in the same way we have, send your contributions to the Firemen's Fund, care of this column.

The response was instantaneous.

Veeck started it with a $1,000 donation. Then came calls from Joe Meegan of the Back of the Yards Neighborhood Council with a $500 pledge, another $500 from attorney Sid Korshak, and $100 from Jim Moran of Courtesy Motors and another $100 from Zollie Frank. For days, by mail and phone, other pledges arrived.

Mrs. W. J. Podbielniak, whose Lake Shore Drive mansion was one of the residential showplaces of Chicago prior to the recent demolition, agreed to open her home to visitors for two days to obtain contributions. Veeck, Meegan, Fire Commissioner Bob Quinn, and executives Pat Hoy, Thomas Beacon, and Rollin Mansfield joined me on a committee to study the needs of the firemen's families and administer the fund accordingly. Attorneys George Rogers and Arthur Morse donated hours of legal counsel.

I had thought our efforts might raise $25,000.

"Nothing of the kind," Veeck had said. "We'll get three or four times that much."

And when the drive was concluded, Veeck had been proved correct. The fund totaled $90,000—enough to provide for the education of all the children orphaned by the fire, and to cover special hardships besides.

Year in and year out, you are told of crime and violence, and commercial and political opportunism in Chicago. You are also told that entertainment stars are vain and selfish, and that newspapers and newspapermen are cynical and hardhearted.

Through these few modest activities of "Kup's Column," however, I hope I have shown that there is another side to the story. I hope I have proved to you that Chicago, show business, and newspaper columns do have a heart—and the heart beats most strongly when it is beating for others.

11. At Random

"Good evening, ladies and gentlemen, and welcome to another session of *At Random* . . ."

Each Saturday night since February 12, 1959, these words have introduced a visit to another favorite stop on my Chicago beat, my late-night TV show, called *At Random*.

As millions of sleepy-eyed viewers know, this is the program on which a distinguished group of serious thinkers and articulate conversationalists in various professions gather for a discussion which literally is "at random." There is no assigned topic. As host, I leave the conversationalists on their own as much as possible. All they do from midnight to about 3:00 A.M. is sit around a low table and talk.

But what talk!

Listeners have taken to napping after dinner on Saturday night so they can stay up until the early hours of Sunday morning without collapsing. They don't want to miss a word.

They hold midnight "At Random Parties." The first three hours are spent in watching the show—and then, for another two or three hours, they continue the discussion they heard on TV.

A Chicago priest has even inaugurated an "At Random Mass." You can attend it right after the show, then "sleep in" for the remainder of Sunday morning!

We were flattered, indeed, to read in Harold Mehling's none

218

too flattering book on television, *The Great Time-Killer*, this passage:

"WBBM-TV has achieved great popularity with Irv Kupcinet's late-night show, a high-calibre, often controversial, usually stimulating talkathon. Kupcinet, a columnist for the Chicago *Sun-Times*, tries to select guests who have something to say and aren't afraid to say it." (And as an aside to Mehling: I have the nasty letters to prove it.)

Hugh Downs was another who was especially kind to our show in print. In his book, *Yours Truly . . . Hugh Downs*, he writes: "With the possible exception of Irv Kupcinet in Chicago, Jack Paar has a greater talent for bringing out the real personality of people than any other interviewer I have seen." These are gracious words, indeed, from a man who has worked at Paar's side nightly for five years, and only guested on *At Random* twice.

It is no exaggeration to say that *At Random* has been one of the wonders in the history of Chicago television. Such shows have been slotted opposite it as David Susskind's *Open End*, Hugh Hefner's *Playboy Penthouse*, and offbeat offerings such as the Caribbean game of jai-alai. But through it all, *At Random* has thrived. It continues to hold the largest after-midnight audience in the Chicago area—approximately one million viewers.

In its first two seasons, *At Random* won two Emmy Awards from the Chicago Academy of Television Arts and Sciences. And because of the show I have been awarded two Emmys, one of them as "Television Man of the Year" in Chicago in 1961.

Its popularity has long since spread beyond the boundaries of the Chicago area. Since early in 1961, through syndication by CBS Film Sales, a ninety-minute version of *At Random* also has been telecast regularly in such cities as Los Angeles, Atlanta, Boston, St. Louis, Milwaukee, Minneapolis, Indianapolis, Dallas, and Portland, Maine.

In the next few pages, let me tell you about some of the many fascinating moments connected with *At Random* since the show began. I think these stories will reveal a great deal, not only about me and my guests, but about Chicago and about television in general.

As befits a simple production built around conversation, *At Random* began simply—with a conversation. Frank Atlass, who was then managing Chicago's CBS-TV station, WBBM-TV, was looking for a new Saturday night program. I previously had appeared for a time on a variety program on WGN-TV, and then on a news-interview-commentary show on WBKB and WBBM-TV and, most recently, I had been on NBC-TV's *America After Dark*, with my fellow columnists Hy Gardner, Earl Wilson, Bob Considine, Paul Coates, and Vernon Scott. Atlass suggested that I drop in to discuss program ideas.

Conversation already was well established on CBS Radio. The newly launched *Open End*, in New York, was finding an enthusiastic audience. No doubt with both of these "talk shows" in mind, Atlass said:

"I'd like to try a conversation show here. But let's not make it a copy. Let's come up with our own format."

Chicago-style TV is traditionally low-budgeted and low-keyed. It was in that tradition that we formulated *At Random*. Variety, spontaneity, and lively, sophisticated conversation—these were to be its keynotes. For the most part I think we have achieved them.

Variety?

The first show featured actor Sidney Poitier, Senator Wayne Morse of Oregon, singer-actor-comedian Sammy Davis, Jr., Congressman James Roosevelt of New York, and actress Ruth Roman. The conversation moved effortlessly from subject to subject— and the subjects included Hollywood, American Presidents, the attitudes of foreign nations toward the United States, race relations, and the water table of North America.

It was Senator Morse who introduced the subject of the water table. Throughout history, he said, civilizations have risen and fallen with the amount of water available to them. Rome fell, in part, because of a water shortage, and the pattern can be traced throughout history. Maintaining an adequate water supply is already a problem in large areas of the American West. And the Senator made it clear that, while the front pages are full of more dramatic news of nuclear weapons and the national debt, much of the real business in Washington involves the careful study and evaluation of such long-range concerns as the anticipated water supply at the turn of the next century.

Nobody could have guessed in advance that such a technical subject would have come up in an informal discussion among this group, and in such a compelling fashion. The diversity of the panel and the fact that no limits were set on the subject matter to be discussed were responsible. Variety helps make the show.

So does spontaneity. Unlike other discussion shows, *At Random* never lists in advance the subjects likely to be covered. We expect the program's information content to be high, but beyond that, we never know what to expect. Conversation is all we are after—witty, free-wheeling conversation that is warm and informal and informed.

Spontaneity cannot be faked. And we don't try to fake it. But there are a few "secrets" which we use to help keep our conversationalists both relaxed and stimulated. These were formulated with the help of my first assistants on the show, producer Jerry Levin and director Phil Ruskin. My present producer, Paul Frumkin, director Ruskin, and I still use these techniques.

One concerns the atmosphere in the studio. On most other programs guests are not brought onto the set until a few moments before sign-on. On *At Random*, our guests are usually seated and talking at least fifteen minutes before the program begins. Normally, guests still are talking when I excuse myself from the group to do the sign-off—and often the conversation continues for a half-hour or more after the show is off the air.

We also use three cameras, two of which are hidden, and we disconnect the red cue lights which customarily indicate at all times which camera is "on." Realizing that it is impossible to know whch camera is "live," everyone tends to forget the existence of the equipment. In this way, extroverts are discouraged from any tendency to "play" to the camera, and introverts are less likely to develop lens fright.

This striving for spontaneity also is one reason that I remain on the side lines as much as possible (which isn't easy when a discussion warms up). And it is also why I don't steer the conversation in a new direction the moment it begins to lag slightly.

For it is often at this point that a guest, sensing that the time is ripe, will change the subject himself—carrying the conversation down an intriguing path that no moderator ever could have planned.

But I don't mean to imply that no planning goes into *At Random*. Hours of preparation precede each show, beginning only a few hours after sign-off the week before. At that time, I begin checking my files and my memory for details on interesting personalities who are likely to be in town the following week. I also consider which resident Chicagoans might be invited to the show, and I prepare a list of potential guests. My producer, Paul Frumkin, does the same, and lists his ideas. On Tuesday afternoon Paul, Phil Ruskin, and I huddle at the WBBM-TV studios to decide on a tentative line-up.

Sometimes, of course, invitations must be tendered weeks in advance. This was the case with a panel of Nobel prize-winners, and later with former Vice-President Richard M. Nixon. And because many of *At Random*'s guests are busy people on tight schedules—especially the dignitaries visiting from foreign countries—acceptances are sometimes not forthcoming until just a day or two before the show.

As soon as anyone becomes a likely guest, Frumkin and I immediately begin doing research on him. In spare moments during the week, during all of Friday evening, and during most of Saturday afternoon and evening, I study this material so I'll have it firmly in mind during the show. It is often a surprise to guests that we know so much about them. But only in this way can we draw the best from each of them, and make the show authoritative.

One other essential ingredient of the show: coffee. *At Random* runs on it—at least two one-pound cans per program. We keep two thirty-two-cup urns operating at all times, not only to refuel those of us on both sides of the cameras in the studio itself, but also to refresh visitors in a viewing room nearby. A huge mound of sandwiches is also consumed during each show.

In spite of all our planning, however, there are anxious moments connected with almost every program. The arrival of out-of-town guests is frequently a cause for worry. Because there is always a chance of transportation difficulties, we never count them present until they are actually seated in the studio. On one occasion, Robert Briscoe, Lord Mayor of Dublin, was due to fly from Ireland and arrive in Chicago a few hours before showtime. At 11:30, the usual assembly time for guests, there was no Briscoe. Finally, just at midnight, he telephoned from O'Hare International Airport. He had just landed, after a trip repeatedly delayed because of weather. He faced a heavy schedule the next day and you could tell from his voice that he was too exhausted to speak to anyone, let alone to one million alert viewers of a three-hour post-midnight TV show. Regretfully we invited him back for a later date and the show went on without him.

Making connections with former Vice-President Richard M. Nixon in May 1961 proved to be even more hectic. It was to be his first visit to Chicago since the Presidential election of the year before. His schedule was crowded and it would be impossible for him to remain in town through Saturday night, so I had arranged with him and the other guests to videotape the show at 3:00 P.M. on Friday. And then, late Thursday morning, one of his assistants telephoned from New York to say that Nixon's schedule had been changed, and could we tape the program Saturday afternoon?

But the station would not be able to handle a three-hour videotape session on Saturday afternoon because its facilities were already scheduled for other programs. I asked Nixon's assistant if we could do it Friday night. But Nixon, it developed, could not possibly be available at any time on Friday. In desperation, I checked back with the studio, and after some complicated rescheduling, we found that we could tape a show on Saturday after all—but only if we started at eleven in the morning and ran over the normal lunch hour. I relayed this news immediately to Herb Klein, Nixon's former press secretary and a good friend of mine, and then I waited while he worked desperately to straighten out the schedule at the other end. Finally Klein phoned back that 11:00 A.M. would be fine. We both started to breathe again.

But not for long: there was then the problem of assembling the other panelists at the new time. As it developed, only two of them could come at the new hour, *Sun-Times* Editor Milburn ("Pete") Akers and Dr. Richard Snyder, of the Political Science Department of Northwestern University. All we could do was to plan the show in two sections, one to start at 11:00 A.M. and the other (without Nixon) at the previously arranged hour of 3:00 P.M.

And even this didn't end the anxious moments! About 10:20 that Saturday, as I was at the station typing out some last-minute material, who should walk into my office but Richard Nixon. Despite his prominence and his busy schedule, there was no way to change the taping schedule again: he would just have to wait around for forty minutes. Apologetically, I tried to explain the situation.

"Don't worry," he said pleasantly. "I know I'm early. I'll just go upstairs for a cup of coffee."

Whereupon, the man who had almost been elected President of the United States borrowed a dime from a TV technician, and enjoyed a leisurely cup of coffee out of a paper cup from a vending machine in the WBBM-TV employees' canteen.

When the time to tape the show arrived, I asked whether there was any subject which he would prefer not to discuss.

"Absolutely not," he said. "Put anything to me that you want to. I'll certainly try to answer."

During the show, as we sat in the same studio in which candidates Nixon and Kennedy had engaged in the first of their "Great Debates," he dodged nothing. In fact, I found him more forthright and natural in manner than in several of his campaign appearances.

"If he had been that sincere and direct when he was a candidate," one viewer wrote me after the show, "I might have changed my mind and voted for him."

Among his most interesting remarks, I thought, were those concerning his campaign. One comment, regarding the TV debates, was that, if he had attempted to avoid them, he would have had more to lose than to gain. Another was that, in the closing days of the campaign, he should have asked President Eisenhower to speak on his behalf in Illinois, rather than in New York. Ike's appearance, he felt in retrospect, might have swung the extremely close Illinois race to him. Incidentally, according to Mr. Nixon, the rumor that General Eisenhower was never wholeheartedly in favor of him was completely unfounded—Ike did everything that he was asked to do during the campaign.

The Nixon show was a great one, when we finally got our schedules synchronized.

But don't get the idea that all the tense moments on *At Random* occur before the show goes on. From experience, I have found that with a spontaneous program such as ours, it is impossible to predict anything that might happen while we are on the air.

Once, when singer-actress Eartha Kitt and Negro publisher John Johnson were on the same program, I noticed that there was a decided coolness between them. After a few pointed remarks had been made, I learned that they had been less than friendly for some time over a derogatory story Johnson's *Ebony* magazine had once carried about Miss Kitt. At the time each had agreed to appear on the show, neither had known that the other was to be present. It was one of the few awkward situations of that type which we somehow hadn't been able to head off by careful research. But, as it developed, the evening ended happily—both the guests were far more friendly to one another when they left than they had been when they had arrived.

Another time, when the show was being telecast from a hotel instead of from our regular studios, a veteran actor managed to tiptoe around our custom of serving nothing stronger than coffee in the cups we provide each guest. He had somehow talked the *maître d'* of the establishment, who was in charge of refreshments, into serving him cupfuls of whisky instead—and soon the actor was almost literally in his cups! We tried to overlook it when he became argumentative, but when he began swearing in discussions with a Russian visitor on the program, alert viewers knew as well as I did that something affirmative would have to be done quickly. Much as I regretted it, we bade him an early good-night.

But some of the unexpected crises on the show represent nothing more than innocent fun. One such surprise occurred in 1961 when my guests included educator Robert M. Hutchins, Edward R. Murrow, and a group of CBS correspondents who had assembled in Chicago that day. One of my secret fears for *At Random* is a deadly lull in the conversation, when neither my guests nor I have anything to offer. Never would I expect such silence from the articulate guests that comprised this panel.

But when I threw out the first question, a sort of warm-up to prime the conversational pump, I was greeted with complete silence. Hutchins shook his head and muttered, "no comment." Murrow had a blank stare on his darkly handsome face. The CBS correspondents—Daniel Schorr of Germany; David Schoenbrunn, then of Paris; Alexander Kendrick of London; Richard Hotellet of the United Nations; Peter Kalischer of the Far East, and Blair Clark, then of New York but now a network vice-president—each shrugged his shoulders as I turned to them pleadingly.

"This," I said to myself, "was the simplest subject I could think of and I can't get any response. Where do I go from here?" Perspiration formed on my forehead but I was chilled inwardly.

Finally, after what seemed an interminable period, Murrow burst into laughter and explained his little gag to the audience. He had suggested to the others not to reply to anything I said, just to cause a few moments of embarrassment. Never did I heave a more welcome sigh of relief than while Murrow did the explaining.

And there was another *At Random* show where Alfred Hitchcock worked a similar gag on his fellow guest, Jack Paar. Confiding to me in advance that he was a bit miffed at Paar, he said, "Now don't worry, but I'm just going to sit there for about an hour and not say a word. Let's see what Paar does about it."

True to his word, Hitchcock did "just sit there," responding to the conversation with nothing more than some occasional mugging of cool assent or cold disapproval. Finally Paar could restrain himself no longer.

"Mr. Hitchcock," he said, "you've been sitting there for almost an hour and you haven't said a word. How come you don't talk?"

Whereupon Hitchcock, with his pixyish grin, explained that it all had been a joke. Paar—who, incidentally, proved to be a bright, witty, and co-operative guest—laughed as hard as everyone else over the gag.

And another time, Carol Channing gave the other guests a bit of a start, although the reason for their reaction was not immediately understood by the viewers at home. Carol had arranged to join our *At Random* party late, as soon as she could get to the studio after her last show at the Empire Room of the Palmer House. Eager to join us as soon as she could, she stripped off her costume, climbed into a red jersey dressing gown, jumped in a cab, and breezed into the studio. Needless to say, several guests did a double take. But Carol knew that she would be on black-and-white TV, where the lipstick-red gown would photograph a stylish black, and that she would be seated behind a table, where the scantiness of her garment would never be seen. The guests were agog, but on the home screens she appeared to be dressed to the nines. As one fellow guest, Marusia, the Hollywood dress designer, described her garb as seen on the monitor: "It was very chic."

Incidentally, a number of actresses specifically request our cameramen not to take extreme close-ups, because under the intense glare of the studio lights, such shots can be extremely unflattering. But the youthful and velvet-skinned Carol isn't one of them. She is one of those to whom no camera angle and no lens distance is detrimental.

But controversy is the ingredient that usually enlivens *At Random*. With such a heterogeneous mixture of guests as ours, some disagreement is inevitable. And within the limits of tastefulness and pace, controversy usually illuminates subjects as no mouthings of mutual admiration ever could. Fortunately, with the caliber of guests we have always enjoyed on *At Random*, there has never yet been a conversation that degenerated into a noisy donnybrook. (Even the drunk actor I mentioned earlier left us with dignity.) Like the mature, well-informed people they are, *At*

Random guests know how to disagree for the stimulation of it, without becoming violent or vituperative.

And there have been some monumental disagreements!

One brilliant controversy involved the Reverend John Banahan, Director of the Radio-TV Department of the Roman Catholic Archdiocese of Chicago, and harmonica-player Larry Adler. Banahan is an unusually articulate spokesman for his faith. And Adler, although I hadn't realized it before the show began, is apparently an atheist.

"How do you *know* there is a God?" Adler challenged Father Banahan at one point.

This set off one of the most stimulating debates I have ever heard on television!

And another time, actress Peggy Cass and Northwestern University political scientist William M. McGovern were face to face across our table. I had known that McGovern was an outspoken political conservative, but I hadn't realized Peggy was such a zealous liberal. She and McGovern were soon clashing over the approach to several controversial issues, in which Peggy, whose love of wisecracks masks an impressive knowledge of history, easily held her own.

Among other provocative political debates on *At Random* was one between Norman Thomas, the eloquent former Socialist Party candidate for President of the United States, and ultraconservative attorney Clarence Manion, formerly of Notre Dame. And still another memorable contest took place between Victor Reuther, brother of the United Auto Workers' Walter Reuther, and conservative Senator Barry Goldwater of Arizona. There was no question of "equal time" in these controversies: the issue was met squarely and openly, and the adversaries were on their own.

One of *At Random*'s many outspoken arguments concerning mass communications and race relations received extensive coverage in *Variety*. This involved an impassioned dispute between playwright Lorraine Hansberry (a former Chicagoan) and movie director Otto Preminger. The issue was whether such Preminger films as *Carmen Jones* and *Porgy and Bess* reinforced erroneous stereotypes of Negroes and thereby retarded progress in race relations. Preminger declared that Miss Hansberry, in believing that such films were anything but beneficial, was a "minority of one." Lorraine, on the other hand, contended that the basic premise in the plots of such pictures was the "exaggerated sexuality" of the Negro and that this misrepresentation not only caused "great wounds," but was also "bad art."

Another *At Random* show that made news was the program featuring Nobel Peace Prize-winners Lester B. Pearson, Phillip Noel-Baker, Sir Norman Angell, and Lord John Boyd-Orr.

But it was my old friend, former President Harry S. Truman, who made what probably ranks as the most significant headline to date to stem from the conversations on *At Random*. It was in December 1960, when Mr. Truman was a guest along with University of Chicago Professor Daniel Boorstin and James McDonald, first United States Ambassador to Israel. Before many minutes had passed, the conversation had swung around to the former President's Korean War dismissal of General Douglas MacArthur. Mr. Truman restated his reasons for his decision with his customary firmness. And then, on *At Random* for the first time, he went on to reveal precisely why it had for so long been his opinion that MacArthur's strategic designs would have led us irrevocably into World War III—MacArthur not only wanted to drop the atomic bomb on Red Chinese territory, but in eastern Russia as well, according to Mr. Truman.

His comments followed a discussion of the reasons why he had ordered the dropping of the first two atomic bombs on Japan in World War II. Our conversation went this way:

"Was there any pressure on you to release the A-bomb again in the Korean conflict?"

"Yes, MacArthur wanted to do that."

"MacArthur did?"

"Yes, he wanted to bomb China and eastern Russia and everything else."

"Use the atomic bomb?"

"Why, of course. That's the only weapon we had that they would understand."

"This was one of the main reasons you recalled him?"

"I recalled him for disobedience of orders. He was in private contact with the Republican minority leader in the House of Representatives, Joe Martin, and he had been warned that the Commander in Chief was still the Commander in Chief."

Both Associated Press and United Press International flashed the story to clients in this country and abroad. Later, when reporters asked Mr. Truman why he had not mentioned MacArthur's alleged advocacy of what amounted to a "preventive war" in his memoirs, the former President replied:

"I didn't want to do MacArthur any damage, but when a question is asked point-blank, I have to answer it."

The next day MacArthur, in a statement issued through his former aide Major General Courtney Whitney, called Mr. Truman's version "completely false."

"The records are available," he said, "and will show that atom-bombing in the Korean War was never discussed either by my headquarters or in any communication to or from Washington."

Mr. Truman's final comment on the subject:

"I'll have no further comment on the controversy. History will take care of itself."

But *At Random* is not primarily a political show. It offers a bit of everything. And inevitably, wherever such literate guests gather, the conversations are laced with innumerable *bon mots* and humorous anecdotes.

Theo Bikel, actor and folk singer, told of what impelled him to leave a position as an agricultural student in Israel for a stage career:

"I was shoveling dung and reciting Shakespeare, and I decided they didn't mix."

Arthur ("Red") Motley, publisher of *Parade* magazine, gave this definition of a committee:

"A group of unfits, appointed by the unwilling, to do the unnecessary."

And actor Pat O'Brien told how his son had won a school prize for an essay on highway safety:

"Drive carefully!" the boy had written. "Don't hit a child! Wait for a teacher!"

But in the long run it is not humor, or controversy, or even the promise of news-making statements that keeps millions of viewers awake long past their normal bedtimes on *At Random* nights: it is that other element—the promise of seeing prominent people as they really are. Because of the varied and freewheeling nature of the conversation, *At Random* reveals these people as few other programs can.

Viewers who heard Bill Veeck discuss research with Dr. Percy Julian, or state his considered opinions on international affairs, social problems, and other subjects can understand why those of us who know him say that the former White Sox president is a most remarkable man. The amount of reading he does is amazing. There is almost no field in which he does not have more than a passing knowledge.

And those who have seen and heard Jimmy Roosevelt in several visits to the show know why he is considered one of the most personable politicians in the United States Congress. He is one of the best-known members of a famous family, but he hasn't an ounce of pomposity. It was highly diverting to hear him tell of how his grandmother would scold his father, Franklin D. Roosevelt, about remembering to dress warmly, even after he was Governor of New York. Or of how Jimmy and his brother Elliot once proposed to horsewhip columnist Westbrook Pegler for something he had written about FDR. Or of how life in the spotlight of the White House needn't "spoil" children such as Caroline Kennedy, if they have wise parents, as he believes Caroline does.

On one show, Jimmy also told an amusing story on his brother John, who was still in college when Franklin D. Roosevelt was inaugurated for the third time. On the night following that inauguration, John accidentally got locked out of the White House grounds. Driving an old jalopy, John arrived at the White House gates well after they were locked at 2:00 A.M. He was challenged by a strange guard, who did not recognize him.

"What do you want?" asked the guard.

"I want to come in," said John.

"Why?"

"I want to go to bed."

"Are you driving that thing?" asked the guard, pointing at the jalopy.

"Sure," said John. "That's my car."

"Look," the guard told him finally. "You might as well face it—you can't come in here if you are driving that thing."

So John Roosevelt spent his father's inauguration night at a friend's house.

"And, you know," said Jimmy with a wink and a chuckle, "I've always suspected that this had much to do with John's deciding to become a Republican!"

And speaking of young Republicans, all viewers who saw the first appearance of Bell and Howell Company president Charles Percy on *At Random*, can well appreciate why he is considered such a dynamic, enlightened spokesman for the moderate wing of his party. That night, former Governor of Utah, J. Bracken Lee, was holding forth on his reasons for favoring abolition of the income tax. With impressive logic and indisputable statistics, Percy so skillfully and so tactfully challenged the arguments of Governor Lee that dozens of letters poured in suggesting that he run for Senator or President. (It is not inconceivable that some day he may do so.)

From the opposing camp, Teamster Union president James Hoffa also made a tremendous impression. It was not that he convinced any skeptical viewers of the rectitude of his dubious associations. But his quick mind, directness of manner, and uncanny memory for figures and detailed contract provisions showed many people that he is a far better executive and a more persuasive speaker than they had been led to believe.

Others who have left indelible impressions on *At Random* audiences include Senator Paul Douglas, with his surprising knowledge of the theater, Dr. Morris Fishbein, General Alfred M. Gruenther, scientist Linus Pauling, University of Chicago population expert Philip Hauser, former Israeli Ambassador Abba Eban, and actor Sidney Poitier.

More than once, viewers have also been surprised to learn of hidden talents or interests among our prominent guests. I know that many were unaware that actor Hugh O'Brian has such a great admiration for Albert Schweitzer that he has gone into the jungles of Africa to visit with the missionary doctor-philosopher. Or that Jane Russell is a dedicated supporter of the overseas adoption organization known as WAIF. Or that idealist Don Murray spent more than two years helping build a "model" town in Italy. Or that Thomas Lanphier, now president of the Fairbanks-Morse Company, quit a $35,000-a-year job with Convair on a question of principle.

It was rather surprising to many viewers, too, that Mort Sahl, who is known as a fast-thinking, fast-talking comedian, said scarcely anything in his first appearance (he more than made amends in subsequent appearances); and that Imogene Coca, generally considered an even more loquacious type, was even quieter. And that fan-dancer Sally Rand revealed that she was reared a Quaker, and spoke with such warm nostalgia about it. And that actor James Stewart, who is an Air Force Reserve General, can speak with such authority on aviation. And that noted con man Yellow Kid Weill is an authority on the World Bank and its handling of monetary reserves.

And many were surprised at the quick wit of my old friend Ed Murrow, whose serious side is the one to which they have been exposed most frequently; at the lack of pretense in the great biographer-poet Carl Sandburg, who unabashedly excused himself during one show to go to the toilet; and at the virtuosity of David Susskind, who has been derided as a moderator by some reviewers, but who is unquestionably an excellent guest.

The late Dr. Tom Dooley deserves special mention. I doubt that anyone on the show has ever moved, inspired, and galvanized our viewers into action as did this slight young man. I'm told that as a result of his appearances on At Random, a number of young people decided to devote themselves to similar overseas work—and enough money was sent to his MEDICO organization to support the operation of two jungle hospitals for an entire year.

When you consider that every At Random program has perhaps half a dozen outstanding guests, you can see that it is all but impossible to pick an "all-star" panel of those who have appeared without omitting dozens of deserving names. Not long ago, however, I was caught off guard and asked to choose a group who would make up a so-called "ideal" *At Random* panel. I named five former guests: Dr. Morris Fishbein, philosophy professor Paul Schilpp of Northwestern University, Jimmy Hoffa, Adlai Stevenson, British biologist Sir Julian Huxley, and Carl Sandburg.

In selecting the all-time classic *At Random* program, much the same dilemma is involved as in singling out "all-star" guests. For this special designation among all our programs, however, I would have to choose what we refer to as our "Darwin show." As anyone knows who saw it, either live or on videotape, it came as close to having everything as any *At Random* show to date.

The occasion was the hundredth anniversary of Charles Darwin's publication of the theory of evolution. The guests were drawn primarily from the distinguished participants in the Darwin Centennial Celebration at the University of Chicago: Sir Charles Darwin, grandson of the naturalist; biologist Sir Julian Huxley; the Honorable Adlai E. Stevenson; former Harvard astronomer Harlow Shapley; and University of Chicago anthropologist Sol Tax.

As Chicago *Sun-Times* reporter Jerry Cohen wrote in his coverage the next morning:

> The program was like a sampling from an anthology to which each of these wise and witty men might have contributed one of his own wisest and wittiest dissertations. It may have been erudite, but it was never dull.

The major issues facing mankind today, the participants agreed, are three: The population explosion; the dilemma of prosperity, by which the rich get richer while the poor get poorer; and the hydrogen bomb.

A typical Huxley comment on the population problem: "When the babies born today are old enough to vote, there'll be a billion more votes. It's appalling! Absolutely appalling!"

Darwin made an eloquent plea for birth control, saying, "The way to tackle the problem is to get the reproduction rate down."

"We need a new international and global policy," agreed Huxley.

So the discussion went, punctuated by such exchanges as one in which it was suggested that Huxley is an agnostic.

"I am an atheist," he answered. "I am not an agnostic!"

And there was outright humor, as when Huxley asked Darwin if he believed that machines had become so far advanced that they one day would write poetry.

"Yes," said Darwin. "A machine will be able to write poetry— but it will be the type of poetry only another machine could enjoy."

Or when someone commented that we have come to expect our schools to be responsible for teaching everything but a course in picking pockets.

"Oh, but they do teach that," said Adlai Stevenson. "They call it banking and finance!"

I find *At Random* a welcome change of pace from my regular routine, but it gives me an opportunity only to skim the surface of ideas and events. I am sure you can understand why I say it is significant that Chicago, which for so long has been berated, underrated, and misunderstood, should be the place where a program on this level originates.

And I am certain, too, that you will agree that its popularity, despite its peculiar broadcast time, demonstrates beyond doubt that people want more out of television than they are accustomed to getting.

And I'm just as sure, as I'm sure that Chicagoan Newton Minow was appointed Federal Communications Commission Chairman, that this added measure of quality is coming to television. I am proud and grateful for whatever part Chicago and *At Random* will prove to have played in bringing this improvement about.

12. Parting Shorts

One thing I learned long ago as an emcee: a good way to get offstage is with a laugh.

This advice holds just as true for writing columns.

And come to think of it, it's not a bad rule for books, either.

So here, from among the thousands of quips and anecdotes my readers seem to have enjoyed over the years, are some of my favorite stories.

They Call It Culture

Quin Ryan tells of the report from France that artist Pablo Picasso had been robbed. But according to local newspapers, Picasso had gotten a good look at the thieves and had willingly sketched them for the local police. Working with his drawing, within forty-eight hours the officers arrested eight gypsies, two horses, a hearse, an accordion, and the Eiffel Tower!

Author Upton Sinclair once was asked what he thought of a certain dull novel. He said he could best answer by citing a friend's experience with the book. During World War II, the friend was carrying a copy in a breast pocket. One day a bullet struck him right over the heart—but he was saved by the book. Not even a bullet could get past the fourth chapter!

236

In the Pump Room a few years ago pianist Artur Rubinstein was telling of his return from an extended tour of the Orient. His first day back, his son, then two, took him by the arm and said, "Play, Daddy, play." Almost overcome at the thought that the child understood he was a concert artist and wanted to hear him play, Rubinstein strode to the piano. But as he was about to start, the youngster tugged at his arm again.

"No," he said, "Daddy, play—play gramophone!"

On one of his final concert tours of the United States, Ignace Jan Paderewski, the famed pianist and Polish statesman, was approached by a grimy bootblack who inquired, "Shine, mister?"

"No," replied the musician, "but if you'll wash that dirt off your face, I'll give you a quarter."

The youngster raced to a hydrant, washed his face thoroughly, then returned to collect his quarter. Accepting it, he hesitated a second, then suddenly handed it back, saying:

"Here, mister, you keep it—and get yourself a haircut!"

Rudyard Kipling, in his day, was one of the highest paid authors in the world, commanding the then unprecedented sum of six shillings per word. One day he received a letter from a practical joker which read:

"Dear Sir. I am enclosing six shillings. Will you be good enough to send me one of your high-priced words."

Kipling replied immediately: "Thanks."

Richard Aldrich was starting a theater group outside of New York and selected George Bernard Shaw's *Pygmalion* as his first presentation. Due to a fund shortage, he cabled Shaw to ask if the playwright wouldn't accept less than his usual royalties.

"Because of our infancy," Aldrich cabled, "we feel entitled to request this reduction."

By return cable, Shaw replied in two words:

"Grow up!"

Stop the Presses

Bob Hope tells how various columnists handled the story of an auto accident in which he was involved.

Drew Pearson: "I predict Bob Hope will see his doctor."

Westbrook Pegler: "Bob Hope, if that's his real name, crashed his car while driving home from a Paul Robeson concert, which he attended with Eleanor Roosevelt and Henry Wallace."

Walter Winchell: "Hope was forced off the road by one of the 250,000 tanks the Russians have patrolling the roads around Hollywood."

Louella Parsons: "Hope and his shoulder have separated after 35 years."

The Christian Science Monitor: "It never really happened."

Cartoonist Bill Mauldin told of two American Indian GIs discussing the war from their foxholes during an air raid:

"The way I figure," said one to another, "when they smoked the pipe of peace in 1918—nobody inhaled!"

This Is War?

On one occasion Admiral William ("Bull") Halsey issued an order to a lieutenant, who replied, "But, sir, that's contrary to Navy regulations." Feigning surprise, Halsey asked the lieutenant to show him the rule in the book on Navy regulations. The lieutenant returned shortly, thumbed to the page governing the order Halsey had issued, and said, "There it is, sir." Whereupon the admiral seized the book, ripped out all its pages, placed the book-covers over his head and replied:

"From now on, *I* am Navy regulations."

During the war, a group of German prisoners being landed in Tunisia pulled up alongside a British destroyer, awaiting further orders. The haughty Nazis, noticing that the English sailors were gazing at them from their ship, suddenly began hurling a stream of invective toward them.

First, they swore at the King. Then they cursed the Queen. Next they loosed a vitriolic blast against Winston Churchill. They even heaped insults on the Duke of Windsor. But through it all, the British boys merely looked at them with amusement. Finally, one Nazi shouted, "The verdammte Ainglish—no spirit!" and spat into the water.

" 'Ere you!" shouted one of the Englishmen. "Mind 'ose ocean you're spittin' in!"

Carlos P. Romulo, hero of the Philippines, may be small in stature (five three), but he has a gigantic sense of humor. Witness this story related by one of his friends, Bob Payton:

Payton was questioning Romulo about the Leyte invasion during World War II and asked if the stories were true about General Douglas MacArthur's wading ashore in water up to his knees, with Romulo right behind.

"Don't believe everything you read," replied Romulo with a smile. "If the water had been up to General MacArthur's knees— it would have been over my head!"

That's Politics

In discussing the problem of trying simply and definitely to say "no" to becoming a candidate for the Democratic nomination for President, Adlai Stevenson told the story of a vicar in a small British town who also had trouble making himself understood. The vicar's wife died suddenly, and he wired his bishop in London:

"Wife died. Please send substitute for weekend!"

It is former Chicago alderman Robert Merriam's story: A candidate in Arkansas was making a house-to-house canvass for votes, but in one home a housewife didn't permit the candidate even to take off his hat before she began berating him.

"You scoundrel, you cheat, you double-crosser!" she exclaimed. "I'll never vote for you. Get out of my house—louse!"

Retreating under the onslaught, the politico took refuge in his parked car. There he drew out from his file of voters the card bearing the woman's name and marked it: "Doubtful."

Publisher Bill Hearst was recalling the 1936 election in which his father, the late William Randolph Hearst, went all-out for the Republicans' Alf Landon—who, in his overwhelming defeat by FDR, carried only two States. A few nights after the election, Bill and his brother Randolph wandered into New York's legendary Club 18, where quick-witted Jack White, the emcee, spotted them. "Well," announced White, "here come Maine and Vermont!"

Rabbi Maurice Eisendrath of New York, winner of the 1961 Gandhi Peace Prize, told of presenting a Torah, the Holy Scriptures of Judaism, to President Kennedy. After the ceremony, Labor Secretary Arthur Goldberg kidded the President about accepting the Torah "without wearing a hat."

"You forget," said Mr. Kennedy. "I'm reformed."

Illinois Senator Paul Douglas, who once led a famous inquiry into government ethics and wrote a book about his findings, was asked to define ethics. He replied by telling of a merchant in New York who was asked the same question by his son.

"Well, it's like this," said the father. "Suppose a man comes into my clothing store and buys a pair of pants. He gives me a new ten-dollar bill. Now, he doesn't know it, but another ten-spot is stuck to it. Son, the ethics is, shall I tell my partner about the extra ten bucks."

During Franklin D. Roosevelt's second term, an Irishman was visiting his priest for some spiritual advice. The priest, after giving the necessary counsel, asked of him, "Now, my good man, is there anything else?"

The Irishman hemmed and hawed, and finally confessed, "I've

got a terrible hate in my heart. I hate Ickes. I hate Wallace. I even hate FDR."

The priest looked at him in astonishment, then asked, "But what about the Supreme Being?"

"I'm sorry, Father," was the reply. "But I hate Eleanor, too."

Former President Truman once gave this reason for his daily, fast-paced walks:

"Any man who expresses himself as freely as I do must keep moving!"

Show Biz

The late stutterin' Joe Frisco, the comedians' comedian, was one of the most quoted in show business. Of many Frisco classics one concerns the time his employer, Charlie Foy, supposedly discovered a turkey missing from the icebox of his California night club. Foy summoned all the help—entertainers, waiters, busboys, everyone—and demanded of each if he knew who had stolen the turkey. When the finger was pointed at Frisco, he stammered, "If y-y-you th-th-think I ate your t-t-turkey, weigh me!"

Joe once borrowed five bucks from Bing Crosby, pleading he was broke and hungry. "If you g-g-give me a f-f-fiver," Frisco promised, "I'll r-r-run right out and b-b-b-buy a ch-ch-chicken for d-d-dinner." Bing forked over the money. Frisco, as expected, raced to the closest bookie. Later Bing inquired about the chicken. Replied Frisco, "He c-c-c-came in f-f-fifth at S-S-Santa Anita."

Then there was the time Frisco was invited to join a society group at a swank address. One of the swank guests imbibed too much and proceeded to knock over a bottle of champagne. The management quickly cleaned the table and the party resumed, but not without a pointed comment from Joe Frisco. "If th-th-this had been a party of b-b-beer drinkers like I travel with," he said, "the s-s-same management would have said, 'Get out—everybody out!' "

On Michigan Avenue one day I accompanied Frisco on a visit to his old Chicago haunts. We paused at the Illinois Athletic Club, where the comedian walked through the lobby without a single nod of recognition. "My, my," he sighed, "how s-s-soon people f-f-forget."

"You once were a member?" I asked.

"N-n-not exactly," he replied. "Th-th-thirty years ago, I was an el-el-elevator b-b-boy."

They remember Joe in Hollywood, too. Once, when Hollywood police were conducting a campaign against jaywalking, Frisco crossed the street in the middle of the block. Immediately an officer pounced on him. Frisco gave him a dirty look and demanded.

"H-h-how f-f-fast was I g-g-going, officer?"

Oscar Levant, attending a private screening of a film in Hollywood, was asked by the producer how he liked it. With typical Levant candor, Oscar said: "I think it's terrible!"

"Who are you to think it's terrible?" retorted the producer.

Replied Levant, "Who do you *have* to be?"

The late George S. Kaufman once invited Levant to spend a weekend at the Kaufman farm in Bucks County. On his arrival, Mrs. Kaufman took Oscar aside, and confided, "I thought you'd be embarrassed about the servants so I tipped them each three dollars and said it was from you."

Levant turned white with rage.

"Damn it!" he shouted. "Why didn't you make it five? Now they'll think I'm tight!"

Levant's mother, who always had great ambition for him, insisted that he devote a certain number of hours daily to the piano. When he eloped the first time, he called her on the phone and excitedly reported, "Mom, I just got married!"

To which Mrs. Levant answered, "Never mind that. Did you practice today?"

Singer Buddy DiVito tells of the frantic patient who rushed to the office of his psychiatrist and screamed, "I have no talent! I can't sing! I can't dance! I can't tell gags! I want to quit show business!"

"Then why don't you quit?" asked the psychiatrist.

"I can't quit," stormed the frantic one. "I'm a star!"

Moss Hart was almost as famous for his faith in psychoanalysis as he was for successful playwriting and directing. (His *Lady in the Dark* was the direct outgrowth of one of his many visits to psychiatrists.) So, when Hart's brother Bernard produced *Dear Ruth* on Broadway and Moss read the critics' rave notices, he couldn't resist phoning his brother immediately and asking:

"Say, who's your psychiatrist?"

Hart, one of Noel Coward's dearest friends, invariably sent a gag telegram to him on every one of his first nights. Once, after racking his brain for an idea, he came up with a plan to send a congratulatory message signed, "Winston Churchill." But the Western Union clerk, after looking Hart up and down and then at the signature, said, "Sorry, but you should know you can't sign Churchill's name to a telegram."

"Whereupon Hart scratched out Churchill's name and wrote, "Moss Hart."

"I'm sorry, sir," said the clerk. "You can't use the name of Moss Hart, either."

"But *I am* Moss Hart," explained the playwright.

"You are?" said the clerk. "In that case, you *can* sign it 'Winston Churchill.' "

Will Rogers was entertaining during World War I when a large middle-aged woman called out, "Hey, why aren't you in the Army?"

Master showman that he was, Rogers wanted everyone to hear the question. "What was that question?" he called out.

"Why aren't you in the Army?" repeated the woman.

"Madam," said Rogers in his unforgettable drawl, "for the same reason that you aren't in the Follies—physical disabilities!"

Alben Barkley, the beloved "Veep," told of a trip to Berlin in 1948 with Bob Hope to entertain GIs. Hope, according to Barkley, talked in his sleep and frequently "mentioned the name Irene." This puzzled Mrs. Hope, also on the junket, and she asked for an explanation.

"Oh, it's just the name of one of Bing Crosby's horses," he replied.

Back home a week later, the telephone rang and Mrs. Hope answered it.

"Who's it for?" asked Bob.

"You, dear," said Mrs. Hope. "One of Bing's horses is on the phone."

Hoosier humorist Herb Shriner, whose folksy, small-town-boy wit probably is the closest modern-day counterpart of the humor of Will Rogers, was recalling his home town in Indiana:

"The girls in our town weren't very pretty. In fact, we had a beauty contest for five years—and never could pick a winner."

Few city folk may have heard of Donald ("Red") Blanchard and the WLS National Barn Dance gang, but for years they have been adored by millions in the rural regions. A sample of Red's humor, from reminiscences about his earlier life:

"Pa wanted me to be a farmer, and Ma wanted me to be a doctor. So they had a nurse put out a pitchfork and a medical book alongside my crib. They figured the one I grabbed for first would decide. It didn't work out that way. I grabbed for the nurse."

Blanchard, when the preacher asked whether he took his wife for better or worse, recalls that he replied:

"I might as well, because I can't do any worse and I don't seem to be able to do any better."

Fred Allen's classic response to the statement, "The show must go on":
"Why?"

And I'll always remember this thought from one of Allen's inimitable lower-case letters:
"remember, as maine goes, so goes the nation. but after spending a summer here i am convinced maine isn't going anywhere."

A Hollywood producer was said to have fired a dozen high-powered press agents within a month. With great trepidation, No. 13 approached him to show the copy he had prepared for the producer's latest movie.

"This picture," the copy read, "combines the poetry of Shakespeare, the suspense of Poe, the wit of Voltaire, and the plot mastery of Dumas. More than an epic, greater than history, it is guaranteed to give you a thrill you'll remember the rest of your life!"

Expressionless, the producer studied the copy a moment, then exclaimed:

"That's more like it. Just simple facts—no overstatement!"

Sam Goldwyn, according to one Hollywood story, was called up by his board of directors some years ago to explain why he was so late getting a story into production.

"I needed a director with imagination," he replied, "and after a long search, the field was boiled down to three prospects. I asked each of them the same question, to see how much imagination he had. The question was, 'How much is two plus two?'

" 'Four,' said the first one.

"The second one—ah, what an imagination—said, 'Three million.'

"And the third—he had the greatest imagination in the world—replied, 'Five million.' "

"Well," asked a board member breathlessly, "which of the three did you hire?"

"The first one," said Goldwyn. "He was my wife's brother."

Brian Donlevy and George Jessel were reminiscing about the late, great John Barrymore when Jessel recalled this incident: Barrymore once visited a haberdashery to purchase a shirt. He selected what he wanted and asked that it be sent home.

"Your name?" asked the clerk.

The actor, taken aback that he was not recognized. replied "Barrymore."

"And your first name?"

Barrymore fixed a cold stare on the clerk, and snapped: "Ethel!"

Jessel, who is so rightly known as America's Toastmaster General (he has emceed some ten thousand banquets in his lifetime), was listening to various speakers extol his virtues at a banquet in his honor in Chicago. As speaker after speaker appeared, piling one compliment upon another, one of the guests noticed that Jessel was beginning to cringe. Tapping him on the shoulder, the guest whispered, "George, I'm surprised that you're so shy. You actually seem embarrassed by all this praise."

"Who's embarrassed?" demanded Jessel. "I'm just thinking how much better I could say all this!"

Max Gordon, the producer who speaks only in theatrical terms, wandered into the Lambs Club in New York seeking an old-time actor he hadn't seen for years. He inquired of the actor's whereabouts from the club manager. "Why, he died a year ago in Kansas City," said the manager.

"Typical of him," replied Gordon. "He *always* died in Kansas City!"

In England, Jimmy Durante was surprised to find a horse named Durante entered in one of London's major races—listed at 100-1 on the morning line. But because Jimmy was in town, a possible omen of luck, so many people wagered a bob or two that the odds were driven down to 10-to-1. Still, the Schnoz, who rarely bets, put down five pounds.

"And whaddaya think this horse does?" said Durante. "It wins by a nose—everybody wants to get into the act!"

Artist James Montgomery Flagg once saw Beatrice Lillie dining with an attractive woman in the Pump Room. Eager to employ the glamour girl as a model, Flagg scribbled a note to Miss Lillie, asking, "Who is that gorgeous creature?"
To which Miss Lillie replied in one word:
"Me."

Red Skelton tells about the studio employee who was desperate for a salary increase. He went in to his boss, then recited a long tale of woe and hard luck.
"He didn't get the raise," says Skelton. "But the studio bought his story!"

Authors often are unhappy with Hollywood's treatment of their novels. And Chicago's Willard Motley is no exception. I asked him which of the two movies based on his books, *Knock on Any Door* or *Let No Man Write My Epitaph*, pleased him more.
"The first one," he said. "In that they kept *two* lines of my dialogue."

After former President Harry S. Truman's celebrated duet with James C. Petrillo at an American Federation of Musicians Convention in Milwaukee, Petrillo was flooded with gag wires from friends around the country. One of his favorites, from Frank Holzfiend of the old Blue Note, said:
"Saw your new combo on television. Crazy, man. Can offer you week at Blue Note—providing you bring same partner."

Shortly before his death, the great Al Jolson told of one of many things of which he was particularly proud:
"I spent two hours with General MacArthur in Japan—and President Truman had only one!"

During a political discussion in Hollywood, George Burns, one of the funniest fellows I know, was arguing that he had eaten better during the Herbert Hoover administration than he did now.

"How come?" asked Groucho Marx.

"Because," snapped Burns, "I had my *own* teeth then!"

Stories about the colorful Tallulah Bankhead are legion. One of my favorites concerns the time my friend Earl Wilson, the Broadway columnist, was interviewing her. Fascinated by her husky, mannish voice, which is many degrees lower than his tenor, he asked if she ever had been mistaken for a man on the phone.

"No, dahling," she cooed. "Have you?"

They're Professional

A patient making his first visit to a psychiatrist was invited to tell all about himself. "Well," he said, "I have a huge home in Lake Forest with four servants. My wife has two minks and a car. My son attends college and has his own car. My daughter also attends college and has a sporty little Jaguar."

Whereupon the doctor cut in and exclaimed, "My goodness, man, what's your problem?"

"Doc, I only earn fifty dollars a week!"

Then there was the psychiatrist who received this post card from a vacationing patient:

"Having wonderful time. Wish I knew why."

Shortly after Dr. Enrico Fermi, the Nobel prize-winning scientist, joined the University of Chicago staff for his highly secret work on the atomic bomb, he was approached by several university executives, who told him, "Now that you are undertaking this mysterious and important work for the government, you undoubtedly will need a secretary. We'll see to it that one reports to you tomorrow."

"But," protested Fermi, "I'm a physicist, not a businessman. What would I do with a secretary?"

"You must have one," the executives explained. "All important people in this country have secretaries."

"All right," said the scientist. Then, without hesitation, he added:

"But I shall need *two* secretaries—so they can keep each other busy."

Bennett Cerf tells about the mouse used for various scientific experiments. He was placed in a missile that went into orbit, and three months later when the nose cone was retrieved he was restored to his cage in the scientific laboratory. Eagerly, all the other mice crowded around him, asking how it felt to be in orbit. Shrugging his shoulders, he said:

"Well, it beats cancer."

The late Coroner Al Brodie was describing a murder victim.

"The man," said Brodie, "was 5 feet 8 inches long."

"Pardon me," said a reporter, "but you mean 5 feet 8 inches tall, don't you, Coroner?"

"When I get them," said Brodie, "they aren't tall—they're long."

Brodie also swore that this happened at a coroner's inquiry:

"You say you shot your husband with this pistol at close range?"

"Yes, sir."

"Were there powder marks on his face?"

"Yes, sir—that's why I shot him!"

At the Clarence Darrow Centennial, Melvyn Douglas told this story:

During the Leopold-Leob case, the press repeatedly called attention to Darrow's slovenly appearance. At first Darrow ignored it. Then one day, tired of such mentions, he stormed into the pressroom and told the reporters:

"My suit is just as expensive as any of yours. My shirts are just as clean. And my ties are just as natty. The only difference is that you fellows take your clothes off when you go to bed!"

And Howard (Vestaglas) Ader knows a minister who bought a used car—but didn't have the vocabulary to run it.

This Is Business?

A wealthy textile merchant visited his physician complaining about insomnia.

"Have you tried counting sheep to induce a sleep?" asked the doctor.

"Have I tried counting sheep?" bellowed the merchant. "Last night I counted 20,000 sheep. From 20,000 sheep I figured I could get 100,000 pounds of wool. From 100,000 pounds of wool, I figured I could get 185,000 yards of material. With this much material, I could make 45,000 overcoats. Listen, Doc. With an inventory like that, who can sleep?"

Colonel Leon Mandel tells of the yokel who made a killing in business and moved to California. There he purchased a lavish twenty-five-room house, equipped with the most expensive furnishings his new-found wealth could afford. An old friend who "knew him when" visited him and immediately was conducted on a tour of the house and grounds, which included three swimming pools.

"The first swimming pool," the owner explained, "has warm water—for my friends who like to swim in warm water.

"The second swimming pool has cold water—for my friends who like to swim in cold water.

"And the third swimming pool has no water at all—for my friends who don't like to swim."

The college-educated young man about to enter his father's fur business decided to tour Europe in search of something new in milady's furs. Returning home, he said, "I've found it. It will revolutionize our business, Papa. It's a brand-new idea—crossing mink with gorilla to get the loveliest fur you ever saw."

"Crossing mink with gorilla?" said Papa. "Son, it wouldn't work. The sleeves would be too long!"

Joseph Schwartz of the Lady Esther cosmetics firm visited his firm's plant in Mexico City a few years ago and had this experience:

A bell, anouncing the morning coffee break, sounded just before lunch one day. On the next day, the bell pealed shortly after the employees reported for work. Curious as to the irregularity of the break, Schwartz asked his plant manager about it.

"Oh," said the manager, "we do have a regular time for the bell—we ring it when the coffee is ready."

"But," said Schwartz, "if the break were scheduled at the same time every day, would not this be more efficient?"

"Ah, but Señor," said the manager. "We cannot do that in Mexico. Imagine the waste of time if the bell sounded at the same hour each day—and the coffee was not ready!"

It happened during a convention. Four visitors were having such a gay time a night-club doorman had to pour them into a cab, then explain to the driver where each was to be delivered. "The one on the left goes to the Morrison," he said, "the one in the middle to the Sherman, the one on the right to the Palmer House, and the one in his lap to the Sheraton-Blackstone."

Nodding in acknowledgment, the cabby drove off. Five minutes later he was back, however.

"Say," he said. "Would you mind sorting these guys again? I hit a bump on State Street!"

"Deep in the Heart of . . ."

Then there was the Texan who died and left his estranged wife three million dollars, with this note:

"She's lucky I didn't cut her off entirely."

And have you heard about the Texan who was so wealthy he had an unlisted phone company?

Or another Texan who was so absent-minded he forgot the Alamo?

And, according to troubadour Chuck Foti, there's a new antique car club in Texas—open to anyone with a Cadillac over one year old.

And sporting goods tycoon Milt Klein tells of the millionaire Texan who decided to take up fishing. He bought a buck-fifty rod, a two-dollar reel—and the Gulf of Mexico.

David Niven left Hollywood for his native England to serve in World War II. Shortly after arriving, he met an old colonel of his regiment. The old campaigner looked at Niven, then remarked, "Why of course I know you. You're Niven. Tell me what you've been doing lately."

"I've been in Hollywood," replied Niven.

"Hollywood? Why bless my soul, never knew we had a station there!"

Two Irish terrorists captured by the British had been sentenced to hang. As it happened, the gallows was located directly over the River Liffey, and by some quirk of fate, as the first Irishman was being hanged, the noose broke. Down through the trap door he slid, and into the river, but somehow he was able to swim for safety. As the noose was knotted around the second Irishman's neck, he pleaded:

"Please, for goodness sake, make sure the noose doesn't break again—I can't swim!"

Democratic Congressman Sidney Yates of Illinois passes along this story of the forty-one-year-old Irishman who tried to enlist in the Army the day following the outbreak of World War II, but was turned down because he was over thirty-five. But, noting the man's disappointment, the recruiting sergeant said, "Look, Pat, maybe you made a mistake in your age. Go home and check your birth record and then come back."

Early the next day, Pat again was on the scene. Smiling, he exclaimed to the sergeant:

"I sure did make a mistake about my age. I *am* thirty-five all right. It's me poor old mother who is forty-one!"

Ray Kroc, of McDonalds Drive Ins, reports that the Ripley cartoon in Moscow is called:
"Believe It—Or Else."

An American and a Russian soldier were arguing about the merits of their countries' respective forms of government.
"I'll show you what democracy is," said the Yank. "I can get a two-week pass from my sergeant and fly to Washington. There I can get into the White House, and with a little luck, I can get to see the President. I even can walk up to him and say, 'President Kennedy, you're a bum.' That's democracy for you!"
"Ho," said the Red. "Under communism you can do the same thing. I can ask my sergeant for a two-week pass, and I can get to Moscow. With a little luck I can get into the Kremlin, and with a little more luck I can get to see Premier Khrushchev. And I, too, can walk up to him and say, so all can hear, 'Premier Khrushchev, President Kennedy is a bum!' "

Chicago labor leader Sidney Lens, after a recent trip to Moscow, told this story of a university student who had been asked to draw a comparison between communism and capitalism.
"In capitalist America," said the student, "there are bread lines and endless slums. People are oppressed by big-money interests, and the country is faced with depression. In Russia, communism has prospered and provided the outstanding scientific achievements of the era. There are no slums. There is no oppression. Production has reached new heights—and by 1970, we'll catch up to America!"

Then there was the devoted Italian father whose son was a contestant on the big-money jackpot program. As the son answered each question correctly, the proud papa beamed and exclaimed from the audience, "That's-a my Tony!" The final question, for the $64,000 jackpot, was a three-part query. The son answered the first two with ease. But on the last part his mind went blank. He couldn't remember who had shot Abraham Lincoln. Finally he had to admit defeat. But not Papa. He stood up and shouted:

"That's-a my Tony—he no squeal on anybody!"

Miscellany

In Fritzel's one day the topic was fast-talking waiters and their humorous sallies at customers, which revived this one:

A waiter on his deathbed was promised by his wife that she would make contact with him in the hereafter. She visited a spiritualist after his death, explained her problem, and requested a seance. Agreeing, the medium said, "Just place your hands on this table, hold it firmly, and while holding it call out his name."

Doing as she had been instructed, the woman called out, "Leo, Leo."

Came a rasping voice from above, sounding just like her late husband:

"Sorry, that's not my table."

A small town, says Quin Ryan, is where you can carry on a long telephone conversation even if you get the wrong number.

Another bit of wisdom from Ryan:
"A fool and his money are invited everywhere."

Definition of home cooking:
Where a man hopes his wife is.

Definition of a modern minute man:
One who can get to his refrigerator and back during a commercial.

Sam Pascal spotted this sign on the window of a gun shop:
"Out to reload."

And Fred Mazzei swears he knows a Communist who furnished his home in Early Un-American.

A businessman picked up his newspaper and turned to the obituary column. There he read his name—Joseph Johanson, age 58, survived by wife, Helen, and three children, Manny, Moe, and Jack. "Why, that's me!" exclaimed the man. "My name, my age, my wife's name, and my three children!"

Wringing his hands in despair, he immediately phoned his partner, and asked him to read the obituary notices. "My, oh my," said the partner. "That's you, all right." Then, after a significant pause:

"Say, Joseph, tell me—where you calling from?"

At a Chicago police station one night, a slightly tipsy gent was hauled in and demanded to know from the desk sergeant why he had been pinched. "You've been brought in for drinking," he was told.

"Fine," said the drunk. "Les get shtarted!"

Two longtime girl friends who hadn't seen each other in ten years met on the street one day. "Gloria," exclaimed the first, "where have you been all these years?"

"Oh," replied the other, pointing to the baby carriage she was wheeling, "you know how it is—married and the mother of this eight-year-old boy."

"He's eight years old and you're still wheeling him in a baby carriage?" asked the first.

Whereupon the youngster lifted his head and said:

"Lady, am I bothering *you?*"

"Bellboy," said the woman in a Miami Beach Hotel, "can I get change for a dollar?"

"Lady," said the bellhop, "at this hotel, a dollar *is* change!"

"I know I'm not as young as I once was," says Red Skelton. "But I still love to chase girls. Only difference now is that I can't remember why I'm chasing 'em!"

Reader Byron Moenter spotted this sign on a firehouse:
"You come to our dance—we'll come to your fire."

The Randolph Street rover boys tell the story of the bookmaker who died. All his pals of the gambling gentry attended the funeral, listening with respectful solemnity as the minister intoned:
"Our dear friend is not dead, he is only sleeping."
Whereupon a voice from the rear boomed:
"I'm laying 6 to 5 he's dead."

Movieman Frank Freeman tells the story of a youngster who came home from Sunday school and told his father the story of how Moses led the Jews across the Red Sea:
"First, army engineers put up a pontoon bridge. Then Egyptian planes bombed the bridge. But antiaircraft gunners shot down the jets, which enabled Moses to lead the people across the water."
"Wait a minute," said the father. "Are you sure that's the way your Sunday school teacher told it?"
"Not exactly," said the boy. "But if I told you the way she told it to us, you'd never believe it!"

Points to Ponder

Newsman Clark Mollenhoff's definition of democracy: Where a person can say what he is thinking without thinking.

Definition of middle age: When your wife tells you to pull in your stomach, and you already have.

Jet planes, according to George Marks, are so fast that he had breakfast in New York, lunch in Los Angeles, and heartburn in Honolulu.

Brotherhood suggestion from Sam Levinson: If you can't love your enemies, at least be a little nicer to your friends.

People are funny. Tell a man there are eight billion stars in the sky and he believes you. Tell him it's fresh paint, and he has to stick his finger in it.

Drivers, remember. Gasoline and alcohol don't mix. Well, actually they do. But the taste is terrible!

A fellow Senator told it to Senator McCarran in an argument over the immigration act that bears McCarran's name:

"I presume it is your position that this country would not be in such a mess today if the Indians had adopted more stringent immigration laws."

The late New York Mayor Jimmy Walker's sage observation on racial tolerance:

"To play 'The Star-Spangled Banner' correctly on the piano, you've got to use the black keys as well as the white ones."

Winston Churchill's definition of a fanatic: A person who can't change his mind—and won't change the subject.

Quote to remember:

"It is a gloomy moment in history. Not for years has there been so much apprehension. Never has the future seemed so incalculable. In France the political cauldron seethes. Russia hangs like a cloud on the horizon. All the resources of the British are sorely tried. Of our own troubles in the United States, no man can see the end."

The source?

Harper's Weekly—of October 10, 1857.

Another worth noting:

"Our earth is degenerate in these latter days. Bribery and corruption are common. Children no longer obey their parents. Every man wants to write a book. The end of the world evidently is approaching."

Source of this one?

Nobody knows. It was carved on a slab of stone in Assyria—in 2800 B.C.!

The late Charles MacArthur liked to sum up his philosophy of life with the words of a condemned man whose hanging he covered as a Chicago reporter. As the man approached the gallows he halted and asked:

"Is this thing safe?"

Let us hope so, friends. Let us hope so.

Index

This book was set in
Electra and Univers types by
Harry Sweetman Typesetting Corporation.
It was printed and bound at the press of
The World Publishing Company.
It was designed by Larry Kamp.